IT'S ALL IN YOUR HEAD!

AMAZING BENEFITS

— OF —

ENDONASAL
CRANIAL THERAPY

& FUNCTIONAL CRANIAL RELEASE

JOHN LIEURANCE, ND, DC

Published by Neuro Alpha LLC

This book is a work that offers health, wellness, and fitness information, and is for educational purposes only. It is not a substitute for, nor does It replace, professional medical advice, diagnosis, or treatment, either directly or indirectly, as a form of treatment for physical, emotional, or medical problems. The author's intent is only to offer information of a general nature to help you in your quest for emotional, physical, and spiritual wellbeing. If you have any concerns or questions about your health, consult with a physician or other healthcare professionals. Do not disregard, avoid, or delay obtaining medical or health-related advice from your healthcare professional due to content in this book. In the event you use any of the information in this book, the author and the publisher assume no responsibility for your actions.

Always speak with your physician or other healthcare professionals before taking any medication or nutritional, herbal, or homeopathic supplement, or using any treatment for a health problem. If you have, or suspect that you have a medical problem contact your healthcare provider promptly.

Information and statements about dietary supplements have not been evaluated by the Food and Drug Administration and are not intended to diagnose, treat, cure, or prevent any disease.

While all attempts have been made to verify information provided in this publication, Revelation Health assumes no responsibility for errors, inaccuracies, or omissions that may appear in this publication. Any slights of people or organizations are unintentional.

Company names and product names mentioned in this publication may have trademarks or registered trademarks of their respective companies and are hereby acknowledged.

BEYOND FASTING

Strategies for Extraordinary Health and Longevity Printed in the United States of America.

ISBN: 979-8-3566331-3-3

Imprint: Independently published

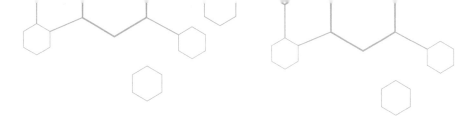

DEDICATIONS

I would like to dedicate this book to the following doctors whom pioneered endo nasal balloon therapy in order to expand the wellness and vitality of human beings:

Nephi Cottam, DC, Dr. Janse J., J Richard Stober, ND & Dr. Finnel F.L.

To William Sutherland, DO, who pioneered cranial therapy itself.

Additionally, I am grateful to have such amazing doctors who I've known along my journey and whom I call my colleagues which have practiced and taught endo-nasal: Adam Del Torto DC, Lewis Arrandt ND, DC and Craig Buehler, DC.

My gratitude to D. Howell, ND who originally taught me basic endo nasal in 1997.

I would like to acknowledge Ari Emmanuel (owner of UFC) for introducing me to Dana White (CEO UFC) who after receiving treatment became inspired to endorse and bring endonasal into the UFC organization. My belief is that this will be a catalyst to bring attention to this relatively unknown and underutilized treatment.

I would further like to acknowledge my staff including Sarah Carnegie, Candace Johnson, Irene Melendez, Brooke Asher, Tara Smith and Daniel Gibson. Also my close friends that supported me Harry Paul, Ben Greenfield, Doyle Bramhall II, Patrick Gentempo, Dan Pompa and all the other people that have been on my journey to share the endo-nasal story.

Lastly, to all of the people that have trusted me and allowed me to stick a balloon up their nose over the last 3 decades. I'm happy to say that all of these treatments worked out for these people and it's those results that keep me pushing forward to be inspired to continue to develop and understand the mechanisms behind this valuable modality.

TESTIMONIAL

Dr John's book on Endo Nasal is the most comprehensive book on the subject & much needed to bring attention to the art & science of this unusual technique. Endo Nasal is one of the most overlooked areas of natural medicine. The way the cranial bones move, particularly the sphenoid bone, act to block the body's ability to heal due to poor CSF flow which circulation of oxygen & nutrients & also proper detoxification of the brain. Dr. John is a teacher & a pioneer in the use of Functional Cranial Release to release that block & provide the body the opportunity to truly heal. This is a technique that both natural medicine practitioners as well as primary care doctor should be fluent in. I have benefited from the treatments personally & I recommend this to anybody to receive.

Frank Shallenberger, MD- Known as the father of Ozone & the original Functional Medicine doctor in the USA. He has the largest holistic newsletter in the world. He is a bestselling author of the book "Bursting with Energy" which the amazing story of ozone and how to use it.

"Dr.John Lieurance has done it again: with each of his books, he manages to delve into scientific and medical concepts nobody else is talking about. In this case a deep dive into Endo Nasal Therapy. Revealing what I consider to be one of the most effective yet underrated physical upgrades one can make to their neurology - and a whole lot more!"

Ben Greenfield- Subversive journalist, author & public figure. One of the original and most prolific Biohacking podcasters. His podcast "Ben Greenfield life is followed by millions of health enthusiast.

ABOUT THE AUTHOR

John A. Lieurance, ND, DC, DABCN (board eligible) - Chiropractic Neurologist and Naturopathic Physician practicing since 1996, Best-selling Author, Lecturer & Scientific Advisor for MitoZen Scientific.

After becoming severely ill with Lyme, EBV and Mold illness, Dr John Lieurance began to explore ways to improve health at the deepest cellular level. His journey brought him to discover the deepest cause of all diseases which is an energy deficiency. This has led him to writing his first book on Melatonin as the core anti-oxidant that supports all systems in the body. His book on Melatonin takes a deep dive into healing naturally and using high dose melatonin along with various other practical healing methods to heal the body and live a longer and more vital life.

His life focus is on vitality, longevity and enhanced consciousness. His interest is in connecting what he calls, "The 3-legged stool": Vitality, Identity & Divinity which is the basis of OutofBoxDoc.com. Using science and ancient wisdom, he aims to connect these dots in his own journey to becoming the best version of himself in this life.

Diving deeply into many healing methods, to discover the deepest and most profound means to activate cellular energy, such as with Melatonin, Methylene Blue, NAD+ as well as Fasting with various nutrients to activate responses. Dr John explores many new paths in the health care world, with his unique & fresh ideas using various delivery systems, such as bullets, mists, liposomes and various protocols he has created.

He attended Parker College of Chiropractic & received his Naturopathic degree in 2001 from St. Luke's School of Medicine. He has practiced Functional Neurology, Naturopathic medicine and Regenerative Medicine, using stem cell therapy in Sarasota for 25 years.

Founder of the Advanced Rejuvenation Center in Sarasota, Florida and developer of the Functional Cranial Release technique - which is an Endo-Nasal Cranial Treatment with the ability to unlock the spinal fluid to allow profound healing of the nervous system.

Dr Lieurance has been involved in multiple clinical trials including investigation into the use of stem cells for Parkinson's Disease, COPD, OA of the knee and hip from 2012-2014. He has a clinical focus on mold illness, lyme disease and chronic viral infections. Using natural eastern and western approaches to healing the true source of disease, which lies in the metabolic pathways that are challenged by chronic inflammation resulting in infections and toxicity.

Books Authored

Melatonin: Miracle Molecule - Amazon

It's All in Your Head: EndoNasal Cranial Therapy – Amazon

Methylene Blue: Magic Bullet - (See MethyleneBlueBook.com)

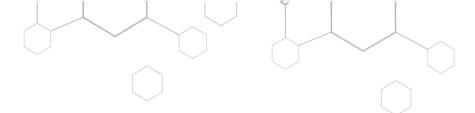

INTRODUCTION

Transform your life with Endo Nasal Cranial Therapy, the most powerful physical adjustment possible to the human body. After practicing Endo Nasal therapy for 30 years & training doctors all around the world, Dr Lieurance includes the newest breakthroughs discovered in his research. Deep diving into nasal breathing, CSF flow, Pineal Health, Brain Health & Emotional storage in deep layers within the cranium. Using expansive pressures to return the skull to its normal, natural position & flexibility Endo Nasal is a powerful healing tool which is little known & not recognized by mainstream medicine. In this book Dr Lieurance breaks down the use of Endo Nasal as well as many healing technologies he uses in his clinical practice to treat a variety of conditions to include Headaches, TMJ, Neurological Conditions, Vestibular Disorders, Sinus and Nasal Breathing & Pineal Function for Mental/Emotional & Spiritual applications. Besides his private practice, Dr Lieurance works using endo nasal therapy with top athletes & the UFC Performance Institute in Las Vegas.

This is a comprehensive book on the benefits of Endo Nasal Therapy that go far beyond just opening the nasal passages. We take a deep dive into how endo nasal is beneficial for a variety of diseases due to its key mechanisms which support a health brain and spinal cord. Endo Nasal Therapy can improve CSF flow & the nutrient delivery to the brain and spinal cord as well as the detox pathways such as the glymphatic clearing mechanism. Using both an activation as well as a structural change Endo Nasal can be used for healing the Brain & Vestibular, ocular & vestibular system. Explore limbic oscillations driven by respiratory cycles within the nasal passage. Explored the history of Endo nasal and the work from world renowned Weston price and how the cranium commonly collapses in industrial living situations versus aborigines, which naturally have wide skulls & pallets. This book is meant for both Lehman & practitioners interested in utilizing advanced cranial therapy. Dr. Lieurance teaches Endo nasal through his institute which you can find at LearnEndoNasal.com.

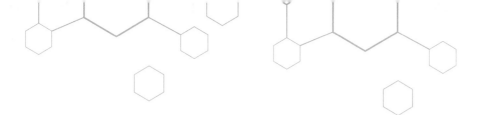

CONTENTS

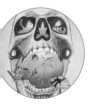

HISTORY OF ENDO-NASAL BALLOON ADJUSTING

HISTORY OF ENDONASAL BALLOON ADJUSTING

Although much of the world's population has never even heard about Endo nasal balloon adjustments, no less cranial therapy, it goes as far back as the 20th century and is effective in the treatment of many disorders. In this book, we will explore how and why cranial therapies have their influence on human health, but for now, you should know that it is through both a structural and neurological influence.

Notable men such as Dr. Stober, Janse, and Finnel, were credited with its development and they left further development to the next generation who has done an excellent work of improving and adapting technology towards its development. [Jordan, 2017]

Writing about the history of endonasal cranial adjusting and Functional Cranial Release will be incomplete without talking about the rich history of cranial therapy from which it came into existence. We will be taking a deep dive into the past and the future of cranial therapy and how endonasal and cranial techniques along with various supportive modalities, which can be utilized to support various conditions and afflictions experienced by humans.

HISTORY OF CRANIAL THERAPY

Cranial therapy is the mother of all cranial manipulations and is a technique used in treating certain disorders by the manipulation of the "mobile" bones that made up the cranium. The history of the development of cranial therapy remains unclear with evidence pointing to the 13th century and the 20th centuries as the time of development

Using the reviews of the work of the Greek Physician, Ligeros, it was evident that Ligeros researched the use of cranial manipulations up to the 13th century and pieces of evidence point to the use of a sort of cranial manipulation in the treatment of disorders by the Bedouins (a nomadic tribe that has existed from ancient Greece). [Ligeros 1937]

The evidence pointing to the 13th century as the time cranial manipulation was first used paled in comparison to the 20th century because the 20th century is the most reported. According to Cottam and Smith Willard Carver, LLB, DC was the first to use cranial manipulation to treat hydrocephalus and brain fever. [Cottam, 1981]

The technique used by Willard was not known and cannot be categorized using the modern-day scheme. Willard himself did not explain the process he used when writing his book called *"Chiropractic Analysis."* Due to this, only a few people were able to get the process of performing the technique using different procedures such as pressure, vibration, and thrusting.

As a result of the slight secrecy in the knowledge of the technique, two physicians, namely (Dr. Nephi Cottam and Dr. Willian Sutherland), would later be credited with the development of cranial techniques.

Nephi Cottam D.C.

Dr. Cottam is referred to as the father of craniopathy, a technique he developed after discovering the power of using cranial manipulation while treating a patient suffering from the lack of sleep. In his book [Story of Craniopathy 1936], he discussed his use of cranial bone alignment to lift the cephalad on the cranial vault, noting how effective the process was when used on patients. With practices and good results, craniopathy spread throughout Europe and the United States of America. [Palmer 2017]

William Garner Sutherland, D.O.

While Cottam was known for craniopathy, Dr. Sutherland's involvement in cranial techniques contributed more to osteopathy. According to him, in the year 1899, he, on careful study of a skull, displayed at an osteopathic school, observed, and deduced that the beveled articular surface of the sphenoid bone indicates that the bone can move by slight adjustment. [Sutherland, 1939]

Dr. Sutherland then started studying the anatomy and physiology of the cranial bones while performing experiments on himself and others. While experimenting, he observed that not only do the cranial bones move, they are also in constant motion due to the action called "the reciprocal tension membrane."

Reciprocal Tension membrane is the tension created by the subtle movement between the sacrum at the base of the spine and the cranial bones. This tension is through the dura matter, which is the firm connective tissue that protects the brain and spinal column.

On the completion of his work, the osteopathic world did not accept his concepts, for example, in the American Osteopathic Association convention that was held in 1932 only seven people attended, and his articles were only accepted for publishing in two papers, and doctors refused to include his cranial concepts in the osteopathic convention that was held in 1940. However, he did not give up until his turning point in 1942. [Sutherland, 1939]

In 1942 during the American Osteopathic Association convention held in Chicago, Dr. Sutherland talked about his cranial concepts with six renowned osteopathic physicians who were astonished, loved, and requested the cranial courses to help with treating various disorders. He would later publish a book *Osteopathy in the Cranial Field* [Wales, Anne L 1990] together with Rebecca Lippincott, D.O., Beryl Arbuckle, D.O., and Paul Kimberly, D.O. The book is currently the standard reference in modern osteopathic cranial concepts. [Sutherland, 1962]

It was from these two individuals' research and advancement in technology that the technique of cranial manipulation diversified into several techniques, one of which is the Endonasal and Cranial Release.

Bilateral Nasal Specific Technique (BNS)

Bilateral Nasal Specific, also known as Nasal specific technique, is a branch of cranial therapy that uses the inflation of balloons to adjust the cranial plates of the skulls, thereby relieving the head of the patient of built-in pressure. The released pressure helps to unwind the body, affects the nervous system, reestablishes the flow of cerebrospinal fluid to the body, and the proper flow of blood to the brain. [Tolmos, n.d]

BNS was developed by notable figures such as Janse J. [Nasal Specific Technique 1947] and Finnel FL [Nasal Balloon Device 1951 & 1954] although it would not have been this popular if not for the work of the USA's Chiropractor, Dr. J Richard Stober, who actively practiced and taught the technique within osteopathic and chiropractic colleges in between 1950-1998 thereby giving it worldwide recognition [Jones 1999]

To understand the concept of BNS, you will need to understand the way the balloon is placed in the nasal passage. The placement is very important since it determines the effect the balloon inflation will have on the bones of the cranium. There are six placements through which the balloon can be inserted into the nasal passage; for example, there is the lower middle and upper chamber or Concha. In the BNS technique, the chiropractor will inflate the balloon in the six chambers in the nasal passages to release the entire cranium in each visit.

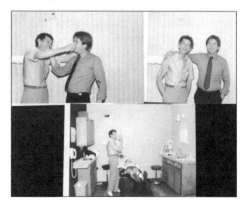

Dr. J Richard Stober

The pure form of BNS continues to be practiced by notable doctors like Dr. Craig Buehler DC, who learned BNS directly from Dr. Stober, and presently teaches and performs the technique, and he further integrated the technique into his Advanced Muscle Integration Technique (AMIT). [AMIT, 2017]

Like the way I have integrated use of the Endonasal and cranial technique in dealing with my patients, Dr. Buehler has found that a healthy, flexible, and properly functioning skull is very important to get the best results for his patients. I have had the pleasure of knowing him. Truly he is a wealth of knowledge with regards to Endonasal techniques and its influence on his work. In 2019 we traded and worked on each other, and both found great benefit to the original work we have both been teaching!

Research into Bilateral Nasal Specific Technique

Research into the bilateral nasal specific technique has yielded many improvements with clinical evidence for the procedures used by the forerunners, like Janse, Finnel, and Stober and the newer generation. The newer generation through skills, technology has been able to develop the technique further. I will divide the research done into the early/late 20th century and the 21st century.

Practice in the 20th Century

The 20th century was a period characterized by a lack of technology, and it was evident in the procedures that Janse, Felipe, and Stober used to raise the sphenoid bone. The period will be based on the recent modification that occurred from the early 20th century to the late 20th century.

1920 -1947

During these periods, the bilateral nasal specific technique was ascribed to only traditionalists and involved the traditionalist inputting a balloon into either the patients' nostrils or the mouth to adjust the cranium plate. However, the procedure was stopped in modern practices because patients were experiencing pain and soreness in the area of insertion. [Jones, 1999]]

1947- Late 20th Century

Stober, Finnel, and Janse did a great job in improving the way traditionalists operate using the technique. Instruments such as Sphygmomanometer and balloon are used to check the pressure exerted by the balloon towards pushing the sphenoid bone. It was efficient in removing the disadvantages of the previous procedure by slowly adjusting the pressure. By adjusting the pressure, the balloon will push against the tissue supporting the sphenoid bone, thereby performing its function. [Jones, n.d]

Practice in the 21st Century

The development of BNS in the 21st century is quite vast and can be attributed to development in technology and more discoveries by the new generation. While some people stuck with the technique, for example, Dr. Buehler, other people such as Dr. Howell (NeuroCranial Restructuring), and I have improved the use of the BNS to treat neurological and functional disorders. It was from intricate studying and practices that I developed the endonasal and cranial technique/functional cranial release.

REFINING ENDONASAL AND ADDING MODERN ADVANCES

Endonasal and Cranial Technique, which is also known as Functional Cranial release is the remodeled version of the Bilateral Nasal Specific I developed to fix health problems at the source by finding the core driver of the disturbance. The source of most disturbances is mostly neurological, and when targeted, the body can then heal itself. In other words, I believe we are as healthy as our brains.

My first encounter with endonasal ballooning is while undergoing nasal adjusting using NeuroCranial Restructuring developed by Dr. Dean Howell, a student of Dr. Stober (like Dr. Craig Buehler). Lewis Arrandt, ND, DC was my first experience receiving endo-nasal. It was such a powerful experience I had to learn more nad become trained in this technique. I could finally breath through my right nostril after many years of not after a broken nose in college.

Lewis Arrandt, ND, DC

Howell found the stress associated with 8 inflations while performing BNS challenging. Since BNS is the process of performing balloon inflations about eight times in the same visit. Howell did this after he found the work of Chiropractor, Dr Jesse Jankowitz, who was using balance

> *Dr. Adam Del Torto who also trained under Dr. Howell, originally in the late 80's, also grew frustrated with many of the limitations with NCR. Shortly after practicing NCR for 2 years, he developed his own version called CFR or Cranial Facial Release. I am certified with Dr DelToro and have assisted in CFR training. Dr DelToro is a brilliant doctor and teacher and has blended the best of a Chiropractic technique called SOT or Sacral Cranial Technique. This technique was developed by the man who invented color photography, Dr. Major Dejournette. It is actually a part of NCR now that Howell was shown by Dr Del Torto about the blocking techniques. Dr. DelToro's CFR is a precise combination of releasing the cranium using external pressures with the hands and also releases to the sacrum prior to the balloon inflations. It is also a 4-day series like FCR. In his advanced practices, Dr Del Torto has also developed methods that combine the use of CFR along with pallet expansion which is a co-treatment with a functional and or a biological dentist.*

techniques in his technique called ABC, Advanced Biostructural Technique. Howell attended one of Dr Jankowitz's seminars and adopted the testing method which he used to determine which exact nasal area to inflate and the best body positions to place the body into while doing the inflation. When I trained with Howell, I had already done extensive training with Jankowitz and was a certified ABC practitioner, so this testing was very familiar to me. We are now able to refine BNS technique where good or better results are achieved using half of the pressure and with only one or two inflations.

After practicing NCR a short period, I began to grow frustrated with many of the limitations such as no other physical adjustment other than the endo-nasal balloon and a mandatory one-hour massage technique.

Functional Cranial Release was born

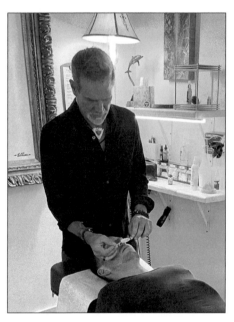

After learning basic endo-nasal technique in 1997 I soon found advanced methods to introduce into my use of endo-nasal therapy with my patients. This catalyzed the development of Functional Cranial Release or FCR. At this time I was studying under Dr Ted Carrick within the Carrick Institute of Neurology and refining the use of Functional Neurology within my practice. I saw a need for further expansion into a better neurological approach and the inclusion of endo nasal balloon adjustments along with Functional Neurology. As a result of this Functional Cranial Release was born as a blend these 2 methods, which I have been teaching for more than a decade now with certified FCR practitioners around the world. Using Functional Neurology means a more functional neurologic exam as well as the use of various methods to bring balance to the nervous system. Keep in mind the nervous system controls the body and it is the master system so balancing this complex network along with correcting the skull, the home of the nervous system, made lots of sense to me. We will dive a little deeper into functional neurology and how I use it for various conditional later in this book.

REFERENCES

1. Jordan, C.A., (2017) Functional Cranial Release [Online] *Available at* https://silo.tips/download/history-of-cranial-therapy# (Accessed 01/08/2020)

2. Ligeros, K. A. (1937). *How Ancient Healing Governs Modern Therapeutics*. New York: G. P. Putnam's Sons

3. Cottam, C., & Smith, E. (1981). *Roots of Cranial Manipulation*. Chiropractic History, 1(1), 31-34.

4. Palmer, D.N., (2017) *Dr. Nephi Cottam and the History of Craniopathy* [Online] Available at https://blogs.palmer.edu/library/2017/01/26/dr-nephi-cottam-and-the-history-of-craniopathy/ (Accessed 01/08/2020)

5. Sutherland, W. G. (1939). *The Cranial Bowl*. Mankato, MN: Author.

6. Sutherland, A. S. (1962). *With Thinking Fingers*. Kansas City, MO: Cranial Academy.

7. Jones D.H. (1999). *Bilateral Nasal Specific A Patients Perspective* [Online] Available at https://docplayer.net/8207828-History-of-cranial-therapy.html (Accessed 01/08/2020)

8. Lieurance J. (n.d) Functional Cranial Release [Online] Available at http://www.functionalcranialrelease.com/ (Accessed 01/08/2020)

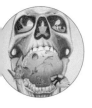

2

FUNCTIONAL CRANIAL RELEASE

INTRODUCTION to FCR

Functional Cranial Release is the process, or better put, the art, and science of utilizing the techniques of endonasal balloon inflation for the correction of tension in the craniosacral system. Functional cranial release perfectly incorporates two different, yet similar techniques to restore normal functioning of the brain and nervous system. These techniques are Functional Neurology and Neurocranial Restructuring. Understanding the role of the brain and the nervous system in the control of the body's response to stress and toxins is critical to understanding how functional cranial release works.

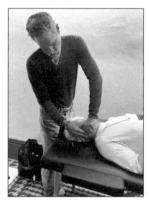

At UFC Performance Institute
treating Cowboy Cerrone

Treating Dr Frank Shallenburger

WHAT FUNCTIONAL CRANIAL RELEASE ENTAILS

Functional Cranial Release (FCR) involves the use of endonasal balloon inflation for the correction of dural torque in the craniosacral system. When dural torque or dural tension is corrected, the flow of cerebrospinal fluid (CSF) improves, and the brain can function much more properly. It involves the use of a combination of functional neurological assessments and treatments to determine the cause(s) of certain kinds of illnesses. FCR combines Functional Neurology to restore the normal functioning of the brain and specific undo-nasal adjustments to restore the normal functioning of the cranium.

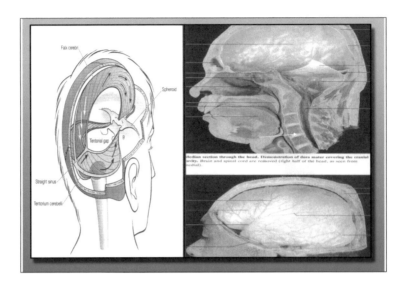

Functional Neurology & How I Have combined it with Endo-Nasal

Developed by Dr Ted Carrick and taught through the Carrick Institute if Neurology, Functional Neurology is the art and science of a natural approach to treating many conditions of a "functionally" challenged brain. Many issues in the brain might not be seen on Computed Tomography (CT), on Magnetic Resonance Imaging (MRI), and might not be from a tumor or stroke. Functional Neurology is based more on function of the nervous system. Many neurological conditions may just be functional, ranging from the way the brain is communicating or firing. Functional neurology works by testing normal nerve pathways and discovering if there are abnormali-

Dr Ted Carrick

ties [Traster, 2019]. The source of many ailments is usually from the clusters of neurons that aren't working properly in various places in the Central Nervous System (CNS). Functional neurology involves the assessment of the central integrative state of the functional units within the CNS and determines whether there are functional anomalies, and where they are [Loewen 2020]. Also keep in mind many structural problems that can be caused by stroke, tumor or trauma can also be treated with Functional Neurology as a superior method compared to using drugs as there are no drugs that can affect specific pathways in the brain. You see functional neurology works on something called neuro plasticity. Neuro plasticity is where the brain creates new pathways. This is how we learn, this is how we experience the world and are able to create memories and thoughts. Using functional neurology, various pathways that aren't working can be circumvented using other similar pathways to allow normal functioning the thus an improved status in various neurological consequences. Some of the work I do with a rare condition called palatal myoclonus is a perfect example of using both endo nasal adjustments in combination with

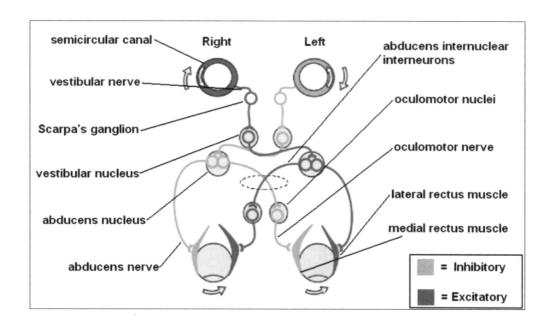

semicircular canal — Right   Left   abducens internuclear interneurons

vestibular nerve —

Scarpa's ganglion —

vestibular nucleus —

abducens nucleus —

abducens nerve —

oculomotor nuclei

oculomotor nerve

lateral rectus muscle

medial rectus muscle

= Inhibitory

= Excitatory

functional neurology and how nothing else may solve this challenge in the way the brain is firing. My work with this rare condition brings me great pride as I have treated more of these cases worldwide than any other physician. I have helped most of them and returned them to a normal life. Endo nasal adjustments will unlock the cranium, allowing for an improved circulatory pattern that's improving fuel delivery along with improved clearing of metabolic wastes. The very same therapy, endo nasal balloons, will also activate the deep areas in the brain stem that are not functioning properly in these cases. I see a need to both releasing and activating the for many if not all of the cases that I treat. Another good example of how important functional neurology can be is that many of these neurologic cases have stiffness and pain with their necks as part of their complaints. It is very common that the vestibular system becomes out of sync whereas the eyes, the inner ear and the neck muscles are not all communicating together normally. This sets up a problem called cervical dystonia. This is where the neck muscles remain tight even when they should not when the neck and the head returned in different directions. Chiropractic adjustments and massage therapy to the neck will never fix this problem. What has to happen in order for these people to return to a normal situation with their necks is to address this reflex called the vestibular ocular reflex or VOR. This is where a very detailed conversation is happening between the eyes, the semicircular canals in the inner ears, and the neck muscles. If you think about it, this is very complex that all of this is calibrated through the central nervous system. These things become out of sync just like the tires in your car can become out of alignment causing extra stress on the tire, wheel and axle. With these types of conditions there is a lot of compensation that causes much stress in the central nervous system. Cleaning these things up with functional neurology can improve cervical dystonia however it takes away a lot of extra work by the central nervous system. This often leaves the brain with more energy to do other tasks and patients usually enjoy more energy and less brain fog and many other benefits that go along with a healthier brain.

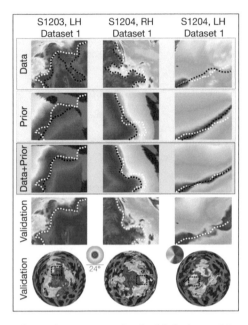

S1203, LH Dataset 1	S1204, RH Dataset 1	S1204, LH Dataset 1

Another critical consideration that functional neurology improves nicely involves knowing where our body is in space compared to where things in our environment are. This is the need for our brain to create grids and maps of both our body and its environment. These maps are held within a part of the brain called the superior colliculus. They are called somato-topic maps and they're extremely important for any type of coordinator movement in our environment. Now this is where things get really interesting. These maps are created through our eyes. When your eyes are functioning normally these maps will continually be updated. The eyes have their own map which is called retinotopic maps. How this works is the eyes have to lock onto various targets in our environment for a brief moment where the eyes need to hold their position. This locked-in position then creates these maps and grids which project from the somatotopic maps to our retinotopic maps. This is continually happening all the time. The problem I see with many of my patients is that they're unable to hold her eyes in any position for even a moment and this will cause problems with these maps. The eyes can also be pulled off of the target through various influences from the brain, usually the vestibular and or cerebellum which creates problems with creating maps as well. There is a simple exercise called eye pinball I like to use where there are accurate eye movements called saccades to memorize targets on a paper which does a great job of updating these maps. I know this is getting very technical, but I think the take-home message here is that there are a lot of pathways that can be disrupted and the use of something like functional neurology can be critical for many neurologic conditions as well as improve functioning with many sports and high level athletes.

The shocking truth I have found through my work is that endo nasal balloon adjustments have a profound impact on the vestibular system. I'll be presenting a study that shows this later in this book. This positive impact through the vestibular system allows me to get more rapid results in the area of functional neurology. In my clinic when I do endo-nasal adjustments and following up with these brain balancing exercises I often see rapid improvements in my vestibular cases. Many of these cases have other specialists that have told them they will have to live with their condition for the rest of their life. Many of the cases I see in my practice have been to dozens of other doctors before they find themselves in my clinic. I'm writing this book not just to get the message out to patients about these powerful treatments but also two other healthcare providers. My hope is that one day these treatments will be more widely available.

HOW FUNCTIONAL CRANIAL RELEASE WORKS AND ITS ROLE IN TREATMENT OF THE BODY & BRAIN

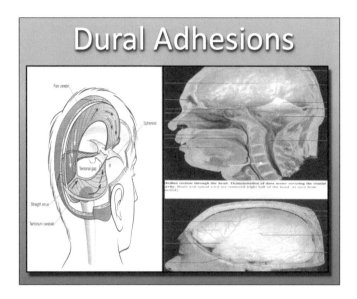

Part of the theory behind the use of Functional Cranial Release (FCR) is the targeting of unstable, fixated dysfunctional parts of the cranium and restrictions in the connective tissue that wraps around the brain and spinal cord called the Dura Mater. The balloon manipulation component is directed towards a specific bone in the center of the skull called the sphenoid bone. The sphenoid bone acts like a central hinge to the entire skull structure. The correct placement of the sphenoid bone allows the remaining parts of the cranium to become balanced, as optimally as possible. When discussing FCR and an endo nasal balloon adjustment, the sphenoid bone must be considered as the main target that the balloon is affecting. The sphenoid bone happens to be an essential structure of the skull because all of the cranium bones (except two -the nasal bones) converge and touch the sphenoid bone.

There are over 30 joints in the human skull, jaw, and face. These joints have stem cells just like the joints where the teeth meet the jaw. Not only are these joints slightly mobile like your teeth, they also allow for change in shape of the entire skull structure. We're going to be diving into this in another chapter but for now I think it's important for you to realize that the skull can change shape and that it has a motion that is necessary for proper health of the brain and the rest of the body.

What FCR does is to decompress and unlock the sphenoid bone and the rest of the cranium. When this is accomplished, proper circulation as well as the clearing of toxins is more efficient, TMJ joint motion is improved, pain in the face and the head can be relieved, and many functional aspects of the brain and central nervous system can be restored. Also, unlocking of the joints in the face and skull helps release restrictions to the connective tissues, which include the dura mater, to release torque or tensions. When this is done, the bony structures increasingly move back to their original shapes and positions and the motion to the skull is restored.

Understanding that the skull moves is crucial to knowing how functional cranial release works. Most people do not really know or get informed about the movement of the skull. The skull is made up of several different bones, and these bones all fit together, just like the teeth fit into the jaw.

As I stated the skull changes shape with time, just like our teeth. This movement of the skull brings about a mechanism that contributes to a pumping action that scientists believe improves the production of the cerebrospinal fluid that bathes the nervous system bringing nutrients such as glucose, proteins, oxygen and neurotransmitters. This fluid and nutrients allow for the proper function of the brain and, in turn, the entire body. Understanding the theory behind Functional Cranial Release depends on knowledge about a connective tissue – the dura mater. The dura mater wraps around the brain and spinal cord where it anchors at the bottom of the spine.

The cerebrospinal fluid (CSF) of the brain and spinal cord acts as a cushion and buffer, preventing the brain and spinal cord from getting injured. The CSF also helps to remove wastes like tau and beta amyloid, drugs, and many other substances from the brain due to its connection to the immune and lymph systems. Also, CSF is responsible for transporting neurotransmitters and nutrients to various parts of the brain. A compressed or distorted skull structure will hamper the rhythmic movement or flow of the CSF, which can lead to the accumulation of metabolic waste products or the lack of required nutrients. The use of Functional Cranial Release to create an optimal, correct skull structure will optimize the flow of the CSF and facilitate the removal of waste products and a more robust distribution of nutrients to the brain and spinal cord.

When the cranial structure collapses, there are several consequences. These consequences range from effects on the oxygenation of the brain and the spinal cord to postural influences, and distribution of the cerebrospinal fluid. Also, since the brain controls the functions of the body, the neural system that controls the entire body is affected. This presents as real-life health problems.

Functional Cranial Release improves nasal breathing and airflow into higher areas within the nostrils. We are going to take a much deeper dive into how breathing through your nose improves oxygen uptake in later chapters. Besides this, as we just described it also improves the normal pumping activity inherent to all humans, that is the cranial rhythm. Both of these actions help to restore the brain's ability to auto-oxygenate. The ability of the brain to oxygenate itself will go a long way in keeping the nervous system healthy.

As previously mentioned, FCR makes use of neurological testing. This kind of testing helps the physician to determine the pathways and the brain centers that might be over-firing or performing at lesser efficiency. FCR incorporates several diagnostic techniques. This involves the examination of:

- Eye movements and reflexes
- Somatotopic Maps and Saccadometry
- Muscles or motor system
- Autonomic Stability
- Circulatory, sensory, and vestibular systems and ability to balance

And more.

WHAT DOES AN FCR TREATENT LOOK LIKE?

Before the commencement, a functional cranial release treatment, the nervous system, and brain structure are examined to ensure that the patient's condition is appropriate for treatment. Then functional neurological examinations are performed. Prior to the treatment a balance test is then carried out to know how the patient is to positioned on the table. This test also tells the exact placement of the balloon.

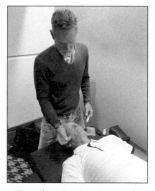

FCR examinations also help to figure out the hemisphericity that is, the balance between the right and left side of the brain. If the brain functioning is higher on one side than the other, it may cause much imbalance. FCR tries to accomplish symmetry in brain hemispheres.

Treating Dr Joe Mercola

Many times, cases will be addressed using the following aspects of physical medicine.

- Specific Adjustments and Functional Brain Exercises
- Soft tissue manipulations of the jaw, neck and around skull.
- Eye and head patterns and eye and head exercises.
- Vestibular Rehab Technique and Work on the VOR or Vestibular Occular Response.
- Canalith repositioning or Eply's Maneuver (often needed)
- Guided meditation prior to the adjustment using a gratitude intention to bring in a spiritual healing mechanism. (more in Chapter 13 on Bliss Release)

Each of these modalities depends on the specific needs of the patient.

FCR is known to fix health issues at the very source. There are differences between trying to manage the symptoms of an ailment and actually correcting the problem. FCR finds the source of the problem and utilizes techniques that help the body to heal itself. Since

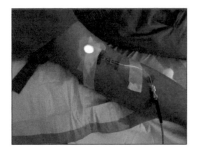

most health problem arises from the brain and nervous system, keeping them healthy will go a long way in keeping the whole body healthy.

The small balloon is gently placed through the nasal passage in a specific area. It is important to adequately determine the specific area because the placement of the balloon affects the sphenoid bone. Functional Cranial Release, therefore, works by adjusting both the bones of the skull but also the release of the deep connective tissues called the dura mater.

In our practice over the years, we've began incorporating many other modalities such as hyperbaric oxygen therapy, CVAC, PEMF, acoustic wave therapy (TRT), regenerative medicine and such as PRP or stem cell therapy to the TMJ, intravenous ozone (RejuvenOX, 10 pass, LumeBlue, EBO3), IV vitamin C, intravenous laser, peptide therapy, a 4-day fasting protocol called MitoFast as well as detox and other various nutritional and naturopathic approaches.

In my practice I often see some of the most complicated cases with afflictions such as Lyme, mold illness, chronic viral infections, toxicity with heavy metals and chemicals, chronic undiagnosed conditions and degenerative neurologic conditions such as Parkinson's, Alzheimer's and TBI. This is why I have to incorporate some of the most advanced techniques available and put them together and very specific ways for each of these different cases.

Don't get me wrong I see my share of simple cases that are chronic sinusitis, simple TMJ or headache cases, simple neck pain patients and many of these cases will do well with just simply the structural component to FCR.

All these combine to ensure that the cranium, and the body returns to its normal state and is functioning at its maximal potential. I will be taking a deeper dive into how I incorporate many of these other alternative and even exotic therapies into my treatments in later chapters.

We have now developed the most advanced system for inner ear regeneration called SunaVae and you can find out more about this at SunaVea. com. SunaVae is a system of inner ear regeneration where the inner ear is injected with stem cells and then a series of laser treatments is directed into the inner ear to repair the damage created by the stress of aging, sound stress injuries and infection injuries which have an impact on the hair cells inside the coclea. Endo- Nasal is a great way to improve circulation and drainage from the head and inner ears through improving lymphatics, cranial rhythm, and reducing dural adhesion's within the cranial structure.

Precautions to Consider

Precautions to Consider When Doing Endo-Nasal Therapy.

- Hemophiliacs
- Patients on blood Thinners
- Nasal Fistulas
- Aneurysm
- Recent Nasal Fractures (w/n 6 wks.)
- Previous Facial Surgeries - Surgical Plates
- Severe Cranial Osteoporosis
- Very high BP (possible hemorrhagic stroke)
- Emotionally unstable patients who can't tolerate procedure
- Allergies to Latex (Although I've not seen this be a problem personally)
- Choanal Atresia's OR Concha Bullosa

REFERENCES

1. Thomas Lim (n.d) Functional Cranial Release (FCR) [Online] https://www.lifesystemschiro-practic.com/functional-cranial-release.html (Accessed 01/08/2020)

2. Lieurance J. (2011) Functional Cranial-Release Explained [Online] https://vimeo.com/19888772 (Accessed 30/07/2020)

3. Loewen J. (2020) Functional Neurology: What It Is and What Patients Need to Know [Online] https://www.cognitivefxusa.com/blog/functional-neurology-vs-neurology-what-you-need-to-know (Accessed 01/08/2020)

4. Traster (2019) What is Functional Neurology [Online] https://youtu.be/8Bx3-N0ZSC4 (Accessed 30/07/2020)

5. Frank (n.d) Neurocranial Restructuring (NCR) [Online] https://www.frankclinic.com/neuro-cranial-restructuring--ncr- (Accessed 30/07/2020)

6. Lieurance J. (2011) Functional Cranial Release Lecture [Online] https://advancedrejuvena-tion.us/dr-johns-lecture-on-functional-cranial-release-on-feb-11/ (Accessed 01/08/2020)

7. Lieurance J. (n.d) How Functional Cranial Release Improves Frontal Lobe Activity In Our Brain [Online] https://www.naturalstacks.com/blogs/news/How-Functional-Cranial-Release-Improves-Frontal-Lobe-Activity-In-Our-Brain (Accessed 03/08/2020)

8. Lieurance J. (2011) Learn Functional Cranial Release [Online] https://vimeo.com/25502433 (Accessed 30/07/2020)

9. Lieurance J. (2011) Dr. John Lieurance Introduces FCR [Online] https://vimeo.com/25789589 (Accessed 30/07/2020)

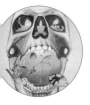

3

RELATIONSHIP OF THE SKULL, TEETH & BREATHING PATTERNS

It's a bit difficult to wrap your head around this subject, no pun intended, until you understand how the skull works and how your teeth realate to a healthy skull. There is a relationship between the skull, teeth, breathing and sleep. Notable men in the field, Dr. Weston Price and Dr. Raymond Silkman where able to see this early on and documented these findings.

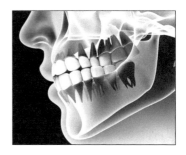

ABOUT THE SKULL STRUCTURE

The skull houses the most important systems in the body, the brain. The brain is the seat of our cognitive part and non congitive part of the nervous (brain) also the endocrine (pituitary gland and the hypothalamus) systems.[Alcamo 2003]

There is a general misconception that the skull is synonymous with the cranium. The skull is not the same as the cranium. It is the bony structure that forms the head of all verte-brates. The cranium, however, is the upper part of the skull. Together with the cranium, the skull contains the movable (mandible). The cranium only has immovable bones.[Alcamo I. 2003] Are they immovable though?

It contains both the freely movable (mandible) and slightly movable (cranium) bones. Twenty-two bones make up the skull. Out of these 22, all but just the two lacrimal bones articulate with the sphenoid bone. [Becker 2020]

The sphenoid bone is one of the most important because it is the central hinge for the movement called cranial rhythm. The skull is a well thought out machine with specific articular surfaces where the bones come together in certain ways to facilitate various types of motion.

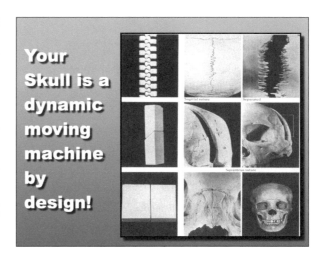

Your Skull is a dynamic moving machine by design!

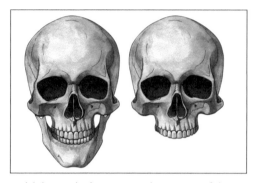

There are eight cranial bones with the most important being the maxilla and the sphenoid bone. The maxilla is important because of its connection with other bones of the skull. It's position is critical in the development of the cranium and tactical bones. [Silkman R. 2006] There are 2 of these on the right and left side and they are the bones that hold our upper teeth and these bones collapse when we mouth breath. The sphenoid bone is important because of its central orientation and importance with cranial rhythm. [Silkman R. 2006]

These sphenoid bone is the most influential bone besides the ethmoid when we perform the endonasal balloon manipulations process. Their flexibility and orientation are critical in the proper development and the overall functionality of the cranium.

These bones come together in 3 different types of fibrous joints: sutures, syndesmoses, and gomphoses. Sutures are found only in the skull and possess short fibers of connective tissue that hold the skull bones in place. Sutures are fibrous joints found only in the skull. [Russell W 2020]

The Mandible

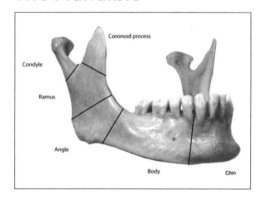

The mandible or lower jaw is the movable part of the skull designed with unique joint movements. One interesting thing about the mandible is that it has both the hinge and sliding joints, unlike other bony structures. [Silkman R. 2006]

The development of the mandible is a critical process in the skull formation. When the lower jaw does not develop well, there is an alteration in its position. The mandible becomes a sunken instead of a protruding. This will, in turn, affect the development of the mandible's joints and the movement of the disc.[Silkman R. 2006]

The Teeth

Teeth have joints as they fit into both the mandible and the maxilla. They are anchored into their sockets within the bony jaws by the periodontal ligaments. This is a gomphosis type of fibrous joint. That's right! Your tooth sits in the bone as a "joint"! We don't think that our teeth have joints like our knee or hip or shoulder, but this is the reality.

It is also the reality that there are multiple joints and articulations throughout the skull. Teeth can move over time and become croocked or become straighter through the use of braces. So can your skull's bones. Of course, this can work either for or against us. This is why a techgnique such as FCR or any other endo-nasal treatment can actually change the shape of your skull and create a healthier skull that's naturally wider so you have better air ways and also works to provide better cirulation of nutrients to your nervous system.

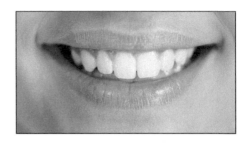

DISORDERS OF THE SKULL & TEETH AND EFFECT ON BREATHING & SLEEP

There are two disorders related to the skull and teeth: cranial collapse and teeth crowding. One is by artificial alteration of the skull shape, while the other occurs due to skull development problems. These disorders are responsible for several health conditions related to breathing and sleep.

In this section, I will discuss the two disorders of the skull, their causes, and a brief explanation of their effects on our health.

Disorders of the Skull and Teeth

The two disorders that I will discuss are cranial collapse and teeth crowding. Cranial collapse is an artificial alteration of the cranium, while teeth crowding is a problem with the mandible development. The two disorders are very important because they can result in conditions such as mouth breathing.

Cranial Collapse

At birth, our cranium is very malleable and has many areas that are not ossified. This allows the cranium to be flexible to fit through the vaginal canal safely.

As I mentioned earlier, the result is a cranium that looks like a fine functioning machine with various joints that articulate and move in

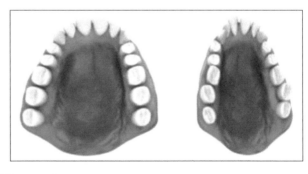

multiple positions, rotations, and sliding motions.

We now also know this is true for the teeth as they fit into the skull, and they are all considered joints.

Most people do not know that the cranium can also move and change its shape. Evidence of this is with an ancient practice of artificial skull deformation.

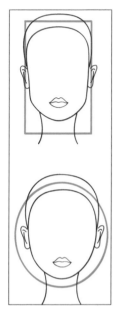

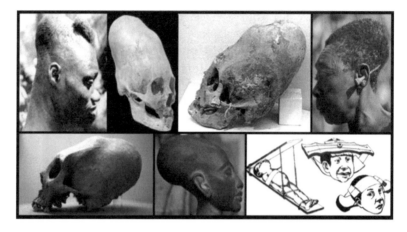

The earliest evidence of skull binding was found in a written record from 400 BC in Hippocrates's description of 'the long head's' (also known as the Macrocephali). Hippocrates believed the practice must have started with them. [Jones S 1923]

Teeth Crowding

When a cranial collapse occurs, the maxillary bone collapses the mouth's roof, or the pallet raises like a tent being raised. It moves up into the nasal passage and also pulls the upper teeth into a narrower position.

The lower teeth will also be affected as they often follow this movement. This results in a situation where you have crowded teeth and a narrow nasal passage.

> ### HIPPOCRATES'S DESCRIPTION ON THE TOPIC OF THIS TRIBE:
>
> *"It is thus with regard to the usage: immediately after the child is born, and while its head is still tender, they fashion it with their hands, and constrain it to assume a lengthened shape by applying bandages and other suitable contrivances whereby the spherical form of the head is destroyed, and it is made to increase in length."*
>
>
>
> *This practice has been seen in many ancient cultures, such as the Mayans, Egyptian, Incan, and Sumerian. Nowadays, it is seen in the Mangbetu tribe. [Agelarakis A 1993]*

After the teeth formation process, there must be a normal alignment of the lower and upper jaw teeth. The proper alignment is visible in the upper jaw's teeth fitting over the lower jaw's teeth and the molar grooves in the upper and lower jaw fitting together.

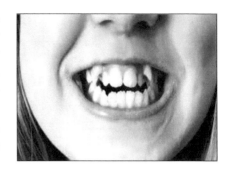

The upper jaw and lower jaw arrangement ensure that our upper teeth cannot bite our lips, and the lower teeth protect our tongue.

Teeth crowding is a condition in which there is not enough space in the mouth for permanent teeth to grow. This lack of space leads to the overlapping of teeth seen as crooked teeth. The severity of the condition can be grouped into three categories, which are:

- *Mild Crowding*

This type of crowding is when the anterior teeth in the upper or lower jaw become slightly rotated.

- *Moderate Crowding*

This type of crowding occurs when two or more anterior teeth overlap in the upper or lower jaw.

- *Severe Crowding*

This is the most extreme case, and it is evident as a severe overlapping of the anterior teeth in the upper and lower jaw.

Causes of Teeth Crowding

Unlike cranial collapse, crowded teeth occur due to an error during the lower and upper jaw development. It is surprising to look at the various causes of these developmental challenges we face in modern civilization.

Modern living brought a host of health problems: *narrowed faces, crowded teeth,* reduction in immunity, and degenerative disease.

When scientists have looked at the Aborigines and our late ancestors, their craniums and pallet architecture were wide. Also, anthropological studies of skulls being dug up demonstrate how much wider cranial structure was. What is it that's happening during our modern life that is contributing to this?

The Type of Food we Eat & Cranial Structural Influence

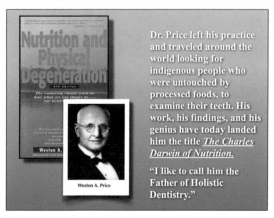

Dr. Price left his practice and traveled around the world looking for indigenous people who were untouched by processed foods, to examine their teeth. His work, his findings, and his genius have today landed him the title *The Charles Darwin of Nutrition.*

"I like to call him the Father of Holistic Dentistry."

Weston A. Price

Based on the type of food we eat, there is a trend in teeth development. In this context, the two types of food are:

—   **Traditional Foods:** These are foods that are grown and free from artificial sugar and other artificial nutrients.

—   **Modern foods:** These are processed foods containing a considerable amount of sugar and other materials.

Weston Price discovered an increase in processed sugar and other poor nutrient-poor content in modern-day foods. People eating modern foods have narrower skull structures compared to those eating traditional food. [Price W. 1938]

The reason for this is because traditional food has more nutrients than the modern ones. Also, the absorption of nutrients by the body is easier, which improves the development of the bones and teeth.

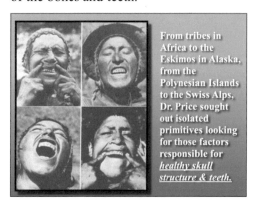

From tribes in Africa to the Eskimos in Alaska, from the Polynesian Islands to the Swiss Alps, Dr. Price sought out isolated primitives looking for those factors responsible for *healthy skull structure & teeth.*

Foods with refined grains and sugars can harm the body. The glucose is so quickly absorbed into the blood, and over time, the body has a hard time clearing glucose. Since glucose has inflammatory and corrosive properties, it can lead to harm.

This is why we work so hard metabolically using insulin to pull and store the blood glucose away in the body. When glucose becomes excessive, we store this as fat.

There are many health consequences downstream from this type of diet, such as chronic allergies, autoimmune disease, inflammatory gut disease, diabetes, neurologic inflammation, and overall poor health. [Della Corte K. et al. 2018]

Effects of Diet on Your Skull

Eating artificial sugar-containing foods is a major cause of teeth crowding, but it can also lead to inflammation in the body. I consider the sinuses and nasal passages as the canary in the coal mine. As far as there is inflammation in the body, often, the sinuses are inflamed.

When there is inflammation through the nasal passage, it creates negative pressure, sums the maxilla into itself, and raises the pallet into the sinus cavity. This then leads to a more restricted and collapsed nasal passage and poor draining sinuses. [Tim Helliwell 2010]

Using the analogy, you're either a swamp or a river. This situation leans more towards the swamp, which, as we know, bacteria, viruses, and other microbes, love a more stagnant wet environment, such as a swamp. This microbial overdrive then causes more inflammation, causing more cranial collapse,  causing more inflammation, and you get the picture. [Tim Helliwell 2010]

Another consideration is that many of these traditional foods, since they are not refined, are still maintained as they were when they came out of the ground. This means that when we chew these raw, natural foods they are harder and will impose more mechanical stress through the teeth, the jaw end of the cranium. This will trigger more activity for cranial bones to develop, and this is another component thought to contribute to the poor development of the modern skull.

Effects of Cranial Collapse and Teeth Crowding

The major effect of cranial collapse and teeth crowding on the body system is mouth breathing. I will explain the concept briefly before discussing it extensively in the next chapter.

Mouth Breathing

Mouth breathing is a process in which people use the mouth primarily for breathing. Using this technique, we do not humidify the air, which is a necessary part of respiration [Harari D. et al. 2010].

Therefore, they show the following signs:

– Chapped lips with a visible vermilion border

– Dark baggy eyes due to the pool up of deoxygenated blood at the dark region

– Short attention span

People using this technique are prone to several conditions because we do not normally breathe through the mouth. Examples of such conditions are sleep apnea, brain degeneration, learning difficulty, poor restorative sleep, Attention-deficit/hyperactivity disorder (ADHD).

REFERENCES

1. Alcamo, I. Edward (2003). "Anatomy Coloring Workbook." The Princeton Review. pp. 22–25. ISBN 9780375763427.

2. Becker C (2020) *"The Skull"* [Online] Available at https://www.kenhub.com/en/library/anatomy/the-skull

3. Silkman R. (2006) *"Is it Mental, or is it Dental?"* [Online] Available at https://www.westona-price.org/health-topics/dentistry/is-it-mental-or-is-it-dental/

4. Russell W., Russell M. (2020) *"Anatomy, Head and Neck, Coronal Suture"* [Online] Available at https://www.ncbi.nlm.nih.gov/books/NBK526011/#:~:text=part.%5B1%5D-,Structure%20and%20Function,the%20skull%20to%20become%20smaller.

5. Price W. (1938) *"Nutrition and Physical Degeneration"* [Online] Available at http://gutenberg.net.au/ebooks02/0200251h.html

6. Della Corte K.W, Perrar I., Penczynski K.J., Schwingshackl L., Herder C., Anette E Buyken A.E., (2018) *"Effect of Dietary Sugar Intake on Biomarkers of Subclinical Inflammation: A Systematic Review and Meta-Analysis of Intervention Studies."* Available at https://pubmed.ncbi.nlm.nih.gov/29757229/

7. Tim Helliwell (2010) *"Inflammatory diseases of the nasal cavities and paranasal sinuses."* Available at https://www.ncbi.nlm.nih.gov/pmc/articles/PMC7172334/

8. Harari D., Redlich M., Miri S., Hamud T, Gross M. (2010). *"The effect of mouth breathing versus nasal breathing on dentofacial and craniofacial development in orthodontic patients."* Laryngoscope. 120(10):2089-93. PMID: 20824738.

9. Agelarakis, A. (1993). *"The Shanidar Cave Proto-Neolithic Human Population: Aspects of Demography and Paleopathology."* Human Evolution. 8 (4): 235–253. doi:10.1007/bf02438114

10. Jones W. H. S., *"Hippocrates of Cos (1923) [ca. 400 BC] Airs, Waters, and Places, Part 14"* Vol. 147, pp. 110–111 http://www.loebclassics.com/view/hippocrates_cos-airs_waters_places/1923/pb_LCL147.111.xml?rskey=NcreTt&result=1&mainRsKey=ZaPSey

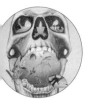

MOUTH BREATHING: A RESULT OF POOR SKULL & TEETH DEVELOPMENT

Quality breathing is among the most important attributes humans need to lead a healthy, vital, and robust life. By breathing, we introduce oxygen into our lungs. The oxygen goes into our bloodstream then to body cells to make energy.

We make energy by converting glucose using oxygen into ATP, the energy currency of body cells. The two most metabolically sensitive organs in your body are the brain and your heart. When breathing becomes compromised, they are the first to show signs of stress.

Breathing is both voluntary and involuntary, controlled involuntarily by the autonomic nervous system. The autonomic nervous system is always hard at work, beating your heart, controlling digestion, and regulating your respiration rate without your conscious effort. Breathing is also voluntarily controlled. Therefore, you can hold your breath whenever you please.

Because of this dual connection, breathing is unique. This can be used to your advantage to strengthen the autonomic nervous system, as we will discuss in this chapter. Many people spend too much time breathing through mouths and over-breathing, and we will take a deep dive into why these are problems and how they can be corrected.

There are structural aspects that provide healthy breathing through your rib cage and pelvis up to your cranium and nasal passages. We already explained a little about the structural side in the last chapter, but we will look into the neurology aspect and its effect on breathing.

We will be looking at the research done by Price Pottenger Nutrition Foundation and the work of both Dr. Weston Price and Dr. Francis M. Pottenger, Jr. The two are both early pioneers in revealing the connection between how we live, what we eat, and our facial bone development.

Dr. Weston Price

Mouth Breathing

As discussed in the previous chapter, improper development of the skull and teeth causes mouth breathing. Normally, breathing should occur via the nose due to some important processes such as humidification and vasodilation that take place when breathing occurs. However, due to some voluntary and involuntary actions, people now breathe via two routes; mouth breathing and nasal breathing [Catlin G. 1882].

The body's anatomy ensures and stipulates the nose as a structure for breathing and mouth for eating. However, it has changed. Many people are now becoming chronic mouth breathers. You might have seen them before, or you might also be one. *They have the following signs and symptoms:*

- Chapped lips with a visible vermilion border

- Dark baggy eyes due to the pool up of deoxygenated blood at the dark region

- Chronically tired and neurologically compromised with a short attention span

Why You Should Not Mouth Breathe
Humidification and Filtering of Particles

There will be no humidification of air passing through the nasal passage if you engage only in mouth breathing. Besides dry air is irritating to our sensitive mucous membranes in our upper respiratory system, when our membranes dry up, they do not function properly.

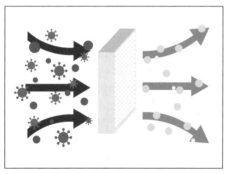

erly. The moisture allows for a clean upper respiratory system and an effective detoxification process [Turowski J., 2016].

We all know that when we get an upper respiratory infection and develop a productive cough, we can clear many of the bacteria compared to a dry environment.

Nasal breathing provides your immune system with an extra layer of defense as it filters mold, allergens, bacteria, and viruses from the air before it enters into the lungs.

Consider this, you have a cat, and it constantly licks its fur. The saliva then dries and then becomes airborne with the dander. If this is floating around the house, and you have a child breathing through their mouth, there might not be a dander filtering. It can easily enter the bloodstream and can trigger an immune response.

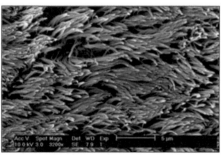

Microscopic view of Nasal Calia

The cells in the nasal passages secrete mucus and have tiny hairlike projections called **cilia**. Usually, the mucus traps incoming dirt particles, and the cilia moved them to the front of the nose or down the throat to be removed from the airway. This process is important to clean the air before it goes to your lungs.

In his book "Hyperventilation Syndrome," Dr. Robert Fried said that the nose would clear these particles within 15 minutes in a normal situation, but if they make it into the lungs, it takes 60 to 120 days to get rid of these particles.

These particles are going to trigger the immune system, which is an inflammatory system. When the immune system is chronically triggered in this fashion, it can lead to autoimmune diseases, multiple chemical sensitivities, nervous system issues, arthritis, asthma, and chronic fatigue.

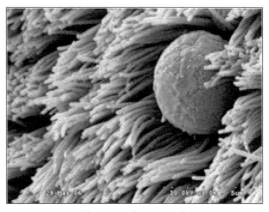

Cilia removing a particle

We also produce a large amount of nitric oxide in our nasal passage through colonies of bacteria that live there. When we breathe in through our nasal passage, nitric oxide compounds circulate through our bodies.

Nitric Oxide Synthesis

Nitric oxide is responsible for increasing arterial oxygen intake observed in people using nasal breathing instead of the mouth breathing.

Nitric oxide functions well here because it is a vasodilator. It relaxes the smooth muscles of the lungs and arteries, thereby increasing oxygen intake. Using nasal breathing maintains our blood vessels and lungs' openness, further enhancing the oxygen that we take in [Yoon Y. 2000].

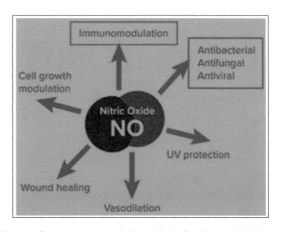

Nitric oxide is also anti-microbial, protecting us from acute and chronic infections. It kills viruses, bacteria, and some parasites. Studies even detected its ability to restrict some SARS coronavirus's growth by inhibiting RNA synthesis and viral protein production [Åkerströ̈m S. et al. 2004].

This has led to research on whether it can be used in treating Covid-19. People who nasal breathe are not as likely to suffer from viral infection experienced by people performing mouth breathing. [Schairer. D et al. 2012]

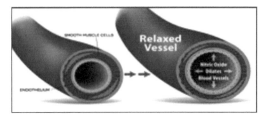

Wider blood vessels mean more oxygen absorption.

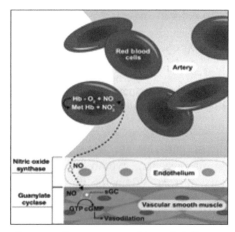

Mouth breathing will also dry out the teeth and gums and decrease saliva production. Saliva is critical to wash away bacteria in our mouths and for neutralizing acid. Without it, tooth decay and cavities increase. Additionally, dry mouth is one of the leading causes of gum disease, leading to other health issues such as heart

Improved oxygen carrying and delivery into your body.

disease. Any chronic inflammation anywhere in the body can lead to health-related problems down the road, and inflammation in the oral cavity is a very common cause of chronic disease in the body.

Over Breathing

Many times, mouth breathers feel like they can get more air through their mouth. Even athletes sometimes primarily ventilate through their mouths when they show signs of air shortage.

The primary trigger for oxygen shortage is an increase of CO_2 in the bloodstream. Red blood cells primarily carry oxygen through hemoglobin, where it is picked up in the lungs to be

carried throughout the body. When oxygen level decreases, CO_2 levels increase in the blood.

There are centers in the brain taking input from carotid bodies, which are nerve bundles in your neck's blood vessels that control how you feel in terms of oxygen shortage.

I find it fascinating that this brain area can be hyper-responsive when this system gets used to having an abundance of oxygen. Breath-holding has been used in athletics, free diving, and many other disciplines to enhance athletic performance. Part of the benefit of pushing the body into an air shortage situation is that it resets these receptors, slowing down respiration.

For the most part, most of us are over-breathing because we are not paying attention to this mechanism, and we are strengthening it. Later in the section, we will talk about various exercises that can reset this and allow you to become more comfortable with less oxygen. Therefore, this behavior will decrease anxiety and normalize a healthier, slower respiratory rate.

In an article called *"CO_2, brainstem chemoreceptors and breathing,"* it is beautifully summed up. "The regulation of breathing relies upon chemical feedback concerning oxygen and carbon dioxide levels." The carotid bodies, which detect oxygen, provide tonic excitation to brainstem respiratory neurons under normal conditions and dramatic excitation if oxygen level falls [Nattie E. 1999].

Feedback for CO_2 involves the carotid body and receptors in the brainstem, known as central chemoreceptors. Small increases in CO_2 produce large increases in breathing." [Nattie E. 1999]

When you breathe through your nose, arterial oxygen uptake increases by 10%. CO_2 in the blood also increases. There is a partial pressure between CO_2 and oxygen in the blood, and CO_2 will stimulate the release of oxygen from hemoglobin so that oxygen can then move into your tissues and cells, providing health and energy. [Nattie E. 1999]

When we over breathe, we do not allow enough CO_2 content in the blood. Therefore, we will have less oxygen being liberated from hemoglobin into our tissues, which leads to lower oxygen utilization. Therefore, if we over breathe, we will reduce the amount of CO_2, whereas CO_2 is vitally important within the body. Therefore, mouth breathers will over breathe and exhale too much CO_2. [Nattie E. 1999]

People primarily using mouth breathing are more prone to various health challenges, as the process is not the normal state of a healthy individual. Some examples that are obvious and well documented in medical and orthodontic literature include: Sleep disorders (which we will discuss extensively next chapter), brain degeneration, learning difficulty, Attention-Deficit/Hyperactivity Disorder (ADHD), and heart disease.

A health strategy to improve nasal breathing is so simple yet is so widely overlooked by many healthcare providers.

Mouth Breathers have lower oxygen for these reasons:

- Lower CO_2 levels that decrease oxygen release from hemoglobin.
- Lower nitric oxide uptake, which constricts the nasal and lung tissue and capillaries throughout the body, lowering the amount of blood and oxygen that can be absorbed through the systems.

Nasal Respiration Entrains Human Memory, Behavior, Limbic Activity & Modulates Cognitive Function.

Breathing links our olfactory system to what's called "Respiratory Rhythms" that draw air through the nose. Slow oscillations from nasal breathing activate at the rate same as breathing (~2–12 Hz). This links the olfactory bulb and cortex through specific phases of the respiratory cycle. These dynamic rhythms are thought to regulate cortical excitability and coordinate network interactions, helping to shape olfactory coding, memory, and behavior.

In a study, they collected intracranial EEG data from rare patients with medically intractable epilepsy, and found evidence for respiratory entrainment of local field potential activity in human piriform cortex, amygdala, and hippocampus. These effects diminished when breathing was diverted to the mouth, highlighting the importance of nasal airflow for generating respiratory oscillations. Finally, behavioral data in healthy subjects suggest that breathing phase systematically influences cognitive tasks related to amygdala and hippocampal functions [Zelano et al., 2016]

This is from the same paper in 2016 "Breathing is a vital rhythm of mammalian life, replenishing the bloodstream with oxygen and eliminating carbon dioxide with essential regularity." Although the respiratory drive is generated by conditional bursting pacemaker neurons in the brainstem (Smith et al., 1991, 2009; Garcia et al., 2011), its pace is not fixed: a variety of emotional and cognitive states, including anxiety (Boiten, 1998), stress (Suess et al., 1980), and exploratory behavior (Welker, 1964; Kay and Freeman, 1998; Verhagen et al., 2007; Evans et al., 2009; Vlemincx et al., 2011; Huijbers et al., 2014), can all modify the rate and depth of breathing. The alternative idea that respiratory phase exerts a direct impact on emotion and cognition, is unknown. The fact that the olfactory system is closely linked with limbic brain regions mediating emotion, memory, and behavior (Carmichael et al., 1994; LeDoux, 2000; Eichenbaum et al., 2007) suggests a robust pathway by which nasal breathing could even shape rhythmic electrical activity in downstream limbic areas, with corresponding effects on cognitive functions.

Alternate Nasal Breathing

Furthermore, the side that nasal breathing is working best or is blocked might matter. In this paper, based on "EEG signatures change during unilateral Yogi nasal breathing" the autonomic nervous system seems to be wired to which nostril one is breathing through."

"Yogic practices suggest, and scientific evidence demonstrates, that right-nostril breathing is involved with relatively higher sympathetic activity (arousal states), while left-nostril breathing is associated with a relatively more parasympathetic activity (stress-alleviating state). The objective of this study was to further explore this laterality by controlling

> *Basically, what they are saying is the that your breathing can be changed through various emotional and physical states such as if your are anxious, then your respiration might increase. If you are calm, your respiratory rate is slower. This is a system that seems to be linked the opposite way as well whereas your breathing can be a trigger to train your brain in certain ways. It is mostly activated through the olfactory sensors, and this means the air must be moving through your nose so that this system works. When it is not, these pacemaker neurons in the brain stem don't get the activation necessary to keep your limbic brain regions mediating emotion, memory, and behavior healthy.*

nasal airflow and observing patterns of cortical activity through encephalographic (EEG) recordings." [Naisi et al., 2022] Just consider if someone had an injury or an abnormality of their nasal passages where they cannot breath through one side of their nasal passage. Like myself where I was only able to breathe through my left side (thank God it wasn't my right as we can see the sympathetics would have been activated

which would be a more challenging action for most people as we are mostly in a sympathetic dominant state anyway).

Calming down the Sympathetic's with Zen.

MitoZen.com sells a nasal spray called Zen Meditation mist and it is based on an Amazonian herb called Mapacho which has a strong burn for a short time after one sniffs it through the nasal passage. It can be done with both nostrils, or just one side if a certain state is desired. I use this product in the clinic for these reasons and most often use the left side activation.

Consider Endo-nasal therapy and how profound this can be for those who have obstruction? Is there a more eloquent way to open the nasal passages than this procedure? It is safe it, takes little time, and the results are very immediate. Consider surgeries, CPAC, and virtually any other method and you should come to the same conclusion that endonasal really holds a valuable place in our healthcare model for these types of cases. I would offer that the vast majority of the population has some sort of collapse of the facial bones which is causing some interference in this system. That's a bold statement to say that the majority of people out there would benefit from an endonasal adjustment, however that is most likely the case. Often, I will see people extremely relaxed yet focused after a treatment with FCR.

Strategies to Improve on Nasal Breathing

Now that we know that we should be breathing through her nose and not our mouth, how do we change this to become more of a nasal breather? There are several techniques available, and it may be best to combine more than one of them for the best results.

First and foremost, the individual needs to be motivated to make this change and understand its consequences. Once we have the involvement and motivation of the individual, then the solution can be possible.

In this section, we're going to discuss taping, CPAP therapy, cranium correction, dietary and food solutions, nasal and sinus hygiene, and various exercises to strengthen the tongue to push back the maxillary bones to widen the skull.

Mouth Taping

One little known strategy to counter mouth breathing is by using mouth taping. While you might be able to correct your breathing technique when awake consciously, you might be able to control it when asleep. I have used this technique with patients successfully for many years, and while it sounded strange to some, it is quite effective and results in much better sleep. There are also chin straps, although I am not a fan of that method.

CPAP Therapy

This therapy uses machines specifically designed to deliver a constant flow of pressure through the nasal passage during sleep. Some CPAP machines have other features as well, such as heated humidifiers. CPAP is the standard of care in our medical system and is NOT the most effective treatment for obstructive sleep apnea. The idea is that mild pressure from the CPAP prevents the airway from collapsing or becoming blocked. [Spafford R., 2017]. The most effective strategy is to address the core causes of the mouth breathing and obstructed nasal airways. This book will give a comprehensive way to work through this problem.

I actually use CPAP as a strategy at one point in my life when I suffered from sleep apnea, but then I did not need it after I received my first endo-nasal balloon treatment. I also addressed food allergies and retrained myself to nasal breath. When using these devices, it can be difficult to get a good night's sleep as they are difficult to forget the plastic attached to your face pushing air. Many patients I have seen over the years suffer poor sleep using them and I have assisted many to get off them for good! They also require a lot of work to keep them clean and sterile and can be a source of biotoxin illness from mold and other pathogens.

Cranium Correction

In the event of considerable nasal passage restriction, consider finding a physician doing endonasal manipulations. And in severe cases, consider power expansion. The use of endonasal and cranial release is useful in the treatment of mouth breathing. *"The procedure involves widening the palate and tilting the head to allow the individual to breathe normally through the nose"* [Silkman R. 2006].

Food Allergies and Proper Diet

There are many different approaches to having a balanced and healthy diet. I have studied them all and have concluded that there is no one perfect solution. Often, it is some sort of rotation with a primary emphasis on some basic principles.

Avoiding Refined Foods

For the most part, we should avoid refined carbohydrates and sugars, vegetable oils (especially when they are being cooked with), dairy, and foods with a high risk of mold contamination, such as peanuts and grains. We should only eat organic produce [Price W. 1938].

Besides glycol phosphate being destructive to the beneficial bacteria or the gut micro-biome, it also has a detrimental effect on the gut's lining. It can lead to leaky gut or increased gut permeability.

Various stressors caused the lining of your gut to lose its integrity. When this happens, various food proteins that are partially metabolized can enter your bloodstream and trigger an immune response. Eventually, these constant triggers will cause the immune system to start mounting a regular defense mechanism against certain foods. This is considered an IgG immune response.

It's not a severe allergy that we see with peanut or shellfish, which manifests immediately as a significant inflammatory reaction. These IgG food sensitivities can be tested through a variety of labs tests. The sensitivities are transient, meaning that your body will reset itself if you avoid such foods for some time [Price W. 1938].

The bottom line is that poor gut health can lead to intestinal permeability and various food sensitivities. This, in turn, can lead to more inflammation in the body evident in restricted nasal passages.

Lectins can also be a significant contributor to inflammation for many people as well. **Lectins** are a family of proteins found in almost all foods, especially legumes and grains. These plants generally produce lectin as a defense mechanism. They are toxic and harmful to individuals consuming them. Consuming **Lectins** will increase gut permeability, inflammation, and autoimmune diseases. For some people, avoiding them can be very beneficial. Cooking can break down a percentage of these lectins.

A ketogenic diet may be very beneficial to someone dealing with a lot of inflammation. Besides being extremely anti-inflammatory, a ketogenic diet can also improve sugar metabolism, weight gain, and neurological health. The ketogenic diet basics involve consuming fats and proteins and a little, if any, carbohydrates. One interesting fact is that our body requires fats and proteins, but we have no absolute carbohydrates requirement. For many, a ketogenic diet is an answer to their prayers, and it is a very safe diet to do when done properly.

Intermittent Fasting

Intermittent fasting is another great strategy for chronic inflammation in the body, where one will restrict eating to a certain level every 24 hours. The idea surrounding this process is that you can't fix the road if there's traffic on it. This means that giving yourself more time throughout 24 hours where food is not traveling through the digestive tract allows it to repair itself and not have to process food continually.

The same thing goes for the liver and kidneys, and pancreas. For thousands of years, fasting has been an important healing strategy in traditional civilization and major religions.

In my clinic, I use three fasting strategies. The first one is what we just described where an individual might restrict their eating to a six-hour or eight-hour window every day, and outside of that time, they will only consume non-caloric substances. Water, coffee, and tea are all allowed as long as there are no cream and sugar additives to those drinks.

The second would be doing a 24 hour fast one day a week where an individual may fast from lunch to lunch. The third, which is more challenging for most people but holds the most benefit, is the 3 to 5 days water fast.

Many times, breathing difficulties can be exacerbated by weight gain, especially around the throat area. This often can be a complicating factor with sleep apnea. I feel between the ketogenic diet and intermittent fasting, they are the best ways to get the body to see fat as a fuel source and start breaking it down and using it as fuel, which leads to less storage of fat as fuel in the body. I have developed a program I call Fast Track Fast. It is a system where I have my patients take 3 phases of supplements that all improve the adaptive signaling of the body from fasting. This adaptive signaling is where all the benefit comes from in fasting. See FastTrackfast.com for more information and an article I wrote on this program. You can also see MitoZen.com and view the fast Track fast Kits we have there.

Nasal and Sinus Hygiene

Often, we don't consider it a ritual to keep our sinuses and nasal passage clean and functioning properly. I have developed a 30-day sinus protocol in my clinic and have found it hugely effective for various health problems. You can find the protocol at OutOfBoxDoc.com. Also, you can email us at Info@mitozen.com and ask for the 30-day sinus protocol. You can also find GlutaStat Mist at MitoZen.com which is the nasal spray used 4 times a day for the 30 days there.

Ask any cocaine user what the quickest route to their brain would be, and they will tell you through the nose. There is a very high absorption rate in the mucous membranes in the nasal passage, which leads directly into your brain and bloodstream.

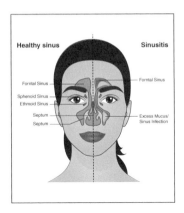

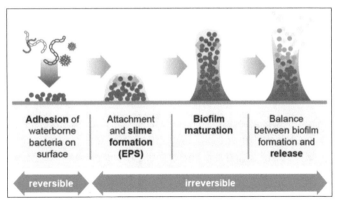

Microbial overgrowth can often occur in the sinus and nasal passage, and these chronic infections secrete toxins. These toxins, also known as endotoxins, are responsible for a variety of diseases [Rawlings B.A. et al. 2013].

They also create a biofilm, which is a sticky substance that protects them from your immune system by harboring them within these sticky protein masses. The problem with these biofilms in the sinuses is that they act as flypaper to collect allergens, pollutants, and mold toxins and spores.

One of the solutions I've seen in the literature for mouth breathers when there is congestion in the sinuses to use decongestants. Keep in mind these decongestants are down-regulating histamine. Histamine is often elevated for a reason, and if we can go upstream, determine the cause and treat that, we will have a much better and safer long-term outcome.[Tim Helliwell 2010]

Decongestants both in the form of nasal sprays and oral pills will never fix the problem. It will only mask the problem and treat the symptom. It is kind of like painting over rust. I've mentioned earlier that the sinuses are like the canary in the coal mine, and if there's chronic inflammation in the body, it can show up with extra blood flow through the sinuses where they get engorged.

Over-breathing can also lead to this if our blood becomes more alkaline. But we could also have an overgrowth of microbes in biofilms or both.

There are three components in my 30-day protocol: a Netti pot, nasal spray, and a nebulizer. A nebulizer is a machine that takes a liquid and puts it into a very fine mist that can then be inhaled and reach the nasal passage sinuses and lungs. A Netti pot is also a device that allows you to flush the sinuses and nasal passages.

The protocol can involve all three, and it depends on how aggressive you want to clear out microbial overgrowth and biofilms from the sinuses and nasal passages. For the milder situation, I can recommend you use a Netti pot once or twice a day.

There can be various anti-microbial substances that can be added to these solutions used in the Netti pot. Things like the GlutaStat solution, colloidal silver, iodine, herbal teas, and grapefruit seed extract can all be added safely as an upgrade to just using only Saline. In my 30-day protocol, we have people use the GlutaStat NS nasal spray outside three times a day. The GlutaStat solution will be nebulized once or twice a day, and then we will have folks use the Netti pot once or twice a day.

GlutaStat is a formula I created, and it is commercially available online at MitoZen.com. It is a powerful yet safe anti-microbial using oregano, sage, clove, Bayleaf, glutathione, NAC, colloidal silver, and a few powerful plant terpenes. Essential oils break up biofilm better than anything you can use and they are also anti-microbial.

A common infection I see in many cases is called MARCoNS (Multiple Antibiotic Resistant Coagulase Negative Staphylococcus) infections that produce an extra sticky biofilm that the bacteria use to protect and hide from the immune system.

This infection is particularly prevalent in Lyme and Mold Illness (CIRS) cases and more often in children. In many cases, with chronic mouth breathing because of a stagnant environment, it might be necessary that there is an intense 30-day protocol and some sort of maintenance until, at some point, the nasal passage opens to provide proper circulation drainage and immune function. Many times, when one first starts this protocol, nasal passages and sinuses might be more inflamed as the body starts to clear these microbes, endotoxins and break down the nasal biofilm. Generally, after a day or two, things improve, so if you attempt this, stick with it.

Get Exercise to Breath Better!

If you are getting any physical activity in resistance training and or cardio, this could greatly affect your body's inflammation, improve sleep, and improve your breathing. What I would recommend is to start with resistive training in the form of what's called super slow training. This is when you do resistive training, usually with machines but you can do it on free weights as well. The key is to go  to total failure. The speed should be such that you hit that failure within 3 minutes. You also don't want to pause at any point and maintain a constant stress to the muscle. This will maximally stress the muscle such that most of the muscle fibers are recruited in the workout whereas only a fraction are in a typical workout. Usually, within 15 to 20 minutes, you can get a very good workout and you can vary your muscle groups and do this 2 times a week only with amazing results.

For Cardio, grizzly bear interval training is among the most effective. What you do is run or cycle at a fast pace or even the fastest you can for 20 seconds and then rest for 10 seconds and do this between six and eight repetitions. This usually only takes 10 to

15 minutes and can be done 2-4 times a week. This strategy is considered high intensity interval training.

Either the super slow or grizzly bear interval is not very time-consuming but doing them 2 to 3 times a week will maintain a healthy body.

Breath Meditation

Meditation can also be a very helpful program to curb mouth breathing and improve nasal breathing. The 36-breath described is a great meditation practice that combines a great breathing exercise with meditation, whereas the focus is completely on only the breath. When thoughts enter the mind, we simply recognize them and refocus our attention back to the breath. This is the point of meditation, recognizing the busy mind and bringing it back to a single point of attention. Don't get frustrated that the mind wanders because this is natural and happens with all of us. With practice,

we get better and better at holding our attention for longer periods. Holding our attention on the breath could be an important part of a program for someone looking to breathe through their nose better as there are many direct and indirect positive health consequences to meditation practice.

Proper Breathing, Over Breathing & Breathing Less to Live Longer and Better!

When I was 11 years old, I woke up in the middle of the night and couldn't breathe. I rushed into my parents' bedroom, desperate for help. They rushed me to the hospital, and that was my first asthma attack experience. Besides having chronic sinusitis as a child, I also suffered severe asthma. I only wish my parents were to have been given this book when I was a child. I would've avoided decades of suffering and health challenges.

Probably the most groundbreaking is the work by the Russian scientist, Buteyko. The idea that many people are not breathing through their nose because their nose is inflamed is no secret. The unique perspective that was first exposed by this Russian doctor is about the buildup of carbon dioxide.

In 1923, Buteyko noted that if you hold your breath, you build up carbon dioxide in the blood, which opens up and decongests the nasal passages. Besides the CO_2 buildup in the blood, other theories support an increase in temperature in the nasal passage when the breath is held and a buildup of nitric oxide. There are probably multiple factors involved, but the bottom line is that the nasal passage becomes less congested when you hold your breath [Bruton A, Lewith GT 2005].

Buteyko's method trains people to slow down their breathing, which results in an improvement in asthma and an opening in the sinuses.

A normal breath should be such that the diaphragm contracts pushing out the belly on the inhale, and the belly is pushed into the spine when you exhale. The diaphragm is the primary muscle of respiration, and often when our bodies are in a stress situation, our breath stays in the upper rib cage, causing stress and tension across the shoulders and in the neck [Wong C. 2020].

Belly breathing or diaphragmatic breathing can be of huge importance to activate a part of your nervous system called the parasympathetic nervous system. I mentioned earlier in the introduction that breathing is both controlled by your autonomic nervous system, which means it's the part of your nervous system that you have no control over, for the most part.

You have two sides to your nervous system, both the sympathetic and parasympathetic. Sympathetic is the fight or flight, and the parasympathetic is the resting and digesting. One of the things I'm sure Weston Price was seeing when he looked at these Aboriginal tribes and saw all of the diseases of modern civilization was the impact of an over activity of the sympathetic nervous system which can be due to chronic inflammation.

The over activation of the sympathetic puts us in a panic state, which decreases circulation to our brain and puts more demand on our cardiovascular system. It does not allow us deep restorative sleep and decreases the circulation and flow of blood to our gut, resulting in intestinal permeability and inflammatory and allergic reaction in the body.

> ## EXPERIMENT
>
> *Let's do this experiment together.*
>
> *Block one side of your nasal passage and take a normal breath, then hold the other nostril and do the same and just notice the difference. Now take a normal breath in through your nose and a normal breath out through your nose and hold your breath while you pinch your nose closed and rock your body back-and-forth gently (you can walk at the same time). Hold your breath comfortably before you start to have air hunger.*
>
>
>
> *Once you begin breathing again, try to control it and slow it down as quickly as possible and repeat this breath-hold for five or six times. Most people will notice that their airway becomes drastically more open.*

We can utilize the voluntary activation of the breath to reach in and exercise the parasympathetic nervous system. Besides strengthening the parasympathetic nervous system when it is more active, it inhibits the sympathetic nervous system. Multiple factors are playing into this as an influence to calm down the sympathetic. It's both voluntary controls, but when we belly breathe, we pool more blood in our abdomen, further stimulating the vagus nerve hardwired to your parasympathetic nervous system [Wong C. 2020].

We need a certain amount of food every day for ideal health. Not too much, not too little. We need a certain amount of water every day, not too much, not too little. We need a certain amount of oxygen for ideal health, not too much, not too little.

Nobody's talking about oxygen and air in this way; however, we have so many stressors changing our breathing patterns in today's world. Processed foods will increase our breathing patterns, as will over-talking, lack of exercising, mental-emotional stress, and nutrient depletion. Toxins such as biotoxins, heavy metals, and human-made chemicals can also trigger stress in the body, which increases the respiration rate.

When we breathe, we are taking in more oxygen, and oxygen is used to make energy. Oxygen is also responsible for oxidation in the body, which is buffered from our antioxidant capacities. If we push our body to process more oxygen than it needs, we increase the oxidation in the body, and there are many diseases and health challenges that will result from over oxidation.

When there is too much oxidation, there will be an increase in cytokines. Cytokines are inflammatory proteins in the body. When it increases, it leads to autoimmune disease, degenerative neurological disease, accelerated aging, fatigue and poor energy, and even cancer [Zhang J. 2009].

EXPERIMENT

I often recommend that all of my patients simply take 15 minutes every day and do the following breathing exercise.

Sit comfortably or lay down. Make sure that your back is straight, and you're not slouched, and your shoulders back. Allow your belly to comfortably relax forward, increasing the curve in your lower back. You're going to begin to inhale at the count of three and exhale to a count of six. This can also be done as a four-second inhale and eight-second exhale.

The important factor here is a slow, relaxed breath where the belly fills up and extends out on the inhale, and the belly is called in towards the lower spine on the exhale.

An animal called a naked mole rat lives deep in the earth and has a very slow respiration rate. This naked mole rat lives up to 30 years old. This is astonishing in light of its cousins, such as normal mice and rats, that only live a couple of years.

They injected these naked mole rats with cancerous cells and found that they were more resistant to cancer. Scientists found that the naked mole rats lived in a very high CO_2 content at a low oxygen content because they are so deep in the ground. The scientist feels that the high CO_2 may be protecting them from oxidative stress making them more resistant to cancer and living longer [Yang Z et al. 2013].

My feeling is that this would translate to humans based on all of the facts taken into account.

Breath Holding Exercises, Hypoxic Training, and how Uncomfortable Stressors can be Game Changers.

Over my 25 years as a physician, I've seen some dramatic changes in medicine as the medical community keep embracing what was once *fringe strategies* to improve health.

Three of these very glaring to me are ozone, cold therapy, and fasting. We have something called a whole-body cryotherapy chamber at our clinic where we cool people down to -250° for three minutes. Besides feeling amazing after the treatment, the therapy stimulates an adaptive mechanism resulting in improved energy production and stress resistance.

Fasting is similar where it allows the body an opportunity to do some housekeeping, it provides a stimulus for the body to become more metabolically flexible to use fat as energy, and lastly, it triggers genes that can lead to one of the most powerful regenerative phasers that researchers have been able to observe.

Lastly, there is ozone, which has been considered very dangerous because it's so oxidative. Ozone is a fused three-oxygen molecule. It is an extremely reactive molecule in the body. When ozone is given intravenously, it produces an adaptive reaction that results in an enhanced immune system and an improved antioxidant buffering system, and it also triggers genes that improve oxygen absorption and utilization in the body.

All three of these are almost counter-intuitive. How often are we encouraged to eat more and to avoid cold exposure? Breathing is the same concept, although our society will often encourage people to take deep breaths and to over-breathe when, in fact, what they need is the opposite.

A man pioneered one of the breathing techniques I have been a fan of for the last five years. He is called Wim Hof or the iceman.

They call him the iceman because he's set world records in his ability to sit in ice water and hike in the snow with only shorts to the top of Kilimanjaro. He was also able to be involved in a study using his breathing technique. There was the neutralization of endotoxins in the body. They also injected him with a toxin that would normally make somebody ill, and Wim Hof neutralizes it through only his breathing [Scott C, 2017].

No doubt that the nitric oxide and CO_2 connection are strong signaling factors for this result. I was able to hold my breath for 5 ½ minutes, which I am very proud of considering my history with severe asthma, much of my childhood and adult life. So how did I do this, you might ask? Well, very simply, I practiced holding my breath. Was it comfortable? No. With my history, particularly with having so many severe asthma episodes, there is a deep fear of being deprived of oxygen. When one holds their breath, besides feeling a panic attack, you'll also start to feel a lot of signaling around the diaphragm telling you to breathe, or you will die. It's one of the more primitive triggers the nervous system has, and it's very difficult to fight against it.

Another strategy I've used is where I've walked, and what I'll do is hold my breath until I hit a certain landmark in my environment, such as a telephone pole. In other words, as I walk possibly in a neighborhood, I might pick a point where I will hold my breath until another point down the road.

There is a great device that I've also used that fits into the mouth called the *Relaxator*. It's a small piece of plastic with a mouthpiece and a dial where you can change the air resistance to flow through the device. This can be placed in the mouth, and it will control and slow your respiration rate. It is a great way to reset the CO_2 receptors and improve breathing patterns. Unfortunately, this is all through the mouth and not the nose.

In 2005, I introduced the ultimate guide to EWOT. This stood for exercise with oxygen therapy and was pioneered by Dr. Manfred von Ardenne out of Germany in the 1930s. Although he called it Oxygen Multi-Step, it is the EWOT principle that he pioneered.

The strategy is now commonly used by many athletes and alternative health practitioners. It involves a large bag filled with oxygen, and the individual will exercise while breathing the hundred percent oxygen coming out of the bag. I'm not a big fan of the basic strategy with only the hundred percent oxygen. I am a fan of utilizing the technology that Live02 has created, where they have retrofitted an oxygen concentrator to fill the lower oxygen to a separate part of this bag. The individual now has a ventilation device covering their face, whereas they can switch from both hypoxic and highly oxygenated air. The protocols

TECHNIQUE

I often recommend Wim Hof's techniques to my patients, and here is the basic technique.

Either sit comfortably on the floor or lay on your back with your arms and legs relaxed. You will take multiple deep breathes in and then relax your breath, allowing the air to leave the lungs.

In other words, there is a deep, forceful inhale, but then there is a relaxation and not a forceful exhale. This can be done through the nose or the mouth. However, it would be preferred to breathe through the nose and out through the mouth.

If this is not easy, then go ahead and do it in and out through the mouth. After you've done about 30 breaths or feel significant tingling in your body, you will then take last deep inhale and exhale completely and hold with the all the air exhaled out of your lungs.

At this point, you want to completely relax every single muscle in your body, noticing any tension in the body and softening it. Try to remain relaxed and calm and hold your breath as long as you can, fighting the urge to breathe and leaning into the uncomfortable sensations as long as you possibly can. Keep in mind you will not die, and you can even monitor your blood oxygen level with an inexpensive finger oxygen monitor device you can buy on Amazon. Sometimes it's fun to see how low you could allow your blood oxygen level to go before the air hunger overtakes you. Some breath instructors would like to bring people down to 85%. I would often use my iPhone and use the stopwatch app, and time my breath holds along with monitoring my blood oxygen for feedback as to how I was progressing. This breath described above should be repeated three times. You should find that your breath-hold time increases dramatically each time you perform the breath. What's happens is that your neurological centers become less and less sensitive to the blood CO_2. This is what happens with cardiovascular exercise as well as these breath holding exercises, you're retraining your central nervous system's tolerance for CO_2.

that I feel are exciting involve exercising with the low oxygen until you land deep into the air hunger, then switching briefly to the high oxygen to recover.

Interval training is a term where exercise will be done in a short bout of intensity followed by a short bout of recovery. Studies have shown that interval training is much more productive than just doing a constant intensity throughout.

Combining interval training with the EWOT using primarily hypoxic air is a fantastic strategy if someone wanted to set this up at their house. Costwise, you're looking at about $3500 to set this up in your home.

One of the simplest methods would be to just practice breath-holding, which can be done anywhere anytime for free.

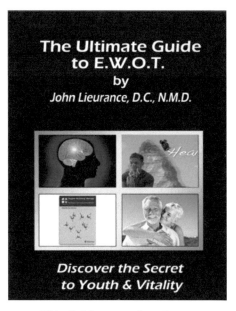

This Guide was written by me in 2005 and might be found at OutOfBoxDoc.com

Mold Exposure and Biotoxin Illness

This section should not be lightly ignored or discounted, as it might be the most important chapter in this book. By filtering through nasal breathing, you will minimize the number of mycotoxins and mold spores that will enter deep into the respiratory system, which, as we know now, can stay up to 60 to 120 days.

If you live in a multi-house, no nasal filtering will prevent the incessant and chronic accumulation and activation of inflammation and immune reactivity in the body. Biotoxins are toxins from biological substances such as from microbes as with bacteria, viruses, and mold. The actual microbe is a biotoxin; however, these microbes will also produce endotoxins, which are by-products [Rosenblum Lichtenstein J.H., et al. 2015].

You could think about it as a large part of these endotoxins. They're excrement or poop. Patients are often subject to chronic exposure to a toxin, whether biotoxin or heavy-metal or human-made chemicals. This chronic exposure then weakens the immune system and allows opportunistic infections to run rampant such as Epstein-Barr virus, cytomegalovirus, and HH V6, just to name a few. Many people also have Lyme disease associated with this syndrome, where Lyme disease can greatly decrease a patient's immune response allowing multiple microbial overgrowths in the body. They call these co-infections. We specialize in the treatment of this because I had my journey and battle with this. Chronically infected with Lyme and a whole host of other co-infections, I was also living in a moldy house. Because of all of these things, I did not know how very sick I was and, at one point, became completely disabled. With no answers in traditional medicine and even in the alternative medicine circles I was searching, I finally diagnosed myself and discovered the secrets of

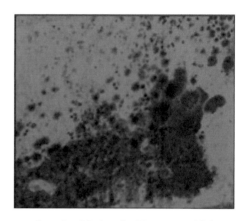

recovering from these afflictions. It is too much to get into in this book. However, if there is interest, please reach out to me through my website OutOfBoxDoc.com. If you think that there is a chance that you're living in a water-damaged building and that mold might be a factor, then this is very important to address; otherwise, all of the things that we talked about will help a little. There will be continued problems, and this situation will minimize the results.

Another great resource is Dr. Richie Shoemaker's website survivingmold.com. If full remediation is not possible using air, you're fine with one that utilizes ozone, and ionizing, and filtering can be helpful. Not sure what you mean. In order to find out if biotoxins are showing up in your body chemically, there are lab tests that you may consider that look at your blood, poop, and urine.

I like to look at some of the blood markers are TGF beta 1, MMP9, hi sensitivity CRP, C4a, Cyrex Array 12, which check a whole family of microbes and several mycotoxins to see if you're reacting to these in your blood. It's worthwhile looking at a viral panel including but not limited to EBV, CMV, HH V6. I also like to look at a T cell called CD57 to see the status of the part of the immune system that destroys microbes. These are the cells that are at the front line in the battle against all microbes.

Often, I see sick people and have not been able to find any answers, and many of these labs will be positive. Patients often make comments that they have been to dozens of other doctors and have mini lab testing performed, but no one has been able to find anything wrong with them. Finally, they have something showing that there is a problem they can begin to work towards correcting and getting their life back. Another important lab test here is the MARCoNS nasal swab discussed in the sinus hygiene section. Please go back and review the section as everyone can benefit from this protocol. If they skip this protocol often, results will be greatly minimized.

Since I have suffered from biotoxin illness and been able to figure out the secrets to recovering, I have had patients fly to me from all over the world for treatment. I was looking for solutions to create treatments that would be as effective as those I provided through intravenous treatments at my clinic. That's when I started to pioneer and develop suppositories liposomal delivery methods and nasal sprays.

I have developed some protocols that utilize these suppositories, ultra-nano liposomal solutions, anti-microbial nasal sprays, and nebulized liquids. Often, there are multiple oral herbal antivirals, anti-fungal, and antibacterial, as well as oral binders to mop up the biotoxins and pull them out of the body. Some of the herbal preparations I like are methylene blue, coptis, artiminesea, allicin, lauracidin, olive leaf extract, oregeno, clove and germanium. Binders I like are BIND, Cytodetox, and Cholestyramine. Information on these protocols can be found at www.ultimatecellularresort.com, and many of the products we utilize are available at MitoZen.com.

I greatly admire that Dr. Dan Pompa has had a similar history to myself with Lyme disease, co-infections, and mold/biotoxin illness. We have worked together to put together some protocols.

One thing that needs to be understood is that these toxins will find themselves deep in the body's cell membranes and fatty tissues because they are fat-soluble and not water-soluble. One of the fat concentrated areas of your body is the brain and nervous system. Besides biotoxins, the nervous system and brain are where many of the heavy metals and some of the chemicals will eventually settle. Since the cell membranes turn over every two years, detoxing these is something that people should consider a more long-term program. It is very important to stop accumulating these toxins by cleaning up the environment if it's moldy and/or getting out of that environment.

Go after any type of infection in the body to minimize the biotoxins from them and allow the immune system to rebuild to keep these infections from getting hold of you again. Using different substances to trigger the release of these toxins and then binding them and safely carrying them out of the body is the science that we have worked hard on for many years to perfect.

Conclusion

There are many factors that make a great argument to have an open nasal passage and to primarily breathe through your nasal passage. We discussed the main reasons for this:

- Improved oxygen absorption through naturally inhaled NO_2
- Increase CO_2 which improves oxygen release from your blood cells.
- Sinus and nasal hygiene for reduced inflammatory response and biotin illness issues.

Ultimately cellular energy is negatively affected due to the cascade of stress that comes from mouth breathing and a narrow skull. Besides toxic sinuses and nasal passages, you also have this spilling over into the gut and absorbing into the blood stream in close proximity to your brain. It's a recipe for disaster as far as ramping up inflammation. Inflammation is at the core of ALL diseases and causes your cellular energy to decline drastically due to the mitochondrial adaption to the inflammation and cytokines. The fixated cranium then blocks the normal cranial motion that keeps CSF circulating and nursing the brain and spinal cord. Since your brain is the most sensitive to poor energy, correcting these issues can be very helpful in the treatment of neurological conditions. For those looking to improve brain function, this is a rich area to get a nice boost to brain power!

In the next chapter we will dive into sleep apnea and how we can apply some of these strategies with breathing and more.

If you're looking for a trained practitioner for this condition then go to www. NasalTherapyBook.com or www.OutOfBoxDoc.com or if you're a clinician wanting to learn how to do endonasal to treat sleep apnea then please go to www.LearnEndoNasal. com

REFERENCES

1. Werman, Howard A.; Karren, K; Mistovich, Joseph (2014). "Continuous Positive Airway Pressure(CPAP)." In Werman A. Howard; Mistovich J; Karren K (eds.). Prehospital Emergency Care, 10e. Pearson Education, Inc., p. 242.

2. Silkman R. (2006) Is it Mental or is it Dental? [Online] Available at https://www.westona-price.org/health-topics/dentistry/is-it-mental-or-is-it-dental/

3. Price W. (1938) Nutrition and Physical Degeneration [Online] Available at http://gutenberg. net.au/ebooks02/0200251h.html

4. Tim Helliwell (2010) Inflammatory diseases of the nasal cavities and paranasal sinuses. Available at https://www.ncbi.nlm.nih.gov/pmc/articles/PMC7172334/

5. Yoon, Y., Song, J., Hong, S. H., & Kim, J. Q. (2000). "Plasma nitric oxide concentrations and nitric oxide synthase gene polymorphisms in coronary artery disease." Clinical chemistry, 46(10), 1626–1630.

6. Rawlings B.A, Thomas S. Higgins T.S, Han J.K (2013) "Bacterial pathogens in the nasophar-ynx, nasal cavity, and osteomeatal complex during wellness and viral infection." [Online] Available at https://dx.doi.org/10.2500%2Fajra.2013.27.3835

7. Bruton A, Lewith G.T. (2005). "The Buteyko breathing technique for asthma: a review." Complement Ther Med. 13 (1): 41–6. doi:10.1016/j.ctim.2005.01.003. PMID 15907677.

8. Wong C., (2020) "How to Do Belly Breathing." [Online] Available at https://www.very-wellhealth.com/how-to-breathe-with-your-belly-89853#:~:text=Diaphragmatic%20 breathing%2C%20sometimes%20called%20belly,diaphragm%20contracts%20and%20 moves%20downward.

9. Zhang J., An J (2009) "Cytokines, Inflammation and Pain" [Online] Available at https://dx.doi.org/10.1097%2FAIA.0b013e318034194e

10. Yang Z., Zhang Y., Chen L., (2013) "Investigation of anti-cancer mechanisms by a comparative analysis of naked mole rat and rat" [Online] Available at https://dx.doi.org/10.1186%2F1752-0509-7-S2-S5

11. Carney, Scott (2017). "What doesn't kill us : how freezing water, extreme altitude, and environmental conditioning will renew our lost evolutionary strength." Potter/Ten Speed/Harmony/Rodale. ISBN 9781623366919.

12. Rosenblum Lichtenstein J.H., Hsu Y., Gavin I.M., Donaghey T.C., Molina R.M., Thompson K.J., Chi C., Gillis B.S., Brain J.D (2015) "Environmental Mold and Mycotoxin Exposures Elicit Specific Cytokine and Chemokine Responses" [Online] Available at https://dx.doi.org/10.1371%2Fjournal.pone.0126926

13. Turowski J., (2016). "Should You Breathe Through Your Mouth or Your Nose?". [Online] Cleveland Clinic Available at https://health.clevelandclinic.org/breathe-mouth-nose/

14. Nattie E. (1999). CO_2, brainstem chemoreceptors, and breathing. Progress in neurobiology, 59(4), 299–331. https://doi.org/10.1016/s0301-0082(99)00008-8

15. Zelano C, Jiang H, Zhou G, Arora N, Schuele S, Rosenow J, Gottfried J, Nasal Respiration Entrains Human Limbic Oscillations and Modulates Cognitive Function,Journal of Neuroscience 7 December 2016, 36 (49) 12448-12467; DOI: https://doi.org/10.1523/JNEUROSCI.2586-16.2016

16. Smith JC, Ellenberger HH, Ballanyi K, Richter DW, Feldman JL, (1991) Pre-Botzinger complex: a brainstem region that may generate respiratory rhythm in mammals. Science 254:726–729, doi:10.1126/science.1683005, pmid:1683005.

17. Smith JC, Abdala AP, Rybak IA,Paton JF, (2009) Structural and functional architecture of respiratory networks in the mammalian brainstem. Philos Trans R Soc Lond B Biol Sci 364:2577–2587, doi:10.1098/rstb.2009.0081, pmid:19651658.

18. Garcia AJ 3rd., Zanella S, Koch H, Doi A, Ramirez JM, (2011) Chapter 3–networks within networks: the neuronal control of breathing. Prog Brain Res 188:31–50, doi:10.1016/B978-0-444-53825-3.00008-5, pmid:21333801.

19. Garcia AJ 3rd., Zanella S, Koch H, Doi A, Ramirez JM, (2011) Chapter 3–networks within networks: the neuronal control of breathing. Prog Brain Res 188:31–50, doi:10.1016/B978-0-444-53825-3.00008-5, pmid:21333801.

20. Suess WM, Alexander AB, Smith DD, Sweeney HW, Marion RJ, (1980) The effects of psychological stress on respiration: a preliminary study of anxiety and hyperventilation. Psychophysiology 17:535–540, doi:10.1111/j.1469-8986.1980.tb02293.x, pmid:7443919.

21. Welker WI, (1964) Analysis of sniffing of the albino rat. Behavior 22:223–244, doi:10.1163/156853964X00030.

22. Kay LM, Freeman WJ, *(1998)* Bidirectional processing in the olfactory-limbic axis during olfactory behavior. *Behav Neurosci* 112:541–553, doi:10.1037/0735-7044.112.3.541, pmid:9676972.

23. Verhagen JV, Wesson DW, Netoff TI, White JA, Wachowiak M. Sniffing controls an adaptive filter of sensory input to the olfactory bulb. Nat Neurosci. 2007 May;10(5):631-9. doi: 10.1038/nn1892. Epub 2007 Apr 22. PMID: 17450136.

24. Evans KC, Dougherty DD, Schmid AM, Scannell E, McCallister A, Benson H, Dusek JA, Lazar SW. Modulation of spontaneous breathing via limbic/paralimbic-bulbar circuitry: an event-related fMRI study. Neuroimage. 2009 Sep;47(3):961-71. doi: 10.1016/j.neuroimage.2009.05.025. Epub 2009 May 18. PMID: 19450692; PMCID: PMC3752895.

25. Vlemincx E, Taelman J, De Peuter S, Van Diest I, Van den Bergh O. Sigh rate and respiratory variability during mental load and sustained attention. Psychophysiology. 2011 Jan;48(1):117-20. doi: 10.1111/j.1469-8986.2010.01043.x. PMID: 20536901.

26. Huijbers W, Pennartz CM, Beldzik E, Domagalik A, Vinck M, Hofman WF, Cabeza R, Daselaar SM. Respiration phase-locks to fast stimulus presentations: implications for the interpretation of posterior midline "deactivations". Hum Brain Mapp. 2014 Sep;35(9):4932-43. doi: 10.1002/hbm.22523. Epub 2014 Apr 16. PMID: 24737724; PMCID: PMC4445359.

27. Carmichael ST, Clugnet MC, Price JL. Central olfactory connections in the macaque monkey. J Comp Neurol. 1994 Aug 15;346(3):403-34. doi: 10.1002/cne.903460306. PMID: 7527806.

28. Eichenbaum H, Yonelinas AP, Ranganath C. The medial temporal lobe and recognition memory. Annu Rev Neurosci. 2007;30:123-52. doi: 10.1146/annurev.neuro.30.051606.094328. PMID: 17417939; PMCID: PMC2064941.

29. Niazi, I.K., Navid, M.S., Bartley, J. *et al.* EEG signatures change during unilateral Yogi nasal breathing. *Sci Rep* 12, 520 (2022). https://doi.org/10.1038/s41598-021-04461-8.

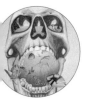

5

SLEEP APNEA: DANGERS OF AND HOW TO TREAT IT WITH ENDO-NASAL

Good sleep is something vital, yet not seen as important by many people. It is an essential process need by people who cherish a healthy lifestyle and well-being. When people lack good sleep, they lack productivity and concentration in their daily activities. People lacking good sleep have a higher tendency to get heart diseases. They also have a lower social and emotional intelligence needed to respond well to scenarios around them. [Joiner W.J. 2016]

Sleep Apnea

As discussed in chapter two, one of the disorders during the development of the skull and teeth leads to mouth breathing, which I discussed extensively in chapter three. Mouth breathing also leads to another called sleep apnea, which I will discuss extensively in this chapter.

Sleep Apnea

Sleep apnea is a severe sleeping disorder in which breathing stops at intervals. The period at which breathing ceases can be a few seconds or minutes, and it occurs intermittently throughout the night. People who I examined suffering from this condition experience a choking or snorting sound when breathing resumes.[El-Ad B. 2005]

Types of Sleep Apnea

There are three major types of Sleep Apnea. The three types show the severity of the condition. [Morgenthaler T.I. et al. 2006]

Obstructive Sleep Apnea

This is the most common type of Sleep apnea, accounting for about 84% of sleep apnea cases. It occurs as a result of the relaxation of the throat muscle. The risk of having OSA increases as body weight and age

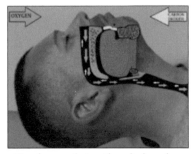

No airway obstruction during sleep.

increase. Also, active smoking tends to increase the risk of having the condition.

Central Sleep Apnea

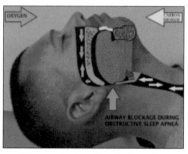

Airway obstruction during sleep.

This occurs when the brain does not send the necessary signals to the muscles that control the breathing process. It is not common as OSA, only occurring in 0.4% of sleep apnea cases. During CSA, the carbon dioxide level and the feedback mechanism supposed to monitor it does not react fast enough. When sleeping, you will not feel the urge to breathe. This will lead to the accumulation of CO_2 in the blood. When breathing begins, it becomes faster before it evens out.

Complex Sleep Apnea Syndrome

This type of sleep apnea occurs when people suffer from both obstructive and central sleep apnea. It is also known as mixed apnea or treatment-emergent central sleep apnea. It occurs in 15% of Sleep Apnea cases. [Khan MT et al. 2014]

Symptoms of Sleep Apnea

The signs and symptoms of obstructive and central sleep apneas overlap, sometimes making it difficult to determine which type you have. [El-Ad et al. 2005]

Bbelow are the most common signs and symptoms of obstructive and central sleep apneas

- After a pause in breathing, people with the condition start snoring loudly.
- When you stop breathing at a particular time (this is from another person's perspective)
- When you gasp for air while sleeping
- Waking up with a dry mouth
- Having a morning headache
- Insomnia
- Hypersomnia
- Short attention span
- Irritability

Health Effects of Sleep Apnea

The effects of sleep apnea result is hormonal disruptions in terms of the release of cortisol, glucose, and fatty acids. It leads to an increase in the secretion of the stress hormone (cortisol) and the synthesis of fatty acids and glucose in the body. [El-Ad et al. 2005]

The secretion of cortisol leads to an increase in glucose in the bloodstream, and when the level of insulin is low, or the individual is under one of the risk factors associated with diabetes, he or she develops diabetes. The increase in cortisol can also lead to weight gain, which is a risk factor for diabetes. [El-Ad et al. 2005]

Sleep apnea is also responsible for increasing the heart rate due to the increase in cortisol secretion. The increased level of cortisol can lead to Cushing syndrome, which is responsible for hypertension.

Treating Sleep Apnea

It will be easy to treat sleep apnea by treating mouth breathing. Therefore, you might see a repetition of the same methods of treating mouth breathing in this section. In addition to this, I will talk about other methods ideal for sleep apnea, such as weight loss and lifestyle changes. [Watson S 2013]

Continuous Positive Airway Pressure (CPAP)

As discussed in the previous chapter, CPAP is the most common method in treating sleep apnea. It is prescribed commonly by our medical care system as the standard of care method for any type of sleep apnea. It works by opening the airways using pressurized air. An individual suffering from the condition wears a facial mask connected to a bedside CPAP machine. [Yu J et al. 2017] This is unnecessary once the underlying causes of the sleep apnea are addressed. This chapter should explain this well.

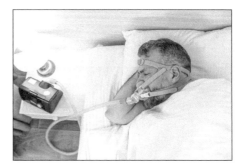

Weight Loss

Excessive weight is a risk factor for sleep apnea. People that are overweight have a large amount of tissue in the back of their throat. This restricts the passage of air while sleeping. According to a study, people who reduce their weight show a reduction in sleep apnea's frequency. [Watson, S 2013]. See fast Track Fast and intermittent fasting as well as ketogenic diet as a solution to weight.

Tongue Exercises to Improve Snoring

One of the symptoms of Sleep apnea is loud snoring, which can be frustrating in some settings. To combat this, many patients look for ways to improve their condition. As we stated earlier, loud snoring is a potentially serious problem related to sleep apnea—however, not everyone has the condition snores. You should check the symptoms as listed in the section above.

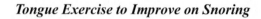

> ### *Tongue Exercise to Improve on Snoring*
>
> *Hold your tongue behind the back of your front two teeth. The spot is just in front of two rough lines on your palate. Press with upward force and hold for 3 minutes. Complete twice daily.*
>
> *Tap tongue behind back teeth to this same point making ‹tut-tut noise. Complete 20 times and repeat five times per day.*
>
> *Move tongue back against the palate, from the spot behind your front teeth. Push against the top of the palate and move towards the back of the mouth. Repeat ten times, twice a day.*
>
> *Hold a spoon at the top of your mouth, or you can also use a paddle pop stick. With force, hold for 2 minutes and repeat two times per day.*

You Should Have a Good Sleeping Hygiene

When I say sleep hygiene, I'm talking about all the different factors revolving around you getting a good night's sleep. A good night's sleep ensures that your body goes into a restorative and regenerative phase.

Let's dive into some of the most critical factors I look at with my patients.

Dark Place of Rest

First of all, your bedroom needs to be completely dark, i.e., you must not allow light to enter. Darkness triggers the release of melatonin and the circadian rhythm to help you go into your sleep phase. The darker the room, the stronger the support for you to have a deep regenerative and restorative sleep. Even little light rays coming from your clocks or a smoke detector or a controller on an air conditioning unit can affect sleep, especially if those lights are green and guaranteed to affect your sleep negatively. Get some black electrical tape and put little pieces over these lights for better sleep conditions.

Get Sunlight in your Eyes

Total darkness is important. However, getting sunlight in your eyes in the morning and even throughout the day is also important. We often protect our eyes from the sun by wearing sunglasses most of the time we're outside either walking or driving to and from work. However, this will prevent our brain from building up melatonin in your pineal gland. The blue and green light spectrum from the sun hitting your eye has a strong influence on you to build up the melatonin released into your body system when you get into total darkness. [Peters B. 2020]

Get Sunlight in your eyes

These are the primary activators for the circadian rhythm for your sleep-wake cycle. You can do this by doing the things listed below:

- Change the lighting in your house so that you have lamps with red lights.

- You should utilize the sun before it goes down so that you're not getting exposure from your indoor lighting in the evening time.

- Get blue-blocking sunglasses if you're going to watch TV or look at your phone or computer at night. Macintosh has an app called Night Shift, which automatically turns down the blue and green light at a certain time in the evening, which can be for your iPhone or your MacBook computer.

Consider Taking High Dose Melatonin

Smaller doses of melatonin 3 to 20 mg can be helpful for sleep. There are also much higher doses of melatonin we use in our clinic for various reasons, as melatonin is the primary antioxidant in the body. Melatonin's rate of absorption is 2.5% in the oral form. Therefore, we sometimes utilize either a liposomal or a suppository form of melatonin because of its fast absorption rate. Occasionally using doses up towards 100 to 200 mg can be helpful to reset the circadian rhythm powerfully. They can also help deal with various stressors we face in modern civilization, including chronic infections, chronic toxicity from heavy metals in the brain, chronic inflammation, and autoimmune conditions. [Auld F. et al. 2017]

Melatonin

Either talk to a healthcare provider about super high physiological melatonin dosing, or you can take a look at MitoZen.com, OutOfBoxDoc.com, and my book that you can find on Amazon called „Melatonin: Miracle Molecule" for more information about the amazing benefits of melatonin.

Keep Your Body Cool

Many studies show that if you keep your body cool, you'll sleep better. Some devices will run water through a mattress, such as cool pads, to keep your body temperature a little bit lower while you sleep.

Getting a pillow that will help keep your head and neck in a proper position is important as well. Things like the Therapillow or the neck nest might be worth checking out.

Bed Elevation

Bed elevation might be something to consider, especially if there is a lot of obstructive sleep apnea involved.

In a study called "The influence of head-of-bed elevation in patients with "obstructive sleep apnea," they were able to considerably decrease the severity of obstructive sleep apnea by elevating the head of the bed 7 1/2° compared to the foot of the bed.

Get out and get some regular exercise to get deeper sleep at night. The best would be to go out and get exercise in the sun sometime between morning and lunch.

References

1. El-Ad B, Lavie P (2005). "Effect of sleep apnea on cognition and mood." International Review of Psychiatry. [Online] Available at https://doi.org/10.1080%2F09540260500104508

2. Watson, S (2013). "Weight loss, breathing devices still best for treating obstructive sleep apnea". Harvard Health Blog. Retrieved 2019-10-21.

3. Khan MT, Franco RA (2014). "Complex sleep apnea syndrome". Sleep Disorders. [Online] Available at 10.1155/2014/798487.

4. Watson, Stephanie (2013). "Weight loss, breathing devices still best for treating obstructive sleep apnea". Harvard Health Blog. Retrieved 2019-10-21.

5. Yu J, Zhou Z, McEvoy RD, Anderson CS, Rodgers A, Perkovic V, Neal B (2017). "Association of Positive Airway Pressure With Cardiovascular Events and Death in Adults with Sleep Apnea: A Systematic Review and Meta-analysis." JAMA. 318 (2): 156–166. doi:10.1001/jama.2017.7967. PMC 5541330. PMID 28697252.

6. Joiner W.J. (2016). "Unraveling the Evolutionary Determinants of Sleep." Current Biology [Online] Available at 10.1016/j.cub.2016.08.068

7. Morgenthaler TI, Kagramanov V, Hanak V, Decker PA, (2006). "Complex sleep apnea syndrome: is it a unique clinical syndrome?". [Online] Available at 10.1093/sleep/29.9.1203.

8. Young T, Peppard PE, Gottlieb DJ (2002). "Epidemiology of obstructive sleep apnea: a population health perspective." American Journal of Respiratory and Critical Care Medicine. 165 (9): 1217–39. doi:10.1164/rccm.2109080. PMID 11991871.

9. Singh H, Pollock R, Uhanova J, Kryger M, Hawkins K, Minuk GY (2005). «Symptoms of obstructive sleep apnea in patients with nonalcoholic fatty liver disease.» Digestive Diseases and Sciences. 50 (12): 2338–43. doi:10.1007/s10620-005-3058-y. PMID 16416185. S2CID 21852391.

10. Werman, Howard A.; Karren, K; Mistovich, Joseph (2014). "Continuous Positive Airway Pressure(CPAP)." In Werman A. Howard; Mistovich J; Karren K (eds.). Prehospital Emergency Care, 10e. Pearson Education, Inc., p. 242.

11. Peters B. (2020) Get Morning Sunlight, and You'll Sleep Better [Online] Available at https://www.verywellhealth.com/morning-sunlight-exposure-3973908#:~:text=It's%20best%20to%20spend%20between,not%20have%20the%20same%20effect.

12. Auld, F., Maschauer, E. L., Morrison, I., Skene, D. J., & Riha, R. L. (2017). Evidence for the efficacy of melatonin in the treatment of primary adult sleep disorders. *Sleep medicine reviews*, *34*, 10–22. https://doi.org/10.1016/j.smrv.2016.06.005

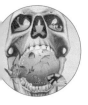

6

CRANIO-SACRAL MOTION: AN IMPORTANT SYSTEM FOR A HEALTHY BRAIN

YOUR BRAIN IS EITHER A SWAMP OR A RIVER

I always say that health is like being less like a swamp and more like a river. Circulation is one of the most important aspects of health and vitality. We're going to be diving into something called the cranial sacral rhythm which has also been called cranial motion. Besides this cranial motion we also have something called the lymphatic system which we're going to discuss. These are Systems utilized by our central nervous system to be more like a river in less like a swamp. Let's take a look at what types of things build up in a "swamp". In our daily activities, we get exposed to many toxins and we also produce toxic wastes

daily. These toxins need to be dealt with. The toxins we are talking about include both endogenous and exogenous toxins. Exogenous (EXO) means toxins we get from our environment, like heavy metals from fish or pesticides from our foods. Endogenous toxins are from the metabolic waste from us making energy, cellular clean up, free radicals, and pro-inflammatory substances released by your immune cells. There are also biotoxions from infections that are much more common than you might think! Your glymphatic and cranial motion are key activators for you to clear these toxins and have a healthier brain.

It is no news that the accumulation of these toxic materials in the central nervous system can adversely affect the functioning of the brain and the entire body. Also, a compressed or distorted fixated skull structure as well as deep connective tissue adhesions will hamper the structured movement or flow of the CSF, which can lead to the accumulation of metabolic waste products or the lack of required hormones and neurotransmitters in essential parts of the brain. Effects of toxins build up in the brain include poor memory, poor sleep, depression, anxiety, , erratic behavior, poor concentration, vertigo, and most of the degenerative neurologic disorders have this as a complicating factor. The ability to get rid of toxic waste substances from the brain and ensure that the brain gets supplied with the right level of nutrients is crucial for brain health.

SIGNIFICANCE OF THE CEREBROSPINAL FLUID

The role of Cerebrospinal Fluid within your brain and spinal cord is to be a cushion and buffer that prevents injury to the brain or spinal cord. As opposed to the previous hypothesis that the CSF slowly trickles through the brain tissues and clears out metabolic wastes gradually, scientists have figured out that this is just a part of the picture. From our discussion on the glymphatic system, we now understand that this system pushes large volumes of CSF very quickly and very deeply into the brain. The movement is much faster than it was previously proposed. With this kind of action, the cerebrospinal fluid transports wastes away from the nervous system under pressure.

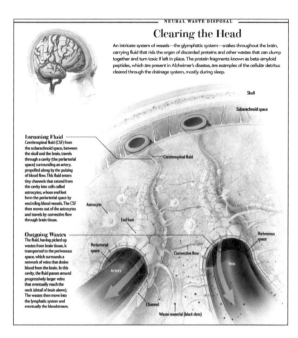

Let me give a quick rundown on how the CSF helps to remove wastes from the brain. A bulk flow process typically moves the cerebrospinal fluid right into the brain tissue via the arterial system. By doing this, it exchanges with the interstitial fluid inside the brain. It then washes through the brain tissue, collecting waste substances which are lying between the brain cells. The CSF then takes the fluid, and waste is picked up from the brain and enters the venous system via the veins within the brain tissue. That means CSF is able to effectively eliminate the waste substances from the brain tissue, via the circulatory system. Besides removing wastes, the CSF helps to distribute several compounds throughout the brain, such as glucose, lipids, amino acids, growth factors, and neuromodulators.

THE CRANIOSACRAL RHYTHM

The ability of the cerebrospinal fluid to adequately flush the brain environment is crucial for brain detoxification, nutrition, and proper brain functioning. There are many different variations of cranial therapy that are specifically aimed at restoring this rhythm. Besides Functional Cranial Release (FCR) which uses endonasal balloons to release and mobilize the cranium, there is also another treatment like Craniosacral therapy. This technique was developed by Dr. John Upledger. Within all of these therapies we are hoping to achieve an improved cranial rhythm leading to enhancing fluid movement within the brain and the spinal cord.

The human upper cervical spine is a critical link for the flow of the cerebrospinal fluid between the brain and the spinal cord. Several studies have shown that there are links

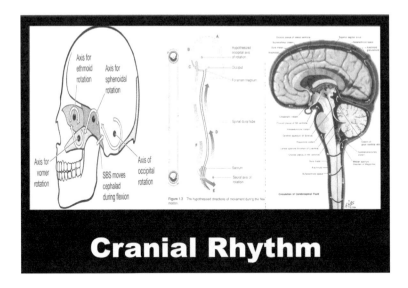

Cranial Rhythm

between craniospinal problems and Alzheimer's, Parkinson's, ALS, and other neurodegenerative diseases. There are chiropractic techniques that are geared directly towards the upper cervical spine. My thoughts are that many of the manipulations and therapies geared towards the upper cervical spine are having their greatest influence on the cranium and the deep connective tissue structures for the dura mater.

I'm sure you're telling yourself, "Hey this sounds great but as this actually been measured?" Researchers Oudhof and Van Doorenmaalen have measured the cranial bone motion directly. They examined the hemodynamic

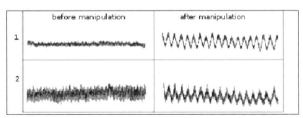

influence on the skull growth. They recorded movement of about 5-10 microns between the bones. This movement was synchronous with the aortic flow and electrocardiogram. Adam et al. also researched parietal bone mobility in adult cats. They analyzed the influence of externally applied forces and changes in intracranial pressure on inducing or restricting parietal motion. A significant level of movement was also observed.

Also, Heisey and Adams described the behavior of total cranial compliance with increased intracranial pressure. At low intracranial pressures, cranial sutures are mobilized, but cerebral fluid and blood volume shifts are primarily responsible for compliance. At higher pressures, fluid shifts are maximized, and cranial bone movement counteracts any further increase in pressure.

With these and many other pieces of research, we can conclude that different physiologic episodes increase intracranial pressure and lead to cranial bone motion. This rhythmic motion is the craniosacral rhythm.

This concept links an involuntary motion of the sacrum between the ilia. The sacrum moves in synchrony with the cranium between the sacroiliac joints. The dural membranes have firm attachments to the sacrum. Then the sacrum is pulled up, and its base will rotate forward during inhalation, and then will lower slightly, and the base will rotate backward during exhalation. It is the dural (deep connective tissues) attachments that link the head to the sacrum, allowing them to move in a coordinated rhythm. (A)

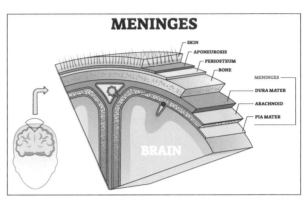

Using endonasal balloons to release these bones in the cranium allowing them to have proper motion structure and function as well as releasing adhesions to the deep connective tissue can have a profound impact on circulation in the central nervous system. It also has a profound impact on your detoxification abilities and your central nervous system. Using endonasal balloons, properly the pressure to the cranial bones, the craniosacral rhythm can be manipulated, leading to the proper flow of the CSF. The rhythmic fluctuations in the cerebrospinal fluid can be improved.

Above is an image from a study showing the improved motion after cranial sacral therapy. Endo-Nasal is much more powerful & it my opinion it may show an even more impressive change.

HOW CRANIOSACRAL MOTION HELPS TO ELIMINATE TOXINS

Cranial Dysfunction does not only obstruct the flow of cerebrospinal fluid but also increases intracranial pressure, causing further physiological problems. For brain detoxification and nutrition to effectively take place, the CSF must be flowing smoothly. What this means is that a general overall higher-pressure status of a dysfunctional skull lends itself to the inability for smooth flowing

cerebral spinal fluid. When the body's cleansing mechanisms breaks down, the central nervous system is exposed to many toxic stressors as well as nutrient depletion stressors. Even if one is relevantly healthy, impaired cerebrospinal fluid flow can fullest potential for health and vitality as well as possibly put you in a risk category for early degenerative neurologic diseases.

When a treatment like functional cranial release is done, the proper release and flow of the cerebrospinal fluid resumes. In turn, the CSF improves the glymphatic flushing of the brain tissues, enhances brain cleansing, helps to remove cellular metabolic waste, biotoxins, chemicals, drugs and toxic proteins such as Beta amyloid, tau, and alpha synuclein.

CONCLUSION

All of these combine to improve the environment and terrain within and around your central nervous system to include the brain and the spinal cord. The body's ability to self-correct itself is enhanced, and a wide range of dysfunctions and diseases can be alleviated. By improving your cranial motion you are going to enhance the function of this "bring in the groceries take out the garbage" phenomenon. You're going to be moving your brain from swamp towards river status. We will dive even deeper into glymphatics in chapter 8. Other things to consider in addition to endo-nasal here are side sleeping may promote more glymphatic motion in the cranium as well as deep sleep as one of the primary activators to the glymphatic system. Transcranial PhotoBiomodulation can be helpful to remove toxins as well. Read more on this in chapter 15. Also see OutOfBoxDoc. com for more suggestions to keep your brain healthy.

REFERENCES

1. https://lifespa.com/detox-brain-cerebrospinal-fluid-csf/

2. https://biomedres.us/fulltexts/BJSTR.MS.ID.003024.php

1. https://www.osteopathyny.com/the-five-components-of-the-cranial-concept/

3. https://www.google.com/amp/s/www.psychologytoday.com/us/blog/resolution-not-con-flict/201606/clearing-the-fog-craniosacral-therapy-aims-ease-dementia%3famp

4. https://www.drhardick.com/glymphatic-system-brain-detoxification

5. http://www.bewellbuzz.com/journalist-buzz/detoxing-brain-health-research-findings-cranio-sacral-therapy-improves-glymphatic-cleansing-brain-tissue/

6. http://stm.sciencemag.org/content/4/147/147ra111 Research publication Science Translational Medicine

7. Oudhof HA, van Doorenmaalen WJ (1983) *Skull morphogenesis and growth: Hemodynamic influence.* Acta Anat 11 7: 181-186.

8. Heisey SR, Adams T (1993) *Role of cranial mobility in cranial compliance.* Neurosurgery 33:869-876.

9. Adams T, Heisey RS, Smith MC, Briner BJ (1992) *Parietal bone mobility in the anesthetized cat.* 1 Am Osteopath Assoc 92: 599-622.

10. Joseph S. Rogers, Philip I. Witt (1997) *Journal of Orthopaedic & Sports Physical Therapy* Downloaded from www.jospt.org on August 25, 2020.

11. Jäkel A, von Hauenschild P (2012) *A systematic review to evaluate the clinical benefits of craniosacral therapy.* Comp Ther in Med 20: 456-465.

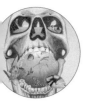

7

PALATE EXPANSION IN CHILDREN & ADULTS

Introduction to Palate Expansion

What we consider to be a beautiful face is generally a wider and more symmetrical face. This is not only achieved through great teeth but also facial and cranial bone structure, in fact, having a more developed (ie wider face, called brachycephali) will give more space for straight teeth, as evidenced through skull examination prior to the industrial revolution. Many of us look at faces and might judge the health of an individual based on how

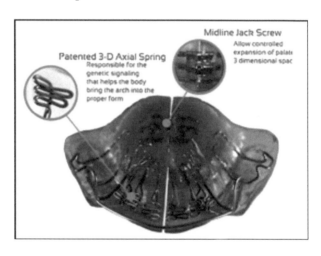

their face presents itself. This chapter is not based on how people can look younger or prettier; however, these facial structures and teeth alignment can also translate into a healthier brain and body. A good set of well-arranged, appropriately placed set of teeth set within a wide palate is the natural state of our facial bones and our teeth. Many of us take this for granted, thinking it comes naturally and commonly for everyone. This circumstance is becoming rarer and rarer as our modern society creates more stressors that prevent this from becoming the natural state of the cranium in the average person. Apart from the proper arrangement of teeth, the shape of the palate or roof of our mouth has a lot of implications when distorted. Besides looking a little less beautiful, some implications are poor cranial rhythm. This results in poor circulation and that swamp situation we keep talking about. Remember in your body things are either Swamp or River Lakes. Things are either stagnant or there is a good circulatory flow. This situation lends itself to nutrient delivery as well as clearing toxins that might otherwise build up and cause disease. Always remember the toxin buildup creates an environment that's favorable to microbial overgrowth. Similar to if you left trash out and rats and bugs started to accumulate fast to clean up and eat what's left over. Science is finding that not clearing many proteins in the brain such as beta amyloid, alpha synuclian, tau and neurofibrillary tangles often are the result of poor detoxification of the brain. Also important is the delivery of oxygen, glucose, neurotransmitters and other vital nutrients important for the health of the central nervous system. Another complication is breathing difficulties such as in sleep apnea of which, narrow palates are associated with, is known for disrupting EEG patterns during sleep, one of which is REM, which triggers the glymphatic system which is our brains lymphatic system that removes the Beta Amyloid plaques. Chronic mouth breathing and poor dental architecture resulting in crooked teeth. Many of us may need to have teeth removed such as wisdom teeth and sadly, bicuspids, to make room for all of the teeth in order to fit into a smaller, more narrow cranial structure. Just think 100 years ago, nobody had to have their wisdom teeth removed. What happened to us as human beings that have set the stage for such a dramatic shift where our cranial bones collapse, leaving us with no cheekbones and restricted breathing through the nasal passage and all of the consequences involved with a locked-up cranium?

This is a book on endonasal balloon manipulations and the technique functional cranial release; however, there is an orthodontic procedure that we will examine. Palate expansion has been performed by orthodontists mainly on children for decades. Dr. James Krumholtz was the first orthodontist to start performing palate expansion on adults (Dr Lieurance, this is not accurate, the first person to do this on adults is Dr Angle, the founder of orthodontics). I had the pleasure of working with this doctor before he passed. Dr. James Krumholtz was a huge advocate of the endonasal technique. He would refer many

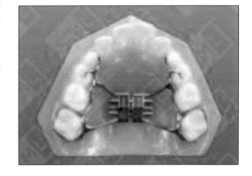

of his patients to have this technique done along with the palate expansion he performed out of his clinic in Boca Raton, Florida. Dr. James Krumholtz even would regularly have these treatments done personally. This chapter examines the history of palate expansion and the benefits it confers both for children and adults and why anyone having this procedure done should consider finding a practitioner to include endonasal balloon and manipulations for faster and more comprehensive results.

What is Palate Expansion?

Palate expansion is an orthodontic procedure of gradual (I agree with this totally, but unfortunately the vast majority of palatal expansion is rapid) widening the roof of the mouth (palate), thereby increasing the perimeter of the dental arch, resulting in the creation of more space in a patient with a narrow, poorly developed palate.[1]

This is often done in children and early adolescents but can also be carried out in adults when necessary.

What are Palate Expanders?

These are orthodontic appliances usually fixed on the teeth (the upper molars) to widen the upper jaw known as the palate. They are also called maxillary expanders.[8] These appliances are uniquely made for each person based on his palate size. Palate expanders come either in fixed or removable forms.

Palate Expansion in Children

Some children have poor or underdeveloped palate resulting in a narrow palate. A narrow palate is associated with many dental and other health challenges in children, which makes dental expansion a necessity. These includes:

Crossbite

This occurs when the lower jaw is wider than the upper jaw resulting in the upper set of teeth fitting inside the lower teeth when biting.[2] This could be unilateral or bilateral. It gives a problem with chewing. This is classic when the maxilla has collapsed which is common when significant change happens due to chronic mouth breathing. The upper palate along with the maxillary bones is almost like a tent. Think about this tent as it widens it will lower the palate and create room in the upper nasal cavity. When it lifts, it pulls in the upper teeth and crowds up into the space in the upper nasal cavity.

Underbite

For a normal dentition, the front upper set of teeth should close directly in front of the lower set of teeth. However, in underbite, the opposite is the case with the front lower set of teeth closing in front of the upper set of teeth. This is the same, in general, as crossbite where the upper palate and maxilla collapse in their relationship to the lower teeth in such a way that the upper palate is smaller and more narrow.

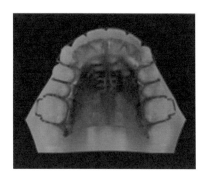

Crowded teeth

Due to a narrow palate, there is little space for the permanent teeth to erupt, resulting in malocclusion or poor alignment of the teeth.[3] Again we have the situation where the upper palate becomes narrow due to maxillary collapse whereas the palate raises up, thus pulling the upper teeth into a more crowded position.

Poor sleep and tongue placement

For those with a narrow, collapsed palate, the tongue does not have enough space to rest in the roof of the mouth resulting in the tongue falling back while sleeping. This causes poor breathing patterns while sleeping where the patient is mouth breathing, which cause the mandible to hinge backwards, along with the tongue, into the throat. Now we have both an obstruction through the nasal passage as well as the throat. Many times, we can also restrict the flow through the throat as well. We need to swallow with our tongue on the roof of the mouth, which then closes our lips, which then allows us to be able to suction breathe through our nose. A strong tongue that is resting behind the upper front teeth is what maintains our cranial structures. For these individuals, besides losing weight, tongue exercises as we described in a prior chapter would be an excellent strategy. Of course, endonasal manipulations and possibly palatal expansion may be beneficial. There are surgeries that will remove the tissue in the throat however I have not seen many people happy with the results from the surgery, conventional UPPP surgery is known to make snorers into silent apnics, and tonsillectomy is a failed technique in adults with OSA. Therefore, I would not recommend it. Often, the side effects are difficulty keeping food down resulting in GERD and many people have reported to me anecdotally that it did not work for their situation. Remember when there is improper nasal breathing, there will be restricted oxygen levels which result in a lack of REM and deep sleep, this is largely due to lowered end tidal CO_2 levels from mouth breathing, which restricts the liberation of oxygen from hemoglobin. This will create a challenge for this very important regenerative process that we go through every 24 hours. Sleep is incredibly important for both children and adults and getting a nice steady flow of oxygen while your body is trying to repair itself is critical. Also recall in a prior chapter we discussed how we absorb nitric oxide through nasal breathing which then allows much higher oxygen delivery to the body.

Sleep apnea

A narrow palate will result in mouth breathing and many times, this results in sleep apnea. Classically in sleep apnea, there will be an irritating, loud sound produced while sleeping due to a falling tongue interrupting the breathing of an individual during sleep.[4] Just like described above, now the individual has lost the airway and both the nasal passages and the mouth. Obstruction of breathing then causes long pauses, starving the body of oxygen. Sleep apnea can cause dramatic stress on the central nervous system and the heart. This has been linked to many health consequences such as heart disease, hypertension, degenerative neurological diseases, chronic fatigue syndrome, poor immune function, attention deficit disorder, autism, and narcolepsy. I would like to even throw cancer into this section because of the dramatic depletion of oxygen every night while sleeping. Considering the work of Dr. Otto Warburg, who won the Nobel prize showing that oxygen and cancer are linked together we can start to connect dots.

Halitosis

Also bad breath can result from a narrow palate, making breathing through the nose difficult. There is compensation where breathing through the mouth resulting in inhalation of unfiltered air and unrestrained access to bacteria, which can progressively result in dry mouth and halitosis. Besides smelling bad, having a dry mouth can favor poor gum health and chronically inflamed gums. Bruxism is strongly associated with poor nocturnal airflow, which compounds the inflamed gums, and can also cause TMJ disorders. Nasty bacteria can begin to develop in the oral cavity, which can then seed into the digestive system. This can lead to many digestive conditions, autoimmune conditions, chronic inflammation in the body, poor immune function, and degenerative neurological diseases. The same thing can happen in the sinus and nasal cavity if one is not maintain in the environment. The same way a toxic mouth can find its way into the brain (is through systemic inflammation making the BBB more permeable) and digestive track so can that situation in the sinuses. I think it's worth knowing in the section that I am a large proponent of an annual 30 days sinus protocol. This is where anti-microbial nasal sprays are used along with natural nebulizing anti-microbial's that are in a protocol. You can find more information about this protocol as well as oral protocols to keep the mouth healthy at www. ultimatecellularresort.com

Poor Cranial Rhythm

We've covered cranial rhythm in prior chapters. It is the ability of the cranium and the sacrum to make subtle movements that allow for your cerebral spinal fluid to be circulated around your brain and spinal cord. These nutrients include oxygen, neurotransmitters, vitamins, minerals, antioxidants, and glucose. It's one thing to get these nutrients into the central nervous system but getting them circulated is the job of this cranial rhythm. Having a collapsed and fixated cranium works against this system, creating blockages that can result in various health problems.

Many of these conditions listed above can be prevented if early intervention with children is achieved. However, it is never too late, as many of these conditions can be reversed with the appropriate care. Obviously, I am a proponent to have both a combination of palate expansion and endonasal balloon manipulations for best results unless it's a mild case that can be corrected with just the endonasal approach.

Dr James Krumholtz

Palate Expansion in Adults

Up until the late 90s, a palate expansion in adults was considered impossible. Dr. James Krumholtz was the first orthodontist I know of to begin using palate expansion with adults. He discovered if he does 25% of what he would do in a child, that he could expand adults as far as he desired and that the adult skull can morph and change dramatically. Dr. Krumholtz was criticized and considered a quack in his time. His work was starting to become recognized before he passed in 2010. Before he passed, he taught his technique to Dr. Singh, who developed a technique called the DNA appliance. Dr. Singh has become quite wealthy and famous for this invention, yet he has given no credit to Dr. Krumholtz. This saddens me greatly because this pioneer, an orthodontist, should be getting credit for this development. Now adult palate expansion is widely accepted in orthodontics, and there are a variety of expanders that are used besides the DNA appliance.

When children with poorly developed palate are left untreated, they progressed to adulthood, and besides having crooked and crowded teeth, they will present with something called the maxillary transverse deficiency. This is a condition in which the upper jaw or palate is narrow, resulting in various forms of malocclusion such as anterior and posterior crossbite and poor facial growth and development.[5] Many of these adults have sleep disturbances, breathing difficulties, especially while sleeping, chronic sinusitis, and sleep apnea. Of course, all of the other complications listed above would be involved in the situation that we've already covered.

Palate expansion has been proven to be successful even in adults in correcting malocclusions, treating sleep apnea, and improving sleep and breathing difficulties in patients.[6] Success has been recorded with the rapid maxillary expansion.[7]

Types of Palate Expanders

The following are the different types of palate expanders commonly used in the correction of palate defects and malocclusions:

Rapid Palatal Expander

Also known as a rapid maxillary expander. It is a fixed type of palate expander used in widening the upper jaw, thereby correcting defects such as narrow palate, crossbites, and crowding. This metallic appliance is fixed to the upper molars on both sides with a turning screw at the center. The screw is turned with a special key each day to create tension between the palatal bones, thereby creating space between for extra bone to grow, resulting in increased width of the palate. Rapid palatal expanders can widen the palate at the rate of 0.5 mm per day. Once the desired expansion is achieved, the screw is locked and secured for 3 to 6 months to allow new bone growth at the available space.[9]

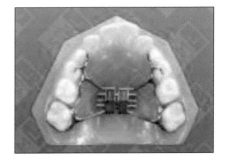

A rapid palatal expander is recommended for children between the ages of 7 and 12 years when the palatal suture is yet to fuse, and much expansion and correction can be achieved. However, it is also sometimes used for adults with some level of success. This technique allows for splitting of the palatal suture, which results in bleeding and clotting, not an ideal situation, especially when considering that RPE is known to have at least a 30% relapse.

Surgically Assisted Rapid Palatal Expander

This would rarely be my first suggestion for any patient; however, in very severe cases, this might be a valid option. The orthodontic profession still considers the skull to be immovable, and the pallet bones fused even though this is not true. The rationale for most facial surgeons is that this would be the first choice for older patients whose palatal bones have "fused" together, and much expansion is required. It is done with a combination of orthodontic treatment and surgical in which the palatal bone is fractured, and space is created for new bone to grow and fill. The appliance is put in place to keep the fractured bone separate during new bone growth and healing. This technique is the exact same philosophy of RPE, but instead of having bands glued to the molars, 4 implants are screwed into the palate, extending into the turbinate space.

In addition to creating space for proper alignment of teeth and mastication, this procedure helps improve breathing, sleep quality, and sleep apnea in such individuals.[10]

My biggest challenge with this option is that you were going to create a lot of scar tissue, and this is likely to make the cranial rhythm challenge much worse even though it may help some of the other aspects of the complication of cranial collapse. Obviously, the recovery can be quite painful as well.

Removable palatal expander

This is usually employed for minor deficits requiring minimal expansion.[11] They are similar to acrylic retainers in appearance, although they are made of chrome. They are recommended more in adults who can comply better with their use.

Examples of Appliances used for Palate Expansion

1. DNA Appliance

This is known as Daytime-Nighttime Appliance or DNA treatment, a form of the technique used in Epigenetic Orthodontics. This device functions by improving the development and function of the palate and nasal structures without using braces.[12] As the name implies, these removable devices are worn during the nighttime while the patient is free during work or school period. This treatment has been highly researched and clinically proven to be naturally effective, totally pain-free, nonsurgical means of remodeling the airway.[13] The following are the benefits of DNA appliances:

- It helps develop the upper and lower jaw into a more desirable form, thereby improving teeth alignment.
- It improves obstructive sleep apnea and snoring.
- It helps in straightening the teeth.
- It enhances facial appearance and balance.
- It improves TMJ symptoms.
- It can be designed for both adults and children.

2. Schwartz Appliance

This is a removable device designed to expand the upper and lower jaw, thereby expanding the arches and creating space to develop permanent teeth. It is the most frequently used removable appliance to develop a narrow arch.[14] It has a small screw at the center of the appliance, which is turned as directed by the orthodontist to effect needed expansion. This device is worn 24 hours a day for optimal outcomes and should only be removed whenever you want to brush, eat, swim, or involve in a contact sport. Schwartz appliance can help correct malocclusions, several crowding, impacted teeth, breathing difficulties, and sleep apnea.

3. Quad Helix Appliance

This is an orthodontic appliance that is used for the expansion of the upper jaw or palate. This appliance can be constructed as a fixed or removable expander and does not require turning to be activated.[15] It is usually attached to the molars by two bands and has two or four active helix springs, which widens the arch of the mouth, thereby creating more space. It works by slowly pushing the teeth out, which ends up widening the upper arch. Quad helix expander can be used in the treatment of narrow palate, crossbite, and crowded teeth.

4. Hyrax Appliance

This appliance was developed by Biedermann, and so it is also known as the Biedermann appliance. It is a high palate expander with its screw positioned high in the palate for greater comfort. The device is made up of stainless steel with bands placed on the first premolars and first molars of the upper jaw. There is a screw at the middle in which the patient can turn as directed by the orthodontist for expansion purposes. Hyrax appliance is used in the treatment of narrow palate, crossbite, and breathing difficulties. If used properly, therefore slowly, when the high vault of the palate is lowered, the expansion screw digs into the palate itself.

Conclusion

The upper jaw or palate not only houses important teeth that complete and compliment our dentition but also serves as the floor of our breathing pathway. Proper development and shape of this important structure are crucial not only to a good smile and mastication but also to proper nasal breathing, sleep, and general health of the brain and body. Then, of course, there is the circulation of nutrients around the brain and spinal cord and all of the benefits related to this important function. A healthy wide palate and cranium will thereby contribute to the overall quality of life of an individual. Indeed, the Maxilla articulates with 8 pairs of cranial bones as well as the septum, and expanding the palate has profound effects on these bones, as does endo-nasal balloon manipulation.

Palate expansion in children and adults may not be necessary for everyone. Endo nasal balloon manipulation, such as utilized with Functional Cranial Release, could be a viable option by itself with both adults and children. I have personally seen dramatic changes in the dental architecture and general health of children using endonasal balloon manipulations. I've seen crowded teeth completely normalize in less than 60 days. See this case I posted on YouTube (https://www.youtube.com/watch?v=u-o8ALukVHQ) I've also treated my fair share of cases with the combination of both palate expansion and endonasal manipulations. And for moderate to severe cases, palate expansion should be something to consider seriously. Of course, best combined with endonasal balloon manipulation to restoring a smile, a wider healthier looking face, sleep, brain function, and an overall more robust and healthy life!

If you're looking for a trained practitioner for this condition then go to www. NasalTherapyBook.com or www.OutOfBoxDoc.com or if you're a clinician wanting to learn how to do endonasal to treat sleep apnea then please go to www.LearnEndoNasal. com

References

1. https://www.jungleroots.com/post/pediatric-dentist-phoenix-what-is-palatal-expansion-and-why-is-it-important

2. https://www.newmouth.com/orthodontics/malocclusion/crossbite/

3. https://www.jungleroots.com/post/why-would-my-child-need-to-see-an-orthodontist

4. https://www.jungleroots.com/post/can-orthodontics-cure-sleep-apnea

5. https://www.scielo.br/scielo.php?script=sci_arttext&pid=S2176-94512017000100110

6. https://www.researchgate.net/publication/51689651_Palatal_expansion_in_adults_The_non-surgical_approach

7. https://pocketdentistry.com/palatal-expansion-in-adults-the-nonsurgical-approach/

8. https://beachbraces.ca/palatal-expansion/

9. https://www.colgate.com/en-us/oral-health/cosmetic-dentistry/early-orthodontics/when-upper-jaw-expansion-benefits-your-child-1014

10. https://pubmed.ncbi.nlm.nih.gov/31815104/

11. https://www.newmouth.com/orthodontics/treatment/palate-expanders/

12. https://www.smilesfromheart.com/p/dentist-Bellevue-WA-DNA-Appliance-p26660.asp

13. https://oralsystemiclink.net/health-care-providers/profile/dr-dave-singh-talks-about-the-dna-appliance

14. https://www.smlglobal.com/upper-schwarz-appliances

15. https://www.panorthodontics.com/appliances-quad-helix/

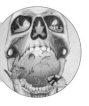

8

GLYMPHATIC'S, ENDO-NASAL & BRAIN CLEANSING

Imagine a train running on coal and spewing black smoke as it rolls down the track. The train is burning coal and the byproduct of it is heat which is turned into mechanical energy that runs the train engine resulting in motion of the train down the track. That waste product is thrown into the air and therefore the train doesn't need to deal with that byproduct of energy production. Imagine if this train was in your body and it was spewing that black toxic smoke into your tissues or into your brain. The human body is a highly metabolic system resulting in the production of waste metabolites AKA black smoke by your cells. This waste must be cleared. How does the body handle this waste and specifically, how does the brain handle this waste? There is a waste removal system we all have throughout the body, and it is

called the lymphatic system. The lymphatic system has been known and widely studied over the years as the body's cleansing mechanism of waste metabolites. The Lymphatics are known as the bodies gutter system. However, of all the body's organs, the Central Nervous System (CNS) comprised of the brain and the spinal cord is known to be devoid of lymphatic vessels.[1] How then does the brain get rid of it waste metabolites?

Over the years, it was taught that the brain cells have an intrinsic way of managing their waste since the lymphatic system is absent. However, recent findings have led to the discovery of a waste clearing system for the brain. This is known as the *glymphatic* system. Although studies are still ongoing to understand this new system better, present

knowledge has shed more light on the importance of the glymphatic system and how it might relate to inflammation due to toxic buildup and even the accumulation of toxic proteins that can choke out all the nerves that make up your brain and spinal cord. Sleep is one of the primary activators of the lymphatic system however cranial rhythm is an important attribute of

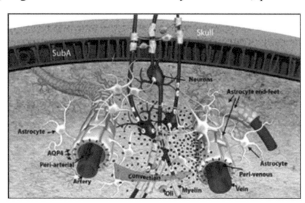

circulation throughout the brain and spinal cord as well. It is important to look at both the toxins being produced, and the rate of toxins being removed. As a result of the dysfunction of either, there is a net accumulation of toxins, which studies show will result in many challenges in the CNS. In this chapter we will look at the glymphatic system, how to optimize it in order to deal with a variety of different pathological conditions in the nervous system and the development of neurodegenerative diseases, and the aging process of the brain.

Let's look into and examine what is known so far about the glymphatic system and its importance.

DISCOVERY OF THE GLYMPHATIC SYSTEM

The word glymphatic comes from two different but related terms which are glial cells and lymphatics. The term was coined by a Danish neuroscientist named Maiken Nedergaard who discovered this system.[2]

Jeffrey J. Iliff et al., in the year 2012 published in the Science Translational Medicine, the pathway describing the glymphatic system.[3] This was done with other researchers like Maiken Nedergaard, Helene Benveniste, and others. Fluorescent tracers and fluorescent-tagged amyloid-beta was injected into the cisterna magna and brain parenchyma of mice, respectively, and they observed the movement of the tracers using two-photon imaging through this glymphatic pathway.

To visualize using MRI, Dr Benveniste developed a 9.4-T system and small molecular weight contrast dye injected into the cisterna magna using an intrathecal catheter.[4] In this way, the glymphatic pathway was studied and described.

THE GLYMPHATIC PATHWAY

Specialized glial cells known as Astroglia are important in the glymphatic pathway. Previously, glial cells were seen as just lowly supporting cells, but now, their functions are better understood. These Astroglia have aquaporin 4 (AQP4) water channels at their end-feet, which enables movement between the Cerebrospinal fluid (CSF) and Interstitial fluid (ISF) resulting in the removal of waste metabolites.[5]

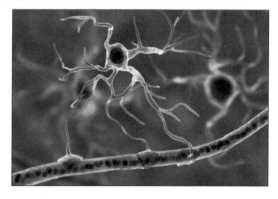

There are three main fluid compartments essential to the working of the glymphatic system.

1. The CSF, which is produced primarily by the choroid plexuses within the ventricles, is the fluid that bathes the brain and the spinal cord. The CSF is separated from the blood by the blood-CSF barrier.

2. The interstitial fluid is the compartment surrounding the brain cells in which waste metabolites from the brain cells accumulate.

3. The blood vasculature, which consists of the arteries, arterioles, and veins that supply essential nutrients and oxygen to the brain cells. The pulsations of these arteries are key to the functioning of the glymphatic system.

The glymphatic pathway runs parallel to the arteries and utilizes the pulsation of the arteries in driving the exchange of waste metabolites between the interstitial fluid and the CSF. This is facilitated by the AQP4 water channels of the Astroglia. This subsequently empties into the lymphatic vessels where the dura connects to the cervical lymphatic vessels and the rest of the body.[6] Consider that the normal physiology of a skull is to provide for a subtle movement of cranial rhythm that keeps cerebral spinal fluid moving throughout the brain and spinal cord as well as the potential to facilitate motion throughout all of the tissues of the brain and spinal cord. We can only conclude that the cranial rhythm and the flexibility of all of the articulations of the cranial bone which all center around the sphenoid bone are important to improve the overall glymphatic system. Let's first dive in to sleep and the glymphatic system.

GLYMPHATIC SYSTEM & SLEEP

Recent studies show that sleep is essential for the clearing of waste metabolites from the central nervous system (CNS) through the glymphatic system. The glymphatic activity is low while awake but high during natural sleep and under certain types of anaesthesia.[7]

Consider both Ronald Reagan and Margaret Thatcher who both wound up with Alzheimer's. Both of these individuals would brag about how they only needed a short amount of sleep each night in order to function as if it was a badge of honor.

Xie et al., first described the connection between sleep and the glymphatic system when he compared CSF tracer's influx during awake, asleep, and anaesthetized mice brains.[8] The study showed that while awake, there was hardly any influx of the tracer into the brain. However, the situation was different during the onset of sleep or induction of anesthesia, in which there was a significant influx of the tracer.

Other studies show that there is a significant increase of up to 60 percent of the interstitial space volume of mice brain while asleep.[9] The increase in volume facilitated an exchange between the CSF and the interstitial fluid. This resulted in better clearance of metabolic waste from the CNS.

Another study by Hablitz et al., proved that glymphatic system activity is not just influenced by sleep but especially by deep sleep.[7] This is because of the magnitude of *slow-wave activity* (SWA) during deep sleep. Slow waves or delta waves are high amplitude (0.5 – 4 Hz) brain waves which are seen on electroencephalography (EEG) during deep sleep.[10]

Hablitz et al., further showed that anesthetics with low SWA anesthetics like isoflurane reduces glymphatic influx.[11] So basically what they found is if they increase high or delta slow wave it increases the glymphatic flow and if they promote a low slow wave it inhibits the glymphatic flow. Now consider many of the drugs that people use to promote sleep. Things like Ambien that will actually inhibit deep sleep. I often tell my patients that if you went up to someone and hit them in the head with a baseball bat and knock them out and you have this person laying on a bed next to someone that was in true deep sleep, they would look the same. However, when each of them woke up they would feel completely different. Many of the drugs being used as sleeping aids will knock you out but they will not necessarily give you the full spectrum of sleep necessary for true health and vitality. There is literally not one prescription medication on the market that has been shown to promote deep sleep.

NEURODEGENERATIVE CONDITIONS AND THE GLYMPHATIC SYSTEM

The discovery of the glymphatic system has brought more light to the pathophysiology of the risk of developing neurodegenerative diseases. Conditions to include Alzheimer's disease, Parkinson's disease, as well as cognitive decline associated with aging. Poor clearance through the lymphatics lead to the accumulation of proteins in the brain such as beta amyloid, alpha synuclein, tau, and neurofibrillary tangles due to the poor detoxification through the glymphatics. Just like the trash not being taken out and the trash accumulates in your kitchen, trash is left throughout the brain tissue choking off many aspects of nutrient delivery and oxygen utilization.

– **Alzheimer's disease:**
Accumulation of amyloid plaques is implicated in the pathophysiology of Alzheimer's disease. Amyloid plaques are aggregates of beta amyloids, which are metabolic by-products found in the brain.[12] The glymphatic system is responsible for clearing beta-amyloid from the brain during deep sleep, thereby preventing its accumulation.

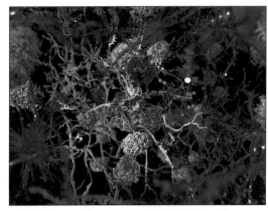

Image Showing Beta Amyloid Build Up Around
Nerves in the Brain

A study carried out on both animals, and humans show that there was an increased level of beta-amyloid in the brain after sleep deprivation.[13] A known risk factor for Alzheimer's disease is poor deep sleep quality. This results in a gradual accumulation of beta-amyloid plaques in the brain.[14]

Improvement of quality deep sleep, could help mitigate the progression of Alzheimer's disease.

— **Parkinson Disease:** A neurodegenerative condition
resulting from the accumulation
of alpha-synuclein protein in the
brain. Researchers believe that
problems with the glymphatic
system might be responsible.
This is because the glymphatic
system helps with the excretion
of alpha-synuclein protein from
the brain.[15]

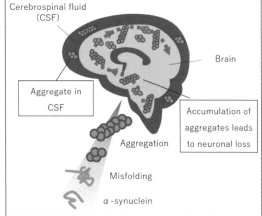

Also, Parkinson's disease is
characterized by disruption of the dopamine pathways of the brain. The dopamine pathways are responsible for the sleep-wake cycles and circadian rhythms;
therefore, a disturbance with these pathways results in sleep disturbances in such
individuals. This could also be responsible for the dysfunction of the glymphatic
system in eliminating the metabolic waste in the brain, including alpha-synuclein
protein. So, the problem with Parkinson's perpetuates the pathology, and more
breakdown and dopamine production leads to poor deep sleep which leads to
more break down in the dopamine system through accumulation of alpha-synuclein protein from the brain.

It's worth noting that it's also important to understand what causes more production of
these proteins in the brain. Science has showed us that these proteins are part of the
immune system in our brain. They are also part of the system that responds to toxins that
get through the blood brain barrier. Besides a leaky blood brain barrier, a toxic influx
from biotoxins, heavy metals, man-made chemicals and chronic infections can all cause
too many of these proteins being produced. Many times, these terrible neurologic conditions are caused by an increase in the production of these proteins and then a decrease
in the clearance leading to a perfect storm. When you throw in the dysfunctional cranial
system which further worsens the clearance of toxins as well as the nutrient delivery
and circulation throughout the brain and spinal cord you really have a serious problem.
Anybody suffering from any neurological condition should seek the advice of a healthcare
practitioner that has been trained to look deeply into these systems, and a comprehensive program in order to address the underlying cause is the most logical approach. The
pharmaceutical companies are working hard to find a molecule that will decrease the
production of these proteins. However, if they are being produced in a response to an

infection, this approach would not be as logical as addressing the infection that's causing the proteins to be over produced in the first place. Simply prescribing a drug for this will inevitably lead to an inferior approach given that most doctors do not have the time in our current insurance model to really dig deeply into a patient's sleep, their cranial rhythm, toxic exposure, and any chronic infections that might be present.

Cranial Therapy Enhances Glymphatic Cleansing

Although glymphatic cleansing is a newly identified process, the concept of a stronger fluid motion through the brain is not new. Cranial therapy pioneer Dr. John Upledger hypothesized his "Pressurestat Model" of fluctuating CSF production within a semi-closed hydraulic system back in the early 1980s. This model of CSF moving under pressure within the dural membranes surrounding the brain and spinal cord was the basis of his evolving research and development of craniosacral therapy. There is now an extensive body of evidence of the health-promoting effects of craniosacral therapy, published by craniosacral therapists among a worldwide network of practicing clinician's.

Dr. John Upleadger

Craniosacral therapy is a gentle, hands-on body therapy that engages with the body's craniosacral system, the interactive physiological environment surrounding and protecting the brain and spinal cord. The focus in craniosacral therapy is encouraging the release of trauma locked within the tissues, improving physiological function, and promoting the body's natural healing processes. Craniosacral techniques restore and enhance fluid movement within the brain and spinal cord and throughout the whole body. During craniosacral therapy, cerebrospinal fluid motion is increased, improving glymphatic flushing of the brain tissues.

Adequate flushing of the brain environment is essential for brain detoxification, nutrition, and a normal range of function. Scientists' recent discovery of the glymphatic system's mechanism affirms Dr. Upledger's earlier hypothesis. Just as importantly, it affirms craniosacral therapy as an effective and established treatment option for enhancing brain cleansing in cases of brain disease or injury and as a preventative measure.[16,17,18]

Dr. John Lieurance performing CranioSacral Therapy After FCR (Endo-Nasal Balloons).

TransCranial & IntraNasal PhotoBiomodulation & Glymphatics

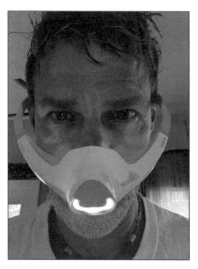 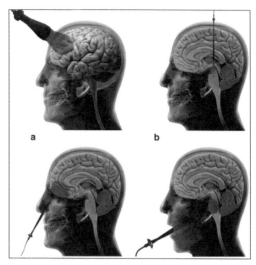

I will dive deeper into this subject in Chapter 15 on PhotoBiomodulation and how it effects the Glymphatics and over all brain. I find Photobiomodulation therapy to cellular energy in the brain and body to be a key upgrade to endo-nasal therapy. This modality has been proven to do the following: Improve Circulation / Blood Flow, Angiogenesis, Synaptogenesis (Neuroplasticity), Increase NeuroTrophins such as BDNF, NGF, & GDNF, increases SOD Antioxidant System, Neuron Progenetor Cells (Stem Cell Activation) and as an Ant-Inflammatory. In Chapter 15, I deep dive into the research and how I use it clinically along with Methylene Blue which further enhances energy production through the same pathways and when combined together can be magical.

Conclusion

In conclusion, the discovery of the glymphatic system in recent years has revolutionized the understanding of the workings of the CNS. Previously, many degenerative neurologic disorders that had the accumulation of these protein tangles was looked at with the filter of 'how can we clear these out of the brain?' Now scientists are starting to see that these are naturally cleared from the brain through the glymphatic system. Anyone that wants to keep their brain healthy and either avoid degenerative neurologic diseases or try to improve these conditions must take a close look at their deep sleep. We know sleep is the most powerful activator of the glymphatic system. We are going to take a close look at sleep in another chapter and how you can improve it to maximize this process. Another aspect that many do not consider is the cranial rhythm. This subtle cranial motion is another factor that allows the movement of cerebral spinal fluid from as far down as the sacrum to up around the brain. Sleep and proper cranial rhythm are both important to look at for proper brain detoxification and protein clearing. Toxic exposure as well as chronic

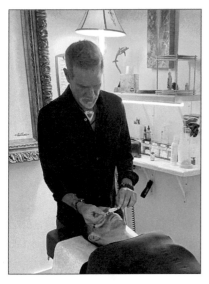

infections must be considered. As we get older our melatonin levels decline which can be a negative impact on deep sleep. It is possible to use both standard and super physiological doses of melatonin which are much higher than what most would suggest in order to create a stronger activation to deep sleep and the glymphatic system. There are acoustic devices such as the one used at the advanced rejuvenation center called the Softwave. Research on trans cranial acoustic therapy to break up these protein tangles is quite promising as well. Transcranial Photobiomodulation using red light (preferable adding in methylene blue/Lumetol Blue) One other modality to consider within the glymphatic conversation is a device called the CVAC. This stands for cyclic variation in adaptive conditioning. This device looks like a spaceship pod where the pressure changes through various set programs. Sessions are usually 20 minutes and at our clinic we utilize this for both lymphatic and glymphatic movement. There are also nutritional strategies that maybe helpful to clear these protein tangles. So much is still to be studied and understood about this new system, and by what is known already about the glymphatic system, deep sleep and cranial therapy may be important therapeutic targets for neurodegenerative diseases and will go a long way in better management of these conditions.

If you're looking for a trained practitioner for this condition then go to www. NasalTherapyBook.com or www.OutOfBoxDoc.com or if you're a clinician wanting to learn how to do endonasal to treat sleep apnea then please go to www.LearnEndoNasal. com

REFERENCES

1. https://www.annualreviews.org/doi/abs/10.1146/annurev-pathol-051217-111018

2. https://www.ncbi.nlm.nih.gov/pubmed/22896675

3. https://pubmed.ncbi.nlm.nih.gov/22896675/#affiliation-1

4. https://www.mdedge.com/neurology/article/114150/alzheimers-cognition/glymphatic-system-may-play-key-role-removing-brain

5. https://www.karger.com/Article/FullText/490349#ref1

6. https://www.medicalnewstoday.com/articles/325493

7. https://www.sciencedirect.com/science/article/pii/S2468867319301609#bib0020

8. https://www.sciencedirect.com/science/article/pii/S2468867319301609#bib0015

9. https://science.sciencemag.org/content/342/6156/373

10. https://www.sciencedirect.com/science/article/pii/S2468867319301609#bib0065

11. https://www.sciencedirect.com/science/article/pii/S2468867319301609#bib0035

12. https://www.sciencedirect.com/science/article/pii/S2468867319301609#bib0090

13. https://www.sciencedirect.com/science/article/pii/S2468867319301609#bib0095

14. https://www.sciencedirect.com/science/article/pii/S2468867319301609#bib0110

15. https://www.sciencedirect.com/science/article/pii/S0149763419300284

16. A Paravascular Pathway Facilitates CSF Flow Through the Brain Parenchyma and the Clearance of Interstitial Solutes, Including Amyloid β | Science Translational Medicine

17. Previously unknown cleaning system in brain: Newer imaging technique brings 'glymphatic system' to light -- ScienceDaily

18. DETOXING FOR BRAIN HEALTH - NEW RESEARCH FINDINGS: CranioSacral Therapy Improves Glymphatic Cleansing of Brain Tissue - Be Well Buzz

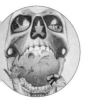

9

FUNCTIONAL NEUROLOGY

I was lucky to have very early on exposure to the study of neurology and various therapeutic applications to treat neurological conditions. My neurology teacher was Dr. Michael Hall and he had an active practice while he was also instructing and soon after became a sought after instructor in the field of functional neurology. Soon after, I begin studying with Professor Carrick through the Carrick Institute of neurology which I have now studied for hundreds of hours over the last 2 ½ decades. What I've seen has been nothing less than a miracle with mini conditions that are thought to be untreatable. Functional neurology is not limited to a specific modality or therapy as much as it is the commitment of evaluating a patient's neurologic system and applying therapies in a rational

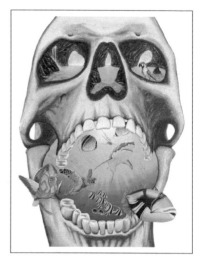

way in order to create neuroplasticity, balance and promote metabolic stability. Fuel supply is very important in functional neurology. It's like if you had a car and it wasn't getting enough gas but you wanted to drive it. You would be out of luck if you didn't have the fuel to run it just like you would be out of luck if you wanted to actively heal your brain but didn't have the fuel in order to perform activities. Balancing the autonomic's in many patients is very critical as this is going to dictate circulation and support fuel delivery

to the brain. In addition to the autonomics, cranial health also plays an important role in fuel delivery to the brain and throughout the various areas of the brain and spinal cord. In this chapter we're going to dive a bit into combining functional neurology with endonasal balloon releases. I believe this combination could be the future of care in an upgraded neurological care model. Breakthroughs in neuroscience have helped us discover that the brain can change throughout a person's lifetime. This is the basis of functional neurology.

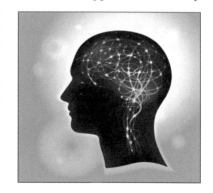

What is Functional Neurology?

Functional neurology is a method that uses an extensive array of therapies and modalities to treat neurological conditions. It is not a technique in the sense that there's a specific set of treatments that one would do. This is more of a deep understanding of the brain and how it can be healed through neuroplasticity when the right signals, symmetry is achieved and both fuel delivery and energy supply are addressed in mini functional neurology practitioners offices. Professor Ted Carrick described functional neurology as a way of returning the human function and increasing it. It involves various brain-based or neurological examinations carried out by physicians to improve brain function [Ted Carrick, 2018].

Functional neurology assesses the body's neurologic, metabolic, nutritional, and biomechanical systems. It uses an integrative approach to examine the interactions of these systems with one another. Functional neurology utilizes brain rehabilitation strategies in the manipulation of brain cells and connections.

Functional neurologists and chiropractors believe that neurotransmitter systems can help improve brain function. Activating the brain cell influences the neurotransmitter systems and promotes new connections with the nervous system. These connections bring about breakthroughs in neurological examinations and treatments.

Careful examination helps a functional neurologist to determine the area of a patient's nervous system that is weak. The functional neurologists can also devise appropriate means of treatment and restoring the quality of the patient's nervous system functions. Generally, functional neurology supports healthy nervous system plasticity through adequate stimulation. It is directed towards protecting the nervous system, but it also helps to activate it to perform effectively.

The Concept of Neuroplasticity

A key to understanding how functional neurology works in neuroplasticity. Our brains are extraordinary, being able to learn new things and create new connections between neurons. Our brains can adapt to new conditions and circumstances with the right stimulations. Neuroplasticity is a term used to describe a vast collection of various brain change and adaptation phenomena [Courtney E, 2020].

Dr. Celeste Campbell described neuroplasticity as the physiological changes in the brain that happen due to our interactions with our environment. The brain develops from time to time, with its connections getting reorganized in response to our changing needs. This dynamic process allows us to learn from and adapt to different experiences [Celeste Campbell, 2011].

Sensory, cognitive, and emotional experiences can modify the nerve connections, which is why they are usually referred to as 'plastic.' The old knowledge of the nervous system was that it was a fixed system. Now, we know that nerve cells can change remarkably.

For example, neurotransmitters and the number of receptors tend to increase if we continue to fire a pathway from one neuron to another. Also, a nerve cell can connect to new neurons or extend to outlying areas. This helps functional neurologists devise ways to help patients recover from traumatic brain injuries and other neurodegenerative disorders. We discussed in chapter 13 how airflow through the nasal chambers can improve neural plasticity as well as utilizing photo bio modulation which we cover in chapter 14.

How Functional Neurology Helps to Treat Conditions

Practitioners of functional neurology make use of neurological and cranial nerve examinations for diagnosis of various conditions. These examinations help us to find the areas in the brain that are not functioning properly. They also help to find treatments that can stimulate those areas for recovery. Functional neurologists use various treatment methods, including transcranial low-laser therapy, diet and nutrition, pulsed electromagnetic field therapy, and more.

Some of the conditions that functional neurology helps to treat include:

Traumatic Brain Injuries

A traumatic brain injury can be caused by several things, such as a violent jolt to one's head or body. Most of the reported traumatic brain injuries occur due to various kinds of accidents to the head. Functional neurologists help find the root cause of imbalances within the brain and body after trauma. As practitioners of functional neurology, we understand the uniqueness of every brain injury. So, we never treat them alike. We combine a range of therapies to rehabilitate and rebalance the nervous system to rebuild new neurons within the brain. By so doing, patients can achieve a well-rounded approach towards healing.

Concussion/Post-Concussion Syndrome

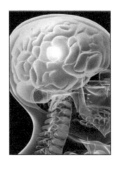

This condition is similar to Traumatic Brain Injury. However, it is a mild type. It is a mild to moderate brain injury directly impacting the head or a sudden rapid movement [Greg Olsen, ND]. It is a complex condition with symptoms that last for several weeks. The functional neurologist treats concussion based on the patient's condition. We make use of specific neurological therapies to aid the brain's functionality. Adjustments that encourage appropriate neuroplastic changes allow the brain to determine the right cognitive and limbic responses.

Vestibular Disorders

The vestibular system includes the inner ear and brain parts that process sensory information involved with eye movement and balance. Vestibular disorders can include vestibular migraine, chronic dizziness, geo-centric vertigo, cervicogenic dizziness, and more.

A functional neurology expert can help with vestibular rehabilitation. Physicians manage peripheral vestibular disorders with treatments like Canalith Repositioning treatment or manual therapy to the cervical spine.

Movement Disorders

Functional neurologists show expertise in treating movement disorders. They devise comprehensive clinical management of Parkinson's disease, Huntington's disease, dystonia, and other related movement disorders.

Practitioners mostly incorporate deep brain stimulation to facilitate the adequate formation and functioning of brain neurons.

Other conditions include:

- Dysautonomia
- Primitive reflex remediation
- Neuromuscular disorders
- Demyelinating diseases
- Ear and equilibrium problems
- Seizure disorders

Study on Endo-Nasal (FCR)& Balance

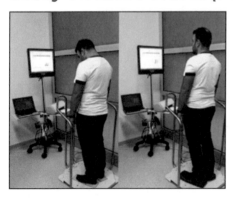

I did this study in 2003 to demonstraight what I was seeing in the clinic with patients balance. Using CDP or Posturography I showed a 30% improvent on balance in 4 days of treatment with endo-nasal.

I am printing this as it was written with my current understanding in 2003 of the mechanisms. There have been some great advances to my understanding of the neurology revolving around endonasal and chapter 13 takes a deep dive into the current viewpoint and research into the mechanisms I feel relate to the results seen in these cases.

Introduction & Definition of Functional Cranial Release

Computer Dynamic Posturography (CDP) is commonly utilized to determine the effects of different sensory conditions on balance. This study utilizes the Bertec Balance Plate to examine the effects of endo-nasal balloon manipulations to the cranial bones has on the vestibular system. Endo-nasal manipulations have been around since 1940's. (5) Introduced by chiropractors and naturopaths for head pain (3) (5) ear and sinusitis care (6) (2) (8) (5). It has been taught in accredited chiropractic colleges as an elective coarse (10) (11) (12)(13) as well as many seminar settings over the years. It has not gained acceptance mainly due to the lack of research and uniform methods. Discomfort to patients can be increased with doctor methods and might cause practitioners to discontinue these treatments even in light of the benefit that some patients receive. Defenition: "The methods of improving the biomechanics of the cranium and improving air flow through the upper nasal chambers through the release of connective tissue restrictions in order to improve oxygenation and circulation of nutrients in and around the central nervous system with the use of latex finger cots through the nasal passage which utilize expansive pressures."

Methods

A series Cranial Release's was performed where the connective tissues that surround the brain and spinal cord called the Dura Mater are specifically released using endonasal balloon inflations.

The patient is first prepared for the treatment using a vibrocussor and Pettibon Multiple Digital toggled MDT adjusting instrument using a proprietary method.

The patient was testing in a standing position using a slight force to determine the automatic correction of the patient when they are pushed into a certain direction in a certain area on the cranium and pelvis. The results are taken into account and this determines the both the position and the placement of the balloon into the nasal concha. The balloon is inflated until the pressure is slightly released and the balloon has passed through just into the throat. I did this over 4 consecutive days.

I conducted a comparative study to observe the relationship between the FCR treatment and improvement in brain function using the Bertec balance platform system. The patient was tested prior to starting any care and on the same day that care was performed and then post testing data was collected the day after the last treatment. The Spectrum of data consists of anterior-posterior sway range and lateral sway range gathered pre and post treatment from a randomized selection of patients who underwent treatment.

Patients were tested in four categories; flat surface (eyes open), flat surface (eyes closed), foam surface (eyes open), foam surface (eyes closed). Within each category the anterior-posterior sway range and lateral sway range was recorded in inches of movement. The area of movement recorded was the range of balance for each patient. Depending on the areas of instability, FCR was then performed to encourage improved brain function in the vestibular, cerebellum and frontal lobes systems.

The gathered data (pre and post) was arranged as a total of all subjects and also divided by gender to show other possible relationships. The mean of the total data was used to provide a visual description of improvement and charted for reference. The mean anterior-posterior and lateral sway was used for each test (Flat SEO, Flat SEC, Foam SEO, Foam SEC) to formulate the area on axis per total and by gender. The bar graph representations are literal interpretations of the data while the area on axis was used to portray balance results as shown via the Bertec balance system. From the mean ranges, the percent improvement per group was calculated and represented in the tables below.

Results

Overall there were significant differences between pre and post examinations. The most dramatic findings were with the Flat Surface Eyes Closed (Flat SEC) and Foam Surface Eyes Closed (Foam SEC) as seen in Table 1. For all subjects there were up to 29% improvement in brain balance compensation while eyes were closed and up to 12% improvement in brain balance compensation while eyes were open.

Report

There appeared to be a stronger relationship between the FCR and Balance exam with the male subjects by a slight margin. The lateral sway range was one variable that had only minor differences pre and post. All results for this were at or near zero percent improvement while anterior-posterior sway range saw larger results.

Subjects had smaller margins of change between pre and post while tested in the balance exam with eyes open. This was true for flat and foam surfaces. When the subjects closed their eyes the difference was drastic. Specifically when discussing the Foam SEC for anterior-posterior sway. Percent improvement proved to be at 29.82% for all patients (27.47% improvement for females and 31.27% improvement for males). Percent lateral sway improvement occurred highest also for Foam SEC with all subjects averaging 22.58% improvement (27.85% improvement for females and 17.48% improvement for males). The area of instability represents the lateral and anterior-posterior sway together. Here the red represents the pre examination for instability and blue is post treatment. Foam SEC for all subjects is represented in figure 4.

We see here that post treatment the area of the sway is less than pre treatment. In figure 8 and figure 12 we see the differences in gender. Where the female subjects found most gains with anter-posterior sway it appeared that male subjects made gains in both lateral and anter-posterior.

Discussion

With sway variability as the measure of postural stability, there was greater age decline in the medio-lateral direction than in the antero-posterior direction (see Teasdale, Stelmach, & Breunig, 1991, for a similar finding)

	ALL SUBJECTS			
	Ant-Post Sway Range			
	FlatSEO	FlatSEC	FoamSEO	FoamSEC
pre	0.25	0.35	0.37	0.57
post	0.22	0.34	0.26	0.40
% improvement	12.00	2.86	29.73	29.82
	Lateral Sway Range			
	FlatSEO	FlatSEC	FoamSEO	FoamSEC
pre	0.13	0.14	0.21	0.31
post	0.13	0.13	0.21	0.24
% improvement	0.00	7.14	0.00	22.58
	FEMALE SUBJECTS			
	Ant-Post Sway Range			
	FlatSEO	FlatSEC	FoamSEO	FoamSEC
pre	0.23	0.32	0.39	0.49
post	0.19	0.30	0.27	0.36
% improvement	17.17	8.79	29.90	27.47
	Lateral Sway Range			
	FlatSEO	FlatSEC	FoamSEO	FoamSEC
pre	0.13	0.32	0.20	0.24
post	0.13	0.39	0.22	0.18
% improvement	0.00	-19.95	-7.20	27.85
	MALE SUBJECTS			
	FlatSEO	FlatSEC	FoamSEO	FoamSEC
pre	0.28	0.38	0.32	0.72
post	0.29	0.32	0.25	0.49
% improvement	-1.52	15.61	22.91	31.27
	Lateral Sway Range			
	FlatSEO	FlatSEC	FoamSEO	FoamSEC
pre	0.12	0.15	0.22	0.44
post	0.11	0.15	0.19	0.36
% improvement	3.66	0.00	12.50	17.48

The first point to note is that despite instructions to give equal emphasis to the cognitive and postural control tasks (`remember as many of the instructions as you can and stand as still as possible'), cognitive activity affected postural stability whereas the reverse was not the case, i.e. postural position had no eåect on cognitive performance. This would appear to contradict a `posture ®rst' principle (e.g. Shumway-Cook et al., 1997) such that where there is competition between tasks, postural control has priority and is therefore maintained at the expense of other tasks.

However, it is clear that postural position can be shown to aåect cognitive performance if more sensitive cognitive tasks and indices are employed (e.g. probe RT in LaJoie et al., 1996b; random digit generation in Maylor & Wing, 1996), or if the postural control task is difficult (e.g. Tandem Romberg position in Kerr et al., 1985).

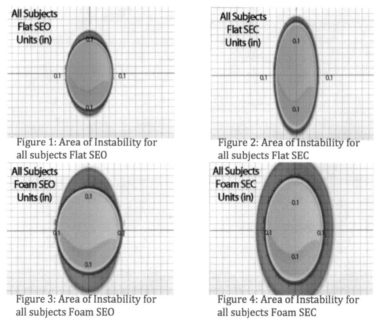

Figure 1: Area of Instability for all subjects Flat SEO

Figure 2: Area of Instability for all subjects Flat SEC

Figure 3: Area of Instability for all subjects Foam SEO

Figure 4: Area of Instability for all subjects Foam SEC

Figure 1 to 4

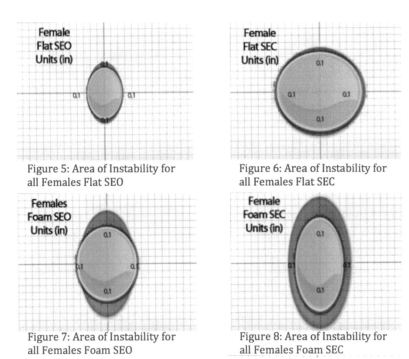

Figure 5: Area of Instability for all Females Flat SEO

Figure 6: Area of Instability for all Females Flat SEC

Figure 7: Area of Instability for all Females Foam SEO

Figure 8: Area of Instability for all Females Foam SEC

Figure 5 to 8

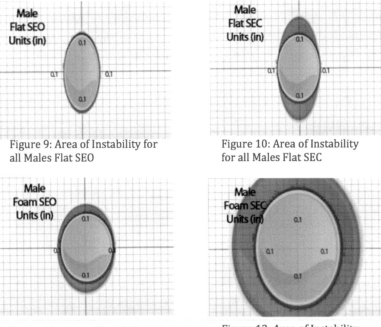

Figure 9: Area of Instability for all Males Flat SEO

Figure 10: Area of Instability for all Males Flat SEC

Figure 11: Area of Instability for all Males Foam SEO

Figure 12: Area of Instability for all Males Foam SEC

Figure 9 to 12

Discussion:

There was significant improvement in Pre and Post Balance Platform results. Percent improvement proved to be at 29.82% for all patients (27.47% improvement for females and 31.27% improvement for males). Percent lateral sway improvement occurred highest also for Foam SEC with all subjects averaging 22.58% improvement (27.85% improvement for females and 17.48% improvement for males).

The idea that FCR helps restore the brains ability to oxygenate itself through both improving air flow through the nasal passage and into higher area's through the nasal passage. Since a significant amount of nitric oxide is produced in the mucosal it is inhaled and supports oxygen absorption into the lungs and on a cellular level. (++) Slight cranial movement called cranial rhythm is a normal pumping action inherent of the skull bones. It is believed to assist in the distribution of nutrients such as oxygen and neurotransmitters that bath the central nervous system maintaining proper fuel delivery to the neurons of the brain. The result is improved cerebellar function and vestibular output. It can be postulated that when the area's of the brain responsible for core stability may have improved resting membrane potential and increased frequency of firing of the neuronal pools. FCR and endo-nasal balloon manipulations are currently not understood well due to the lack of research into the subject. The results in the study suggest that these methods have a positive effect on brain function and balance. It would be beneficial to do a larger population and examine other aspects of brain function that FCR is effecting.

John Lieurance, DC, ND

As mentioned in the beginning of this section these were the original writings by me in 2003. Please reference chapter 13 regarding some of the more contemporary viewpoints on how endonasal might be affecting the vestibular system.

Functional Neurology and Endonasal Technique

Some people believe that functional neurology is somewhat outside the scope of chiropractic modality. This notion is, however, far from the truth. In fact, it is central to everything we do as chiropractors. Combining our knowledge of functional neurology, craniosacral motion, and endonasal technique helps us devise to more effective means of improving brain function.

As I have mentioned earlier, functional neurology utilizes brain rehabilitation strategies to manipulate brain cells and connections. Chiropractors who make use of the endonasal techniques include neurological testing in their practice. The neurological testing helps such a physician determine the brain centers that may be overfiring or performing at a lower rate.

From this perspective, we can notice that chiropractors have always worked with the nervous system. Our work has always dealt with removing subluxation and improving the nervous system's function and performance. Most of our works involve adjustments to the functional parts of the brain and spinal cord. Therefore, we can refer to ourselves as functional neurologists.

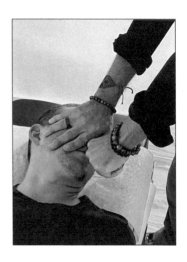

Several of my works and the works of many other chiropractors have proved the statement I made above. Some of my chiropràctic adjustment works involve the pre-frontal cortex, impact brain plasticity, reduce pain, and remove joint dysfunction. All these are due to my knowledge of functional neurology.

According to research, the changes that we see in the brain after spine adjustment occurs in the pre-frontal cortex. The pre-frontal cortex's effects explain the improvements seen in sensorimotor function, better joint positioning, improved muscle strength, and better mental ability. These changes help individuals to perceive the world around them accurately. This research presents solid pieces of evidence that chiropractic adjustments help the brain process information [Heidi Haavik et al., 2016].

Let's take a look at Attention Deficit Hyperactivity Disorder (ADHD) as an example. Pediatric researches show that low axial tone is one of the major factors for ADHD. It makes sense to say that influences on the pre-frontal cortex can, in turn, influence ADHD. A physician who has a well-grounded understanding of functional neurology and endonasal technique can help manage this condition.

Such a physician will be able to harness the vestibular system's function to improve the spine's tone. Hence, develop the cortex by increasing afferent feedback to the pre-frontal feedback. Our ability to link functional neurology with our knowledge about chiropractic practice helps us serve our patients better.

Photo-Bio-Modulation to Enhance NeuroPlasticity.

Photobiomodulation therapy is helpful within Fuctional Neurology to enhance NeuroPlasticity through its enhanced cellular energy in the brain and body. Otheer benefits include: Improve Circulation / Blood Flow, Angiogenesis, Increase NeuroTrophins such as BDNF, NGF, & GDNF, increases SOD Antioxidant System, Neuron Progenetor Cells (Stem Cell Activation) and as an Ant-Inflammatory. In Chapter 15, I deep dive into the research and how I use it

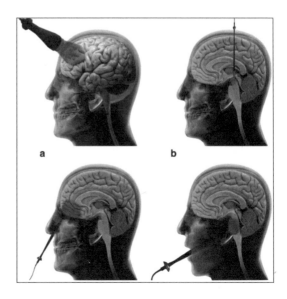

clinically along with Methylene Blue whoch further enhances energy production through the same pathways and when combined together can be magical.

What are other ways to support the nervous system?

 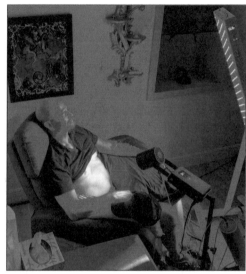

For neurological conditions, besides FCR, our clinic uses treatments such as IV therapies using ozone, methylene blue with light therapy, oxygen therapy using CVAC, laser therapy, PhotoBiomodulation, stem cells therapy, NAD+ therapy, Fasting (Fast Track Fast), Detox programs and testing and treatment for chronic infections of EBV, CMV, HHV-6, Lyme and Lyme (CIRS/Biotoxin illness).

Conclusion

Functional neurology can be a fairly complicated and difficult treatment for many doctors due to the extensive training and the vast knowledge required to understand how to apply this therapy to specific conditions. I have personally spent over two decades studying this work and still feel like a newbie. I have been humbled and honored to observe Professor Carrick work on many complicated neurologic conditions that have been considered untreatable. I've seen many of these cases have remarkable responses functional neurology. I personally do not see functional neurology as the Silver bullet to fix all conditions however it is necessary to bring balance back to the central nervous system as far as how it's firing through various pathways. I see the application of using endo-nasal balloon releases with functional neurology as an extremely powerful way to improve the health, functionality, endurance, fuel delivery through CSF through cranial rhythm.

In Chapter 14 we will get into depth regarding concepts on how endo-nasal might effect the brain through: the default mode network, Stimulous processing through the trigeminal pathways, pacing the cortical oscillatory activity or neural oscillations and the ascending reticular activating system (ARAS) and Locus Coeruleus (LC).

Consider Strategies to improving "the metabolic ceiling" through the approaches in chapter 10 on Neurological Fitness.

If you're looking for a trained practitioner for this condition then go to www. NasalTherapyBook.com or www.OutOfBoxDoc.com or if you're a clinician wanting to learn how to do endonasal to treat sleep apnea then please go to www.LearnEndoNasal. com.

References

1. https://spinalresearch.com.au/functional-neurology-what-is-it-and-where-is-the-evidence/

2. https://positivepsychology.com/neuroplasticity/

3. https://www.brainline.org/author/celeste-campbell/qa/what-neuroplasticity#:~:text=Answer%3A,our%20interactions%20with%20our%20environment.

4. https://www.askdrolsen.com/concussion-diagnosis-and-recovery-with-functional-neurology-podcast/

5. http://www.hindawi.com/journals/np/2016/3704964/

6. https://carrickinstitute.com/citv-37-case-review/

7. Lelic, D, Niazi, IK, Holt, K, Jochumsen, M, Dremstrup, K, Yielder, P, Murphy, B, Drewes, A and Haavik, H (2016) *Manipulation of dysfunctional spinal joints affects sensorimotor integration in the pre-frontal cortex: A brain source localization study.* Neural Plasticity, Volume 2016.

8. Meyer AL, Meyer A, Etherington S, Leboeuf-Yde C (2017) *Unravelling functional neurology: a scoping of theories and clinical applications in a context of chiropractic.* Journal Chiropractic and Manual Therapies, retrieved fromhttps://doi.org/10.1186/s12998-018-0198-7 on 29th October 2020.

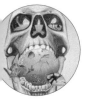

10

NEUROLOGICAL FITNESS & ENDO-NASAL UPGRADES

In this chapter we are going to be discussing various upgrades to an endo-nasal clinical protocol. *Many of the suggestions in this chapter are not meant to be performed without consulting your healthcare provider first.*

Metabolic Medicine, the future of medicine.

Metabolic medicine may be the future of medicine as it is an "upstream" aspect of health that is at the root of most all diseases. Our current pharmaceutical-based medical system is a broken system. It has failed miserably as we have more disease here in the U.S. than many countries, and while we possess most of the medicines, we are still much sicker than most countries with far less "modern" pharmaceutical-based health care. The bottom line is our drugs are killing us. The idea that we can "cure" disease by giving a certain molecule (drug) for certain conditions has shown to be like painting over rust leaving the patient as the victim to only need more drugs for side effects of the first drug. Your body is a self-healing, self-regulating, and intelligent organism which contains all it needs to be healthy and vital. It's not about chasing genes either because your genes fail due to a poor stress response which is caused by poor metabolic capacity within your cells. Many human diseases involve abnormal metabolic states that interrupt normal physiology and lead to tissue and cellular disruption. When you get to the top of the mountain where the stream begins you have *metabolism* and the ability to make adequate energy with as little waste as possible. This is a new health paradigm for treating disease which will allow the body with its innate wisdom to figure out the complexities with its newfound spark for

> 66
> *Many human diseases involve abnormal metabolic states that interrupt normal cellular energy. This is almost always created through excessive inflammation which shut down mitochondrial function. The result is a loss in normal physiology which then leads to tissue and cellular disruptions. These disruptions can be unique to each individual based on their genetics and environmental influences as well as the vectors of stressors which are regulating the inflammation.*

life. Not only does this medicine work but it addresses the cause of many conditions. In this chapter, we will dive into how to use the science of metabolic medicine to gain better results with endo-nasal releases. In order to fully understand how metabolic medicine works you need to have a base of knowledge of the mitochondria.

Mitochondria & Neurological Wellness

In this section, we will dive into the mitochondria, where you convert glucose and oxygen into energy through something called the electron transport chain. This is where electrons are moved through a chain of chemical reactions to produce what is called an exothermic reaction. Basically, moving electrons creates energy your cells utilize to do work, like keeping up with all of their functions. Just like a train which burns coal to produce energy that drives the train down the tracks, your cells burn sugar. And just like the train produces toxins that are released when the coal is burned in the form of smoke, your cells also produce a toxic by-product called oxidation. The ability of the mitochondria to stay healthy and continue to efficiently make energy hinges on its ability to neutralize these harmful byproducts. Antioxidants are the primary method the mitochondria use to do this. Melatonin is produced by every mitochondrion and is the primary way that the mitochondria neutralize the stress of oxidation. Consider your brain is 2% of your bodyweight, however, it consumes 20% of the overall energy. Your central nervous system is incredibly demanding and requires a high total energy supply. When that starts to run low, both your heart and your brain, which are the two most metabolically sensitive organs, will begin to show signs of stress and disease. Making your mitochondria more efficient is the name of the game to improve all aspects of health, vitality, and lifespan. There are some great ways to do this through the cytochrome pathway. We will cover a way to access all 4 cytochrome pathways in this chapter. Also, later in this chapter we will discuss strategies to improve mitochondrial function through something called autophagy and mitophagy. It is important to fully understand how stress and cytokines work at the cellular level to appreciate some of my methods.

Stress, Cytokines & Melatonin.

All stressors lead to one outcome which is inflammation. Whether it's a sunburn, an infection, or even intense exercise, there is a specific set of cytokines that are responsible for the inflammation that occurs, which in essence, is cellular stress. When that inflammation or the cytokines become too overwhelming for the

cell to deal with, it switches its energy production method from moving electrons in the mitochondria to a very primitive way of making energy called aerobic glycolysis. The problem with aerobic glycolysis is that it only produces 10% of the energy that is otherwise created through the electron transport chain. This is what chokes off the energy reserves with COVID-19 when a patient

goes into a cytokine storm that typically leads to death due to acute respiratory distress syndrome[1]. I wrote a book called *Melatonin: Miracle Molecule*. You can find information on this at melatoninbook.com. In this book, we discussed how melatonin has been shown to enhance the health of virtually every system in your body. There is a large body of research that supports the use of high dose melatonin for a variety of different diseases. When you consider that the brain and the heart are the two most metabolically sensitive organs in the body, it is easy to understand that melatonin may improve the function of the central nervous system and support many people looking to improve the health of their brains.

Stress & The Neurological Ceiling.

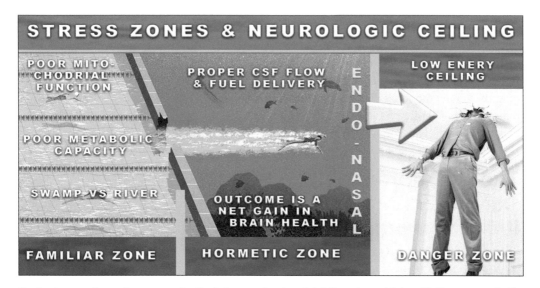

In the image above factors on the far left are mitochondrial function which will dictate metabolic capacity or the ceiling that will become limiting when there becomes too much demand on the nervous system.

Therapeutic Approaches to a Healthy Nervous System

Whenever we want to create strength or activate a healing response in the body, it is always through stressors acting on all your genes where your body responds, and you get a net gain in health. The zone you benefit most from is the hormesis zone. The familiar zone is too little to activate any changes and the danger zone is when it's too much activation or stimulation. The metabolic ceiling is what limits the hormetic zone's outer boarder. By supporting the autonomics' mitochondrial function and circulation (fuel delivery and detoxification), you can have a positive effect on how far you can push into the hormetic zone before hitting the danger zone. You can see how beneficial this would be if you had a neurologic condition and you were looking to improve and broaden the amount of activation to the brain. The nervous system is a bit different than if you were to train the muscular system in the sense that you would want to push it beyond your abilities to full exhaustion to best activate the strengthening effect that exercise has on your muscles. With the brain, it's much better to stay below the ceiling and only push

the neurology just above the point where the system is comfortable yet outside the familiar zone. One of the things that drives neuroplasticity more than anything else is a new and novel experience. When I say the familiar zone, it's not necessarily things that are familiar to you as much as it's describing the amount of energy that the system can utilize before crashing. In training the brain, it is better to do small doses frequently versus the muscular system that can be done once a week. I'll often have my patients do neurologic exercises every 1 to 2 hours while they're awake.

The Cytochrome Complex. What is it & why would you want to know about CCO?

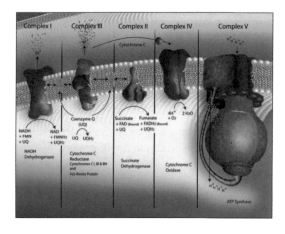

The cytochrome complex consists of cytochrome I-VI and is a small "heme-protein" found associated with all of your mitochondria. It belongs to the cytochrome c family of proteins and plays a major role in cell apoptosis (cell death) and is an essential component of the electron transport chain, where it actually carries an electron. It primarily transfers electrons between Complexes III (Coenzyme Q) and IV (CCO). Since the cytochrome complex is a component of the electron transport chain in mitochondria; it helps your mitochondria shuffle those electrons along which allows it to make energy.

In the study, "Interplay between up-regulation of CCO and hemoglobin oxygenation induced by laser," the author describes how this process using red-to-near-infrared light can stimulate cellular functions for physiological or clinical benefits[2]. The mechanism of LLLT is assumed to rely on photon absorption by cytochrome c oxidase (CCO). This is the machinery within the mitochondrial respiratory chain that catalyzes energy metabolism.

Luke Storey receiving LumeBlue IV protocol (IV Methylene Blue & Silver with PhotoBiomodulation with red light both on IV bag as well as IV laser using LumeStem system- after receiving endo-nasal (FCR).

Red Light Therapy & Photo-Bio-Modulation.

I use Photobiomodulation therapy regularly in my practice to enhance cellular energy in the brain and body as well as improve circulation, angiogenesis, synaptogenesis (neuroplasticity), increase neurotrophins such as BDNF, NGF, & GDNF, increase SOD Antioxidant System, neuron progenitor cells (stem cell activation) and as an anti-inflammatory. In Chapter 15, I deep dive into the research and how I use it clinically along with Methylene Blue which further enhances energy production through the same pathways, and when combined together, can be magical.

Nebulized Glutathione

Glutathione is a sulfur helix that has a number of positive effects in the body. It is considered a master antioxidant in the body and is produced through the liver, primarily. Besides having antiviral support[3], it is also one of the primary ways that we detox chemicals out of our body. Glutathione also has an anti-inflammatory and calming effect to both the body and the brain. I have been using nebulized glutathione along with my endonasal treatments for over 2 decades now and have found them to be very synergistic. I will often give the patient nebulized glutathione after their treatment. Using Glutagenesis in a nebulizer helps to improve neurological status through its calming and modulating effects.

NAD+ & Neurological Fitness

First, let's discuss why you might want to supplement w*ith NAD+. NAD+* or Nicotinamide Adenine Dinucleotide. NAD+ is a sister to Niacin, which is a vital vitamin that you cannot live without. NAD+ is a critical coenzyme found in every cell in your body, and it is involved in hundreds of metabolic processes. Maintenance of an optimal NAD+/NADH ratio is essential for mitochondrial function. The maintenance of the mitochondrial NAD+ pool is of crucial importance. From plants to metazoans, an increase in intracellular levels of NAD^+ directs cells to make adjustments to ensure survival, including increasing energy production and utilization, boosting cellular repair, and coordinating circadian rhythms. By the time we are middle-aged, levels of NAD^+ will have fallen to half of the youthful levels. In recent years, several studies have shown that the treatment of old mice with precursors to NAD^+ can greatly improve health. Observed effects include increased insulin sensitivity, a reversal of mitochondrial dysfunction, reduced stem cell senescence, and lifespan extension[4].

Euler-Chelpin, in his 1930 Nobel Prize speech, says, "NAD+ is one of the most widespread and biologically important activators within the plant and animal world[5]."

NAD+ levels are related to the expression of NF-κB, and low-grade inflammation is a primary driving force of aging[6]. A possibility is that addressing inflammation is the answer to slowing the aging process. Doctors in the know, and scientists in the field, all conclude that molecules that maintain NAD^+ levels, will allow people to celebrate many more anniversaries. Inflammation is not just linked to aging but is present and involved in almost all disease processes.

NAD+ levels naturally decline with age, and various stressors can deplete your NAD+ at a more rapid rate. Poor restorative sleep and alcohol use are the top two stressors that deplete NAD+; however, any stressor will drain away NAD+. The "Stress" categories include anytime you have a higher energy demand, immune activation due to infections stress, mental stress, emotional stress, physical stress, structural stress, electromagnetic (EMF's) stress, and chemical stress. We cannot avoid these completely, and so, inevitably, our NAD+ levels will be taxed, creating a need to replace NAD+.

In this article, *"Why NAD^+ Declines during Aging: It's Destroyed," the author states, "NAD^+ is required not only for life but for a long life...the decline of NAD^+ during aging, with implications for combating age-related diseases*[7]*. "*

I don't advocate ignoring underlying stressors driving inflammation and only supplementing with NAD+ but rather approaching it from both sides. You can receive an NAD+ via an IV because it's not possible to absorb it orally. These intravenous therapies of NAD+ are extremely expensive. I am an advocate for the use of suppositories as the best route as they absorb slowly into the bloodstream just like or better than an IV; there's no side effects like there are when you're running an IV of NAD+ so it's much more convenient and considerably less expensive. We use the product in NAD+Max which is sold in both an oral liposomal as well as suppository form from MitoZen.com. The dosage is comparable to what you would get at a doctor's visit with an NAD+ IV. Also, it is not smart to supplement NAD+ or NAD+ precursors like NMN or NR every day as it will support senescent cells which we will get into soon, so it's best to pulse NAD+ 3 to 5 times a week. Warning: According to this study, boosting levels of NAD+ may make senescent cells more aggressively inflammatory[8]. It's smart to only take NAD+ 3-5 times a week or pulse NAD+ and not to take it during your fasting windows.

Fasting, Autophagy & Mitochondria

Mitochondrial dysfunction is a hallmark of metabolic decline (vitality) during aging[9]. You're constantly replacing your old, weak, dysfunctional mitochondria with new, healthy mitochondria or "mito". The population of all the mito of a given cell constitutes your *Chondriome*. Like your MicroBiome, we have a healthy pool of them or an unhealthy pool, which dictates how functional they are. The average cell in your body has between 1,000-2,000 mito. Again, they turn over as they get old. They are recycled, and it's a process mediated through gene expression ruled by **mTOR**.

The mTOR pathway is a central regulator of metabolism (vitality) and physiology (function)[10]. Without getting too deep into mTOR, let's just leave it at the fact that when mTOR is inhibited, we shift into a cleaning and recycling phase where we see Autophagy and Mitophagy.

Autophagy is a Latin word that translates into "self-eating." Autophagy is the body's way of cleaning out damaged cells in order to regenerate newer, healthier cells[11].

Mitophagy is the selective degradation of mitochondria by autophagy. It often occurs to defective mitochondria following damage or stress[12].

Remember all the types of stress? These ALL have an impact on the demand for Mitophagy to be activated through mTOR! So, what activates mTOR and Autophagy? Fasting is the primary activator of this process! We will revisit this soon, but first, we need to talk about senescent cells. What are senescent cells, and how do they have a detrimental effect on health and life span? They accumulate, due to poor Autophagy (which normally removes and recycles them).

Cellular Senescence, Zombie Cells & How to Recycle Them Into New Cells.

Cellular senescence is an irreversible cell-cycle arrest mechanism that acts to protect against cancer[13].

Basically, cellular senescence is a permanent state of sleep a cell goes into. This state is associated with a release of inflammatory products and higher energy consumption, pulling it away from your healthy cells. They are zombies in the literal sense!

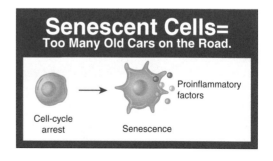

Production of pro-inflammatory cytokines and chemokines are emerging as a common feature of senescent cells irrespective of the senescence-inducing stressor or mechanism.

Cultured cells usually reach senescence within several weeks after exposure to senescence-inducing stressors but remain viable for months after that[14].

This means these "zombies" will float around spewing inflammation and sucking the life out of your body by deferring vital energy that would normally be going to healthy cells.

Another consideration here is ozone therapy which we use intravenously in our clinic. Ozone works through hormetic activation in the body which results in very powerful autophagy and mitophagy responses. I will often have my patients do ozone during their fasting phase. There are home units you can purchase and do rectal installations that are very powerful. There are also saunas that can be purchased that deliver ozone quite efficiently. Methylene blue such as in Lumotol Blue is also a substance that activates autophagy and can be taken during fasting. Remember care needs to be taken with this substance because it amplifies antidepressants or MAO inhibitors.

Plant Extracts Which Inhibit mTOR & Activating Autophagy.

There are a few extracts worth mentioning that have been reported to inhibit mTOR signaling. Apigenin, a family member of flavonoids, is abundant in fruits (oranges, apples, cherries, grapes), vegetables (onions, parsley, broccoli, sweet green pepper, celery, barley, tomatoes), and beverages (tea, wine)[15]. Cryptotanshinone is one of the major tanshinones isolated from the roots of the plant *Salvia miltiorrhiza Bunge* (Danshen)[16]. Another helpful extract is Curcumin (diferuloylmethane), a natural polyphenol product of the plant *Curcuma longa*[17]. Fisetin might be the more powerful of all polyphenols, is in the family member of flavonoids, and occurs in fruits and vegetables, such as strawberries, apples, persimmons, and onions[18]. Indoles are natural compounds in cruciferous vegetables such as broccoli, cauliflower, cabbage, and brussels sprouts[19]. Isoflavones, a class of flavonoid phenolic compounds, are rich in soybean[20]. Quercetin, a polyphenolic compound, is mainly from tea consumption, onions, red grapes, and apples[21]. Pterostilbene, from blueberries, is another one. Resveratrol, a natural polyphenol rich in red grapes and red wine suppresses mTOR signaling as does Tocotrienols, members of vitamin E superfamily[22]. Finally, it is worth mentioning that many other natural products, such as caffeine, epigallocatechin gallate (EGCG, in green tea), celastrol, butein, capsaicin, and β-elemene (a class of terpenes such as Beta Pinene from the pine tree family) can all inhibit mTOR and upregulate autophagy.

You can't possibly get all of this or even a fraction of the dosage of each of these plant extracts in a standard diet or even eating lots of the plants high in them. Research shows that, for example, curcumin can't absorb well. You need to take piperine to aid in its absorption and even then, very little is absorbed compared to what you ingest. This is why delivery methods other than oral might be considered to get the most robust autophagy and mitophagy. Finding a quality product that has liposomal formulations is good and suppositories which bypasses the first pass in the liver and enzymes in the stomach and intestines makes this a superior delivery which might rival an IV infusion as per its absorption!

What about After the Fast?

Post fast or the re-feeding is as important as the fast. This is where you would want to activate mTOR which means growth, repair, and stem cells. Amino acids, especially leucine, are the primary activators of mTOR, which you want to activate at this point to increase the growth and repair after your fast. Below is a typical recommendation I will have for people after fasting.

- A supplement high in leucine like StemTOR, PerfectAmino's and a diet high in protein during this phase will activate mTOR! Deer antler velvet and Rhodiola are also contained in StemTOR which further enhance mTOR. Take StemTOR 2 x a day for 2-3 days following your fast.

- Perfect Amino's 4 scoops per day. 5 grams per scoop. Best to take 15-20 grams a day for 2-3 days following the fast.

How to take all this information and use it for Fasting. Introduction to the Fast Track Fast.

Example of how the Fast Track Fast™ protocol can be accomplished with MitoZen. com's: **NAD+Max™, Lucitol™ & StemTOR™**

NAD+Max™ is a combination of both precursors to NAD+ (Nicotinamide Riboside / NR 250mg and Nicotinamide MonoNucleotide / NMN 250mg) as well as Nicotinamide Adenine Dinucleotide / NAD+ 500 mg. Available in suppository and liposomal delivery.

Lucitol™ is a blend of polyphenols: Fisetin, ECGC, Resveratrol, Quercetin, Apocynin, Ginkgo Baloba, Lutein and Curcumin. This stack is intended to support a senolytic (senescent cell clearing and recycling) effect through Autophagy as well as activate Mitophagy.

Available in suppository and liposomal delivery.

StemTOR™- Leucine, Rhodiola and HMB suppository.

You can either use suppositories or the liposomal version of these products. Liposomal delivery is a way to wrap the contents inside a liposome so that it is more easily absorbed. Suppositories are a rectal delivery method that can be very powerful. The substance bypasses the first pass in the liver and digestive enzymes so the nutrient stays intact and is slowly released over 5-6 hours making it highly absorbable and gives the body a chance to pull the nutrients deeper into our cells where they are needed. Both have superior absorption versus standard oral routes of administration. The suppositories give an added benefit due to its slower release, allowing for a more prolonged peak plasma level in your blood. Sometimes stacking both NAD+Max™ suppository and a Liposomal formulation result in an even stronger NAD+ dosing.

Below is a suggested program I have used in my clinic. You can substitute these suggestions with other products if you choose.

PHASE 1- Monday & Tuesday

NAD+ Loading Phase.

After breakfast - take (1) NAD+Max™ Suppository or 10 mls of NAD+Max Ultra Liposomal

After lunch - take (1) NAD+Max™ Suppository or 10 mls of NAD+Max Ultra™ Liposomal

**you can take two suppositories at once, which will give even more NAD+ in your loading phase.

PHASE 2- Wed & Thursday-

Cleaning / Autophagy / Senolytic Phase (This can be done with or without a fast).

I suggest a 24-36 hour fast such as a lunch to lunch fast (A full 3-day fast can be done here also).

Take (1) Lucitol™ suppository, or 10 ml of Lucitol Ultra™ Liposomal, twice a day.

Consider ozone therapy such as a rectal insufflation or drinking ozonated water.

PHASE 3- Friday & Saturday-

Regeneration, Stem Cell Production, Cellular Growth Phase.

Take (1) StemTOR™ suppository twice a day. mTOR signaling taken in the post fast phase.

Up your dietary protein intake and also supplementation with perfect amino's at 15-20 grams a day.

Dosing schedule example using senolytics during a 24-36 hour fast:

Wed: Mid-Day and Evening - *Take (1) Lucitol™ suppository or 10 ml of Lucitol Ultra Liposomal.*

Thurs: Morning and Mid-Day - *Take (1) Lucitol™ suppository or 10 ml of Lucitol Ultra Liposomal.*

Phase 3 Optional Upgrade #1: Stem Cell Support.

Stem cells are also vulnerable to becoming senescent. This is a real problem in regenerative medicine today. We are one of the first clinics to begin using stem cells for our patients here in the US, and for example, if we would aspirate some bone marrow from your pelvic bone then place those stem cells into your knee joint, only a certain percentage of those would survive and the others would become senescent, essentially becoming

useless. Stem cell survival is a real problem for doctors like us and we use techniques to provide a better "home" or an environment that would provide the stem cells more support to proliferate and differentiate to repair and regenerate your body. There are a few substances that have been shown to be great support to stem cells. CoQ 10 and Fucoidan are two of my favorites! CoQ 10 is a powerful anti-oxidant and Fucoidan is a polysaccharide from brown seaweed. Evidence for both Fucoidan and CoQ-10 in the prevention of stem cell senescence is clear, which allows more stem cells to do the regenerative work on your body. CoQ10 has shown to protect stem cell aging and mechanisms of cell senescence are inhibited by CoQ10[23]. Fucoidan rescues mesenchymal stem cells from cellular senescence and increases stem cell proliferation through the regulation of cell cycle-associated proteins[24]. CoQ-10 has poor absorption orally, so a suppository route can allow much higher bioavailability of CoQ-10. There are benefits to using these nutrients post fast so that when your new stem cells are released, more of them will survive. We have a product called StemZen in in our practice that comes in a suppository that is very high in fucoidan. It may make sense to support this for a week or two after any type of stem cell therapy and/or extended fasting protocol.

Phase 3 Optional Upgrade #2: Microbiome Swarming Support.

The Role of Fasting & Melatonin on Microbiome Health & Swarming

Poor quality gut microbiota is highly associated with both acute or chronic diseases, in particular digestive disorders including inflammatory bowel disease, liver cirrhosis and colorectal cancer, and thus is responsible for the unrelenting increase in so-called diseases-of-affluence[25]. Fasting can be a great way to reset your microbiome through a healthy stress called hormesis. Fasting has been shown to improve obesity and multiple sclerosis in experimental models through restoring gut microbiota[26, 27].

Microbiome swarming is used to stimulate more growth of the good bacteria. Using melatonin supplementation may be the answer. Your gut produces 400 times more melatonin than your brain[28]. Gut melatonin is the main activator of microbiome swarming which is the primary signaling for the good gut bacteria to grow in numbers.

One research study, 'Human Gut Bacteria are Sensitive to Melatonin and Express Endogenous Circadian Rhythmicity,' published in the PLoS One in 2016 has stated that "Melatonin specifically increases the magnitude of swarming in cultures of E. aerogenes, but not in Escherichia coli or Klebsiella pneumoniae[29]." The swarming appeared to occur on a daily basis by the body's circadian rhythm synchronized perfectly in the presence of melatonin[30]. This study focused on assessing the impact of the body's circadian rhythm on gut health. Circadian rhythm is the fundamental property of most eukaryotes including humans, animals, plants, and even fungi. In vertebrates, like humans, the digestive system expresses a strong circadian pattern hard linked to melatonin. Recent studies suggest that the gut flora, which is composed of trillions of healthy bacteria is regulated primarily by the circadian clock of the body. And this circadian rhythm, in turn, is regulated by how much melatonin is secreted in your body at specific times.

I have used larger than typical melatonin dosages in the 100-200 mg to activate microbiome swarming. Using melatonin in a suppository makes sense for this action as the microbiome primarily exists in your large intestines so placing the melatonin there may lead to more of a swarming effect. Sandman™ suppository is our 'go to' product as an optional upgrade to the Mito Phase™ during the post fasting / re-feeding phase. This can be taken for 2 days up to a week or longer post fast as microbiome support.

Advanced Options for PHASE 3- Friday-Saturday

Microbiome Swarming Activation & Microbiome Probiotic Support, Nutrient Support for new Stem Cells to prevent senescence.

Take (1) Sandman™ suppository at bedtime. High dose 200 mg melatonin.

Take (1) ProbioMax™ suppository twice a day. Spore Based Probiotic & Butyrate.

Take (1) StemZen™ suppository twice a day. CoQ10 & Fucoidan

So, what's the answer? How do you clear these senescence cells from the body?

It happens to be the same process involved with Autophagy and Mitophagy, where mTOR is involved. Fasting and senolytics are the best answer to clean, clear, and recycle these "zombie" cells. This is why we stack the most powerful senolytics on the planet with a 24-hour lunch-to- lunch fast that can be done each week or pulsed as directed by your health care provider. A long 3-day fast is suggested for a more powerful effect. The microbiome should also be considered within this process as the fasting phase is a positive stressor to the good bacteria and can allow for a positive effect to your microbiome post fasting. Adding a good spore-based probiotic, butyrate and a high dose melatonin are excellent ways to support this and even give it a boost. Your microbiome has a circadian rhythm just like you do and when "gut melatonin," which is 400 times higher than within the brain[31] is raised during sleep, it is a powerful activator to something called "swarming". One study, 'Human Gut Bacteria Are Sensitive to Melatonin and Express

Endogenous Circadian Rhythmicity,' stated a human signaling that powerfully affects gut microbiome is the secretion of melatonin into the lumen of the intestine. Another study showed that melatonin specifically increases the magnitude of swarming in cultures of E. aerogenes (good bacteria), but not in E. coli or Klebsiella (bad Bacteria)[32]. This swarming is how your microbiome regenerates. Taking a very high dose of melatonin such as 200 or more mg for a few days may be of benefit. Keep in mind, oral melatonin is only 2.5% absorbable[33]. Suppository or liposomal delivery would make better sense. Suppository would deliver the melatonin directly to the large intestines where your microbiome lives! We will speak on melatonin again soon. Butyrate and probiotic's can be given rectally as a suppository which has a huge advantage as it's placing the substances right where it is needed.

If you are looking to be better, think clearer, have more energy and function at a higher level, these two aspects of health that lead to better and stronger Mito can't be ignored. Restoring youthful NAD+ levels, using cellular clean up and recycling such as Autophagy and Mitophagy can be a great strategy to add to any neurological program and endo-nasal series. The Fast Track Fast is easy to do and tolerated by most. The Phase can be done once a week four days a month, or less, if a less aggressive approach is desired. Some people start with once a week and might consider this

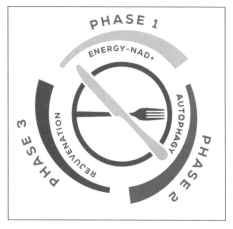

for a few months to a year. Others might do a couple of months a year as a maintenance. Before you start this protocol, consult your health care provider, and use their guidance.

Fast Track Fast is a common program I will run my neurological cases through, and I have seen much better results with using fasting this way. If you have a difficult time with fasting, then consider supplementing with exogenous ketones like BHB or Ketone esters. It's about becoming metabolically flexible and having the option to gain energy through fat and protein via ketosis.

Below is the D.E.R.R. approach I use in my clinic.

You will notice many of these treatments are aimed at three basic goals:

1) **DETOX**- Detoxification of the liver, gallbladder, and gut. Deep cellular detoxification by clearing toxic build up within the cell membrane.

2) **ELIMINATE INFECTIONS**- Finding and eliminating microbial overgrowth.

3) **RESTORE CELLULAR ENERGY**- Metabolic Therapies- Improving mitochondrial function.

4) **REGENERATE**- Repairing what is possible to do so using regenerative medicine with stem cells. VSELs, Peptides, Nutritional methods like Fasting, Oxygen Therapies, and PhotoBiomodulation.

This is a list of some of the therapies we use in my clinic.

IV therapies using ozone, oxygen therapy using CVAC, PhotoBioModulation, LumoBlue (IV Methylene Blue with IV laser & CVAC) laser therapy, LumoMed Inner Ear Therapy, hyperthermia, stem cells therapy, NAD+ therapy, Fasting (Fast Track Fast), Supporting BDNF, Detox programs and testing and treatment for chronic infections of EBV, CMV, HHV-6, Lyme, Mold Illness (CIRS, Biotoxin illness).

In addition to these, I emphasize a liver, gallbladder, gut cleanse using binders, as well as an initial 30-day sinus protocol followed by proper sinus hygiene.

Two of the most common suggestions I have with new patients in my clinic are to do a 30-day sinus protocol which we discussed in other chapters along with taking binders to mop up all of the toxic buildup that is circulating in your bile. The product called BIND is excellent and I generally will have people take 3 to 4 of those before bed as the first couple of hours of sleep is a time where your gallbladder releases a lot of bile. In the morning is another good time to take a binder especially after drinking some lemon juice. For more difficult cases that have biotoxin illness associated with them and mold exposure, they will need to look at a prescription binder called Cholestyramine. Find my 30-day sinus protocol here.

BDNF & Neuroplasticity

BDNF enough stands for brain derived neurotrophic factor. BDNF supports the survival of neurons and brain cells, promotes synaptic connections between neurons, and is essential for learning and long-term memory storage[34]. BDNF is low with Alzheimer's and dementia[35]. Some scientists think that boosting BDNF levels could help preserve their brain function. Other evidence suggests the higher your BDNF, the lower your risk of Alzheimer's and dementia.

Hot sauna's can be helpful to stimulate your body to release BDNF through something called heat shock proteins. Cold therapy does the same and can be accomplished with cold plunges or cryotherapy. Exercise, sleep, and nutrition can all effect your BDNF levels. The stress hormone cortisol has a negative effect on BDNF. BDNF helps you to learn, adapt, and supercharges neuroplasticity.

These are some considerations to raise BDNF.

- Get proper exercise 3 or more times a day. I like blood flow restriction training along with super slow resistive style training. Cardio is the form of sprint interval or grizzly bear intervals.

- Avoid processed foods with vegetable oils and consuming too many sugars.

- Eating plenty of high-quality protein can help your brain stay healthy as you age. One reason is that amino acids, the building blocks of proteins, are necessary for the production of neurotransmitters--including BDNF. I personally like essential amino acids such as in Kion Aminos. Dark chocolate, blueberries, and extra-virgin olive oil are high-polyphenol foods that are proven to increase BDNF and support brain health.

- Extended Fasting. Similar to carb restriction, ketosis and beta-hydroxybutyrate production could be one reason extended fasting windows (at least 48 hours but better 3-5 days) can increase BDNF while shorter fasts don't do it as effectively. I created the Fast Track Fast protocol. You can read my article on this here.

- Get quality sleep. Make sure you're not getting light pollution when the sun goes down. Use blue blocking glasses at night and limit electronic devices. Turn off WiFi at night, get sun in your eyes during the day and many people might consider supplementing with melatonin.

- Use techniques to reduce stress like meditation, breathing exercises like Wim Hoff style, Soma, or fire breath. Do things you love to do and laugh more and connect with your true self through being in silence and avoid always being busy and adrenalized. Hot yoga would be a great way to increase BDNF!

- Take mushrooms like Lions Mane. Animal studies show that lion's mane mushroom extract supports brain health by stimulating the creation of two important compounds: nerve growth factor (NGF) and brain-derived neurotrophic factor (BDNF).

- Sauna or Cold therapy through heat shock proteins.

- Semax peptide enhances BDNF. It's been shown in animal studies to increase BDNF These can be found as a nasal spray. Occasionally MitoZen.com will carry one called NeuroMax. You need to call and ask as it's a special order.

Enhancing BDNF along with Endo-Nasal and/or Functional Neurology are great ways to optimize and support the brain to make positive changes through neuroplasticity.

What are the Stressors we face today?

There are a lot of stressors we face today that our parents did not have to deal with. In this section, we will discuss some of these ideas to stay healthy and vital. There are now thousands of toxins in our environment and saturating our bodies. EMF or electromagnetic stressors can affect our circadian rhythm, cellular energy, and cause microbes to be multiple times more virulent. For hyper adrenalized states, we use technology to become ultra-productive causing  a constant busy state. Poor nutrient content in our food and super bugs whether genetically created or due to antibiotic resistance, are additional concerns. Light pollution such as not getting enough sunshine during the day and getting too much blue and green light in the evening, is triggering a daytime response affecting our circadian rhythm. I personally think that the pharmaceutical industry is poisoning us. I would put this as a stressor as many of my patients are taking more than 10 prescriptions. Doctors pushing polypharmacy on their patients is widespread and this could be leading to many diseases we are yet to discover. Then, there is poor water quality. We simply need to do more to stay healthy these days!

Conclusion

As you can see after reading this chapter there are a lot of various therapies and modalities that can be combined with an Endo nasal treatment. In my clinic, we often create custom protocols for patients based on how they present as well as various lab findings. In this chapter, we have presented many things that you can do at home. I always recommend people work with a healthcare provider whenever they start any type of program like discussed in this chapter. There are a few things more important than neurological fitness. It is essential to keep your brain and central nervous system healthy and contained within a structure that supports it, meaning in your skull. All of these therapies work better when the cranium has its proper motion, also call cranial sacral motion because it delivers nutrients and carries out metabolic wastes. Remember you're either a swamp or a river and increasing glymphatic circulation is important for a healthy central nervous system. Remember the glymphatics are activated primarily during deep sleep so pay close attention to the discussion on high-dose melatonin. You can also go to the website melatoninbook.com for more information on the book *Melatonin: Miracle Molecule*. And also, please note all of these therapies we discuss work much better when you are getting proper sleep. So, track your sleep and make sure you're getting enough R.E.M. and Deep Sleep to support your brain. Looking at a lot of these modalities one might think that it can get a little extreme. Consider all of the stressors that we have in today's world which makes it more important for us to take some extra precautionary steps as well as integrate some rituals into our daily routine such as 10 minutes of red-light therapy in the morning with a device like the MitoLight. Using ozone at home directly, methylene blue such as Lumetol Blue, BDNF enhancing substances, and Fasting with Fast Track Fast are all great options to enhance your health through what I call upstream therapies. These are therapies addressing metabolic conditions especially through the mitochondria. Many types of treatments and modalities are what I called downstream whereby they address genes or enzymes or certain chemistry in the body. I

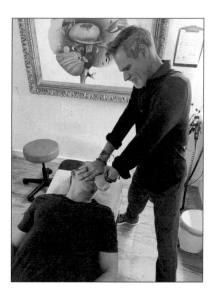

like to go as upstream to the core of what is disturbing the health and vitality at a cellular level. Remember the body is an amazing machine. It is self-regulating, self-healing, and has innate intelligence, and when given the right energy can do a much better job than throwing chemistry at it. Metabolic medicine addressing the mitochondria and the energy reserves in the body is the most powerful medi-

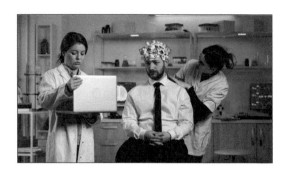

cine available and when combined with endo-nasal releases can restore health in the way nothing else can offer. When you address the function of the nervous system through functional neurology you have what I consider to be the ultimate situation to recover from a condition or simply be at your functional best.

References

1. Reiter, R. J., Sharma, R., Ma, Q., Dominquez-Rodriguez, A., Marik, P. E., & Abreu-Gonzalez, P. (2020). Melatonin Inhibits COVID-19-induced Cytokine Storm by .Reversing Aerobic Glycolysis in Immune Cells: A Mechanistic Analysis. *Medicine in drug discovery*, *6*, 100044. https://doi.org/10.1016/j.medidd.2020.100044

2. Wang X, Tian F, Soni SS, Gonzalez-Lima F, Liu H. Interplay between up-regulation of cyto-chrome-c-oxidase and hemoglobin oxygenation induced by near-infrared laser. Sci Rep. 2016 Aug 3;6:30540. doi: 10.1038/srep30540. PMID: 27484673; PMCID: PMC4971496.

3. Lana JFSD, Lana AVSD, Rodrigues QS, Santos GS, Navani R, Navani A, da Fonseca LF, Azzini GOM, Setti T, Mosaner T, Simplicio CL, Setti TM. Nebulization of glutathione and N-Acetylcysteine as an adjuvant therapy for COVID-19 onset. Adv Redox Res. 2021 Dec;3:100015. doi: 10.1016/j.arres.2021.100015. Epub 2021 Aug 8. PMID: 35425932; PMCID: PMC8349474.

4. Yamaguchi S, Yoshino J. Adipose tissue NAD$^+$ biology in obesity and insulin resistance: From mechanism to therapy. Bioessays. 2017 May;39(5):10.1002/bies.201600227. doi: 10.1002/bies.201600227. Epub 2017 Mar 15. PMID: 28295415; PMCID: PMC5469033.

5. Hans von Euler-Chelpin – Biographical - NobelPrize.org

6. Covarrubias AJ, Perrone R, Grozio A, Verdin E. NAD$^+$ metabolism and its roles in cellu-lar processes during ageing. Nat Rev Mol Cell Biol. 2021 Feb;22(2):119-141. doi: 10.1038/s41580-020-00313-x. Epub 2020 Dec 22. PMID: 33353981; PMCID: PMC7963035.

7. Schultz MB, Sinclair DA. Why NAD(+) Declines during Aging: It's Destroyed. Cell Metab. 2016 Jun 14;23(6):965-966. doi: 10.1016/j.cmet.2016.05.022. PMID: 27304496; PMCID: PMC5088772.

8. Nacarelli, T., Lau, L., Fukumoto, T. *et al.* NAD$^+$ metabolism governs the proinflammatory senescence-associated secretome. *Nat Cell Biol* **21**, 397–407 (2019). https://doi.org/10.1038/s41556-019-0287-4

9. Srivastava S. The Mitochondrial Basis of Aging and Age-Related Disorders. Genes (Basel). 2017 Dec 19;8(12):398. doi: 10.3390/genes8120398. PMID: 29257072; PMCID: PMC5748716.

10. Srivastava S. The Mitochondrial Basis of Aging and Age-Related Disorders. Genes (Basel). 2017 Dec 19;8(12):398. doi: 10.3390/genes8120398. PMID: 29257072; PMCID: PMC5748716.

11. Glick D, Barth S, Macleod KF. Autophagy: cellular and molecular mechanisms. J Pathol. 2010 May;221(1):3-12. doi: 10.1002/path.2697. PMID: 20225336; PMCID: PMC2990190.

12. Ding WX, Yin XM. Mitophagy: mechanisms, pathophysiological roles, and analysis. Biol Chem. 2012 Jul;393(7):547-64. doi: 10.1515/hsz-2012-0119. PMID: 22944659; PMCID: PMC3630798.

13. Lee S, Lee JS. Cellular senescence: a promising strategy for cancer therapy. BMB Rep. 2019 Jan;52(1):35-41. doi: 10.5483/BMBRep.2019.52.1.294. PMID: 30526771; PMCID: PMC6386234.

14. Chen H, Li Y, Tollefsbol TO. Cell senescence culturing methods. Methods Mol Biol. 2013;1048:1-10. doi: 10.1007/978-1-62703-556-9_1. PMID: 23929093; PMCID: PMC3873382.

15. Huang S. Inhibition of PI3K/Akt/mTOR signaling by natural products. Anticancer Agents Med Chem. 2013 Sep;13(7):967-70. doi: 10.2174/1871520611313070001. PMID: 23272914; PMCID: PMC3775843.7.

16. IBID

17. IBID

18. IBID

19. IBID

20. IBID

21. IBID

22. IBID

23. Zhang D, Yan B, Yu S, Zhang C, Wang B, Wang Y, Wang J, Yuan Z, Zhang L, Pan J. Coenzyme Q10 inhibits the aging of mesenchymal stem cells induced by D-galactose through Akt/mTOR signaling. Oxid Med Cell Longev. 2015;2015:867293. doi: 10.1155/2015/867293. Epub 2015 Feb 18. PMID: 25789082; PMCID: PMC4348608.

24. Lee JH, Yun CW, Hur J, Lee SH. Fucoidan Rescues p-Cresol-Induced Cellular Senescence in Mesenchymal Stem Cells via FAK-Akt-TWIST Axis. Mar Drugs. 2018 Apr 6;16(4):121. doi: 10.3390/md16040121. PMID: 29642406; PMCID: PMC5923408.

25. Vijay, A., Valdes, A.M. Role of the gut microbiome in chronic diseases: a narrative review. *Eur J Clin Nutr* **76,** 489–501 (2022). https://doi.org/10.1038/s41430-021-00991-6

26. Boziki MK, Kesidou E, Theotokis P, Mentis AA, Karafoulidou E, Melnikov M, Sviridova A, Rogovski V, Boyko A, Grigoriadis N. Microbiome in Multiple Sclerosis; Where Are We, What We Know and Do Not Know. Brain Sci. 2020 Apr 14;10(4):234. doi: 10.3390/brainsci10040234. PMID: 32295236; PMCID: PMC7226078.

27. Albosta,M.Bakke,J.Intermittent fasting: is there a role in the treatment of diabetes? A review of the literature and guide for primary care physicians. Clin Diabetes Endocrinol, 2021; 7, 3-3. Doi: https://doi.org/10.1186/s40842-020-00116-1

28. Bubenik GA. Gastrointestinal melatonin: localization, function, and clinical relevance. Dig Dis Sci. 2002 Oct;47(10):2336-48. doi: 10.1023/a:1020107915919. PMID: 12395907.

29. Paulose JK, Wright JM, Patel AG, Cassone VM. Human Gut Bacteria Are Sensitive to Melatonin and Express Endogenous Circadian Rhythmicity. PLoS One. 2016 Jan 11;11(1):e0146643. doi: 10.1371/journal.pone.0146643. PMID: 26751389; PMCID: PMC4709092.

30. IBID

31. Bubenik GA. Thirty four years since the discovery of gastrointestinal melatonin. J Physiol Pharmacol. 2008 Aug;59 Suppl 2:33-51. PMID: 18812627.

32. K. Paulose, Jiffin; M. Wright, John; G Patel, Akruti; M. Cassone, Vincent (2016): Swarming behavior in E. aerogenes is induced by melatonin and occurs with a circadian frequency.. PLOS ONE. Figure. https://doi.org/10.1371/journal.pone.0146643.g001

33. Waldhauser F, Waldhauser M, Lieberman H, R, Deng M, -H, Lynch H, J, Wurtman R, J: Bioavailability of Oral Melatonin in Humans. Neuroendocrinology 1984;39:307-313. doi: 10.1159/000123997

34. Weinstein G, Beiser AS, Choi SH, Preis SR, Chen TC, Vorgas D, Au R, Pikula A, Wolf PA, DeStefano AL, Vasan RS, Seshadri S. Serum brain-derived neurotrophic factor and the risk for dementia: the Framingham Heart Study. JAMA Neurol. 2014 Jan;71(1):55-61. doi: 10.1001/jamaneurol.2013.4781. PMID: 24276217; PMCID: PMC4056186.

35. Passaro A, Dalla Nora E, Morieri ML, Soavi C, Sanz JM, Zurlo A, Fellin R, Zuliani G. Brain-derived neurotrophic factor plasma levels: relationship with dementia and diabetes in the elderly population. J Gerontol A Biol Sci Med Sci. 2015 Mar;70(3):294-302. doi: 10.1093/gerona/glu028. Epub 2014 Mar 12. PMID: 24621946.

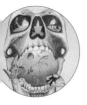

11

INNER EAR REGENERATION: ENDO-NASAL, LASER & STEM CELL THERAPY

Over the last 20 years I have been able to fix things that have been considered incurable. Hearing loss and tinnitus are two of them that achieve good results with endo-nasal therapy. Particularly, when endo-nasal is combined with a few modalities like naturopathic care, stem cell therapy, laser therapy, and ear protection. Keep in mind that a proper functioning cranial is flexible and moves in a rhythm flushing oxygen and nutrient rich CSF that bathes the central nervous system and thus, keeps it free of toxic build up and delivering "groceries". I like to say, *"Bring in the groceries and take out the garbage."* Circulation is not just limited to the CSF and direct blood supply to the brain and ears, it is also lymphatics that will clear fluid from tissues. You have two key systems that work with the inner ear. Lymphatics that drain down through the neck and also the glymphatic system, both of which are the primary gutter system that waste follows to be cleared from tissues in the brain and

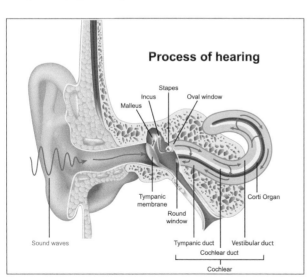

Process of hearing

Stapes
Incus
Oval window
Malleus
Tympanic membrane
Round window
Corti Organ
Sound waves
Tympanic duct
Vestibular duct
Cochlear duct
Cochlear

inner ears. In this chapter we will be covering a few key therapies and strategies specifically for the inner ears to support recovery from afflictions to the inner ear such as vertigo, Meniere's disease, tinnitus and hyperacusis. Using endo-nasal balloons in combination with advanced therapies can be what I call the entourage effect which is 1+1 = 4. In this chapter, we will dive into some of these modalities and why it makes sense to use them in conjunction with an endo-nasal treatment regime.

To understand how these treatments work, you need a good understanding of hair cells.

Hair cells in the inner ear are the nerve cells that allow us to perceive sound waves. They are essential for our balance, hearing, and proper brain function. Without them, we would be deaf and disoriented. If hair cells are damaged in any way, we suffer permanent hearing loss or debilitating balance disorders. We are finding these insufficiencies are also intimately connected to our brain function and can cause issues with proper coordination of the eyes and movement of the body. Since the autonomic nervous system is also wired through these pathways, function of the gut, heart, liver, kidneys, and bladder can all suffer with issues from your hair cells. With these little cells being so important, you would think they would be a major area of new medical breakthroughs… but it's not when compared to other areas of medicine!

What are hair cells?

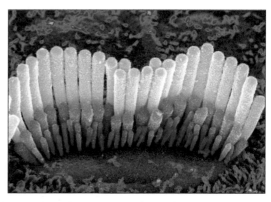

Under a microscope, these cells look as though they have a tiny hair protruding from them. Hence the name "hair cells". Stereocilia are the organ made of hair cells, and they bend in response to sound or other mechanical influence. There are two types: auditory and vestibular. Auditory hair cells, which detect sound, are located in the cochlea of the inner ear. Movements of the stereocilia are transmitted to the brain and interpreted as sound. Our sense of balance is also made possible through vestibular hair cells. These are located in vestibular organs. Loud noises, ototoxic drugs (drugs which damage the hearing), Lyme disease, and other bacterial and viral infections, as well as trauma can all damage hair cells.

Laser Therapy & Photo-Bio-Modulation for the Ear

We discussed Photo-bio-modulation in detail in chapter 7. If you modulate your inner ear structures to support them to be stronger and more resilient, they will function better and can even repair damage. Laser therapy is the use of specific and concentrated light beams to promote cellular repair and vitality. Laser therapy, just like red light, involves the activation of the mitochondrial respiratory chain using the cytochrome complex. The healing effects of laser therapy through low-level laser or photobiomodulation, refers to the use of the energy within the laser to enhance cellular functions for clinical benefits. If you haven't yet, please review the cytochrome complex and how light works to improve energy production within the mitochondria. Lumomed is a protocol created by Dr Kaiser in Germany. He and his father have pioneered the use of laser for inner ear conditions over the last 30 years. I was introduced to Dr Kaiser by a mutual patient whom I did FCR for Meniere's disease. She had great results with FCR

for her balance issues, however, limited benefit to her tinnitus and hearing. In my practice's experience, balance was improved much more rapidly and consistently with the endo-nasal balloon releases along with functional vestibular-based neurological therapies. She was so excited with her results after traveling to Germany from the US to receive the LumoMed protocol. She told me if I integrated the LumoMed with FCR that I would have the most cutting-edge program in the world for inner ear treatment. It wasn't until a few years later I happened to be in Germany and posted on Facebook when this patient responded to my post and told me that I was very close to Dr. Kaiser's clinic in Baden, Germany. I called Dr. Kaiser and was welcomed to his clinic for a meeting. We agreed to bring LumoMed for use in my clinic in Sarasota, Florida and we are the first USA-based center.

LumoMed Inner Ear Protocol

LumoMed uses a special high-powered laser, which puts out 25,000 Joules. It's generally conducted over a 2-3 week period where daily laser treatments are given to each ear. The therapy lasts about 1 hour with 30 minutes for each ear. Ten to twenty treatments are needed in a general series. A pre and post audiometric exam is conducted and we often observe statistically significant improvements in hearing. I

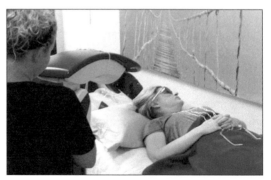

LumoMed laser therapy being performed to our patient's inner ear.

do not find the vertigo cases do well with only the LumoMed where the integration of endo-nasal and functional neurology are important in these cases. The LumoMed seems to speed this process up and is complementary through supporting the inner ear. The laser supports the energy through the mitochondria as well as enhanced lymphatic drainage from the inner ear.

Amon Keiser, ND
LumoMed Founder

Remember your either a swamp or river and a river is much cleaner and free of microbes. Tinnitus is a common inner ear condition that is often caused by damaged hair cells. Due to the central integration of the sound through the inferior colliculus located within the brain stem, tinnitus can become a problem due to the sensory mismatch from the ear to the brain. This is why tinnitus takes longer to see results using LumoMed. Sometimes 4-6 months are needed.

Stem Cells for Inner Ear Health

Dr Minbo Shim & Dr John Lieurance

Recently there has been numerous conversations about both LumoMed and ShimSpot treatments combined together in a treatment called SunaVae. Both Dr. Kaiser and Dr. Shim are excited about the potential of their combining their individual treatments for the inner ear and its potential for an even more advanced result. As mentioned above, LumoMed is a series of laser treatments and ShimSpot is a safe and effective injection of stem cells into the inner ear. Combined, they become SunaVae Therapy.

I have been focusing on inner ear regeneration for many years. By seeking out the best options for treatment, I can regenerate the inner ear for tinnitus, hearing loss, hyperacusis, and balance disorders due to inner ear damage. With COVID and vaccine injuries so prevalent now, this combination has come at the perfect time to support all who suffer damage to the inner ear. The beauty of these two together is not a new way of thinking as an approach to the regeneration of cells. For the past 25 years, the staff at Advanced Rejuvenation and his medical staff have been performing this combination with orthopedic care such as with knees and shoulders. Using stem cells along with laser holds much promise. Stem cells ultimately result in healing of tissue and reduction in inflammation. The laser draws them into the area that is being injected. Stem cells are fragile,

and there is a risk called senescence which means they go to a permanent state of sleep. This is the major focus of many studies to improve stem cell results by scientists working in the field of regenerative medicine. Laser in the spectrum of 660nm is the secret used with SunaVae, and Methylene Blue is also used to further improve the activation of the stem cells by the laser. See Dr. John's on Methylene Blue at www.MethyleneBlueBook.com for more information on this medicine called the "Magic Bullet."

Dr Shim & Dr Lieurance doing clinicals in 2022.

Advanced Rejuvenation has been working to put together the most cutting-edge therapies for the treatment of inner ear health. Currently, we are focused on the combination of regenerative injections into the ear (ShimSpot), laser to the inner ear (LumoMed); a program we call the "Sensory Rejuvenation Protocol," specific lifestyle modifications, nutritional support, and removing all triggers causing inflammation in the nervous system and/or the inner ear.

STUDIES ON LASER FOR INNER EAR CONDITIONS

HARVARD STUDY: Biostimulation of inner ear cells with light.[1]

JOURNAL OF BIOPHOTONICS: PhotoBioModulation reduces inflammatory cytokines and markers of oxidative stress in cochlear hair cells.[2]

Here Are Some Study Results From Dr. Shim On His ShimSpot Treatment:
These results are based on patients treated with ShimSpot.

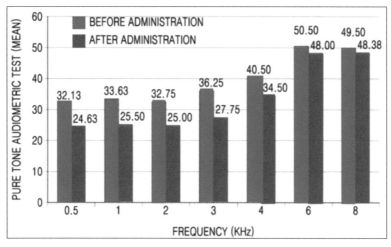

The statistic results are more realistic than dramatic. The better results are within the most meaningful range which is where conversation takes place, and they are statistically significant.

Treatment Result of Sudden Hearing Loss:

A 37-year old Female.

PRP Injections with ShimSPOT x 7 over a 1-month period.

Here are her results:

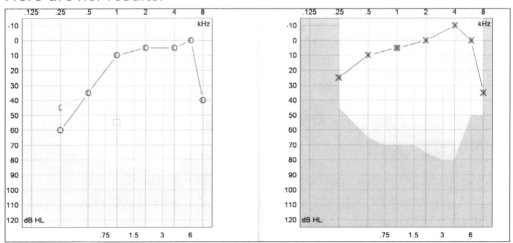

Before

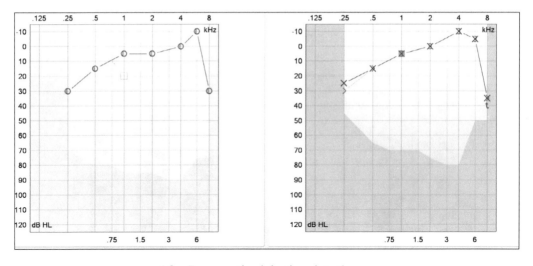

After Regenerative injections into the ear.

Her hearing is now normalized!

SunaVae only requires 2-3 stem cell injections. The injection is painless and only requires you to lay for 30 minutes afterward. LumoMed will be performed shortly after the ShimSpot injection. An IV or an oral preparation of Methylene Blue will be administered each day one received LumeMed. A series of 5-10 treatments of LumeMed laser therapy over a 1-2 week period is suggested. LumoMed is a series of laser treatments. Each lasts an hour, and they are done daily for 1 or 2 weeks for the 5-10 treatments. Folks who travel from out of town can receive 2 treatments per day however this isn't as ideal as receiving one treatment a day. A home laser is suggested to provide laser support at home after the clinic treatments. A follow up visit for laser and or a stem cell booster may be necessary is some cases at 4-6 months. See SunaVae.com for more information on this treatment.

Importance of Ear Protection & Inner Ear Regeneration.

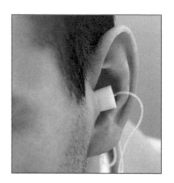

Stress is the inner ears' nemesis. Mental-emotional stress seems to bring on inner ear disease such as vertigo, tinnitus, and hearing loss. Reducing these stresses is emphasized with my patients, however, there is a stress that the ears never get a break from. Consider a runner and how the knee joints take on physical stress due to the constant pounding each time the foot strikes the ground. The inner ear has a different stress; everyday there is sound stress. If you had a knee problem and you came into my office, I would suggest a runner to switch to cycling or working out on an elliptical machine which has far less impact stress to the knees. Think about the inner ear and how it never gets a chance to rest as it is constantly processing sound even while we sleep. How do we give these hair cells a break so they can use the energy they would normally use to process sound to repair itself? The answer is simple. Avoid loud environments and wear ear protection. I suggest that ear protection be worn for a few hours each day or as long as can be tolerated during a program to heal the inner ears. This allows a deep relaxation to the inner ear cells which reduce the stress and burden of supplying the mitochondrial energy to process that sound. This can be combined with what I call "Sensory Rejuvenation Protocol" to support the maximum benefit from the LumoMed, endo-nasal, and any other therapy that you might consider. Next, we will dive deep into the Sensory Rejuvenation Protocol.

The following section will have some repeat information form my Fast Track Fast as it is an identical protocol however the language within the description and a few studies have been added.

Sensory Rejuvenation Protocol
The Amazing Weekly (6-Day) Protocol to Invigorate Your Inner Ear and Overall Energy Reserves.

"Sensory Rejuvenation Protocol" is a technique to invigorate your inner ears. This is done through improving and renewing your mitochondria. One third of your body weight is made up of the mitochondria within your cells. These little structures convert glucose and oxygen to create energy. This energy is needed to run every aspect of all your cellular functions, including your inner ear. They keep your brain running, your hormones secreting hormones, your heart beating, your lungs absorbing vital air, your immune system functioning to protect you from all the viruses, bacteria, and molds in our environment, your gut absorbing nutrients, and your ears working 24/7.

Your mitochondria create the energy needed for all functions of the body. You should appreciate your mitochondria and take care of them, but we don't always get practical ways to do this. Our Sensory Rejuvenation Protocol provides a way, based on science, for you to care for your mitochondria. Taking care of your mitochondria will make positive changes in your health and longevity, including your hearing and inner ear health! Studies show mitochondrial function can greatly impact the quality and length of your life. A worthwhile effort indeed! We will dig into a few technical subjects such as autophagy, mitophagy, cellular senescence, Methylene Blue and NAD+.

Sensory Rejuvenation Fast™ is a six-day program where the first two days are focused on Cellular Energy loading with NAD+ and methylene blue (Lumetol Blue™). The next two days are focused on activating autophagy and mitophagy with the senolytics in plant polyphenols (Lucitol™), and the final two days are focused on generating stem cell growth with StemTOR™. It is optional to make the fasting phase a 24- hour fast from lunch to lunch."

Phase 1: Cellular Energy Loading Phase with NAD+ & Methylene Blue

There are 2 molecules that are important to provide cellular energy, NAD+ and methylene blue. NAD+ (nicotinamide adenine dinucleotide) is a sister to niacin, a vitamin you cannot live without. NAD+ is a critical coenzyme found in every cell in your body, and it is involved in hundreds of metabolic processes. Maintenance of an optimal NAD+/NADH ratio is essential for mitochondrial function. The maintenance of the mitochondrial NAD+ pool is of crucial importance.

From plants to metazoans (multicellular animals), an increase in intracellular levels of NAD$^+$ directs cells to adjust to ensure survival. These NAD+ mechanisms include increasing energy production and utilization, boosting cellular repair, and coordinating circadian rhythms. By the time we are middle-aged, levels of NAD$^+$ will have fallen to half of our youthful levels. In recent years, several studies have shown that treating older mice with precursors to NAD$^+$ can greatly improve health. Observed effects include increased insulin sensitivity, a reversal of mitochondrial dysfunction, reduced stem cell senescence, and lifespan extension.[3]

Here are a couple of studies on NAD+ and Hearing Loss. Short-term NAD+ supplementation prevents hearing loss in mouse models[4]. Vitamin Supplement with NR, a precursor to NAD+, Successfully Prevents Noise-Induced Hearing Loss[5]. Euler-Chelpin, in his 1930 Nobel Prize speech, says, "NAD+ is one of the most widespread and biologically most important activators within the plant and animal world."[6]

NAD+ levels are related to the expression of NF-κB[7], and low-grade inflammation is a primary driving force of aging. A possibility is that addressing inflammation is the answer to slowing the aging process. Both doctors and scientists in the field conclude that molecules that maintain NAD$^+$ levels allow people to celebrate many more anniversaries. Inflammation is not just linked to aging but is involved in almost all disease processes.

NAD+ levels naturally decline with age, and various stressors can deplete your NAD+ at a more rapid rate. Poor restorative sleep and alcohol use are the top two stressors that deplete NAD+; however, any stressor will drain NAD+ levels. When there is immune activation due to infections, mental, emotional, physical, structural, electromagnetic (EMF's), or chemical stress, there is a higher energy demand. This demand taxes our NAD+ levels, creating a need to replace NAD+.

In this article titled, "Why NAD$^+$ Declines during Aging: It's Destroyed," the author states, "NAD$^+$ is required not only for life but for a long life...the decline of NAD$^+$ during aging, with implications for combating age-related diseases."[8]

I don't advocate ignoring underlying stressors driving inflammation and only supplementing with NAD+, rather it is best to approach it from both sides. You might be looking at the future of medicine.

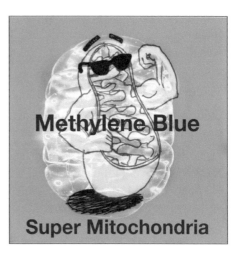

Methylene Blue (MB) is the second molecule used in Phase 1 of our Sensory Integration Fast™. MB is a brilliant blue salt that was first used as a dye. It improves mitochondria respiration and may very well be a magic bullet within metabolic medicine. MB provides energy to the electron transport chain by recycling electrons, and it works through the cytochrome complex. This shifts your cells into a very efficient energy production.

Methylene blue is anti-inflammatory, anti-microbial, mitochondrial enhancing, and neuro-protective, showing promise in treatment of diseases such as stroke, Alzheimer's disease, and Parkinson's disease[9]. Both MB and NAD+ can be used together or separately with good results. You can find more information about NAD+Max™ and Lumetol Blue™, our MB product, at MitoZen.com.

Phase 2 - Autophagy, Clearing & Cleaning

Mitochondrial dysfunction is a hallmark of metabolic decline (vitality) during aging[10]. We are constantly replacing our old, weak, dysfunctional mitochondria with newer and healthy mitochondria. The population of all the mitochondria of a given cell constitutes your Chondriome. Like your microbiome, we either have a healthy bacterial pool of mitochondria or an unhealthy pool. This will dictate how functional they are. The average cell in your body has between 1,000-2,000 mitochondria. As cells get old, they are recycled, through the gene modulation process ruled by **mTOR**.

The **mTOR** pathway is a central regulator of metabolism and vitality[11]. When mTOR is inhibited, we shift into a cleaning and recycling phase where we see autophagy and mitophagy. Autophagy is a Latin word that means "self-eating." Autophagy is the body's way of cleaning out damaged cells to regenerate newer, healthier cells[12].

Mitophagy is the selective degradation of mitochondria by autophagy. It often occurs in defective mitochondria following damage or stress[13].

Remember all the types of stress? These ALL have an impact on the demand for mitophagy to be activated through mTOR! Fasting is the primary activator of this process, and methylene blue will further activate autophagy and mitophagy. Poor autophagy, which leads to the accumulation of senescent cells, has a detrimental effect on health and life span. The goal is converting these senescent cells into fresh, healthy cells.

Cellular senescence is an irreversible cell-cycle arrest mechanism that acts to protect against cancer[14]. Basically, cellular senescence is a permanent state of sleep a cell goes into. This state is associated with a release of inflammatory products and higher energy consumption, pulling it away from your healthy cells. They are zombies in the literal sense!

Production of pro-inflammatory cytokines and chemokines is emerging as a common feature of senescent cells irrespective of the senescence-inducing stressor or mechanism.

Cultured cells usually reach senescence within several weeks after exposure to senescence-inducing stressors but remain viable for months after that[15].

These "zombies" will float around, spewing inflammation and sucking the life out of your body, by deferring vital energy that would normally be going to healthy cells. In this study scientists found fasting reduced hearing loss through autophagy. *The Antioxidative Role of Autophagy in Hearing Loss*[16].

So, what is the answer? How do you clear these senescence cells from the body?

It happens to be the same process involved with autophagy and mitophagy, where mTOR is involved. Fasting and senolytics are the best answer to clean, clear, and recycle these "zombie" cells. This is why we stack the most powerful senolytics on the planet with a 24-hour lunch-to- lunch fast that can be done each week or pulsed as directed by your health care provider.

Phase 3 - Stem Cell Activation

In Phase 3, the body (and your inner ears) are ready for growth and repair through the activation of mTOR. mTOR positively regulates cell growth and proliferation by promoting many anabolic processes, including biosynthesis of proteins, lipids, and organelles such as mitochondria[17].

Growing new mitochondria is called mitochondrial biogenesis, and mTOR activates this very powerfully!

Mitochondrial metabolism and biogenesis are both regulated by mTOR activation[18].

Protein is the most effective activator of Phase 3. I suggest you increase your protein intake with highly absorbable forms of protein such as fish, chicken, and steak at each meal. In addition, I recommend supplementing with quality essential amino acids, the building blocks of protein. Perfect Aminos is a highly absorbable form of protein, and it's well tolerated by most. Four scoops per day is the recommended amount. The amino acid leucine, in particular, activates growth and repair. We have a product called StemTOR™ which activates mTOR. StemTOR™ is very bioavailable and a great way to get leucine into your blood stream. In addition to leucine, there are a few nutraceuticals that have been shown to be great activators of growth and repair, including the following:

HMB- Hydroxymethylbutyrate is a powerful activator of mTOR. Studies indicate supplementation with HMB shows a significant increase in the anaerobic peak power, average power, maximum speed, post-exercise lactate concentrations, and a significant increase in fat-free mass and a reduction in fat[19].

Rhodiola- Rhodiola encourages a healthy response to physical activity and mental/emotional stress by supporting stress hormones such as cortisol. Rhodiola enhances the anabolic effects of training and exercise and minimizes the catabolic (tissue breakdown) effect of the high stress hormones, cortisol.

Sensory Rejuvenation Protocol:

Purpose: Amplifying Regeneration to the Inner Ear.

- *Build back cellular NAD+ levels & increase MB for mitochondrial support.*
- *Assist the autophagy & mitophagy signaling response using Senolytics.*
- *Stimulate a growth phase via stem cell and hormetic response.*
- *Stimulate microbiome swarming and bacteria diversity post-fast.*

PHASE 1 (Days 1-2) - Methylene Blue & NAD+ Loading to Support Mitochondrial Health & Cellular Energy.

(Can be helpful leading into a fast for strong autophagy signaling).

1. Take NAD+Max™ and Lumetol Blue™ Bar (1/2 bar). Two suppositories of NAD+Max per day for 2 days & ½- ¼ Bar (40-80mg). (NAD+Max™ liposomal can be used in place of the suppository.)

PHASE 2 (Days 3-4) – Lucitol™ and Lumetol Blue™ to Maximize Autophagy.

1. Do a minimum of a 24-hour fast. Extended or intermittent fasting works at different signaling strengths.

2. Consume senolytics like fisetin, quercetin, and resveratrol which can be taken as liposomal and suppositories for better absorption. Use MitoZen's Lucitol™ Ultra (10 ml 2 times a day for 2 days) or Lucitol ™ Suppository (2 times a day for 2 days).

3. Methylene Blue can also be taken to promote autophagy. MitoZen's Lumetol Blue™ can be taken once a day during this phase. ½- ¼ of Bar (40-80mg) is a typical dose per day.

4. Exercise can promote autophagy.

5. Consume foods, spices, and teas to promote autophagy like ginger, coffee, green tea, elderberries, turmeric, ginseng tea, garlic, chaga, reishi, pomegranate, and Ceylon cinnamon.

6. Use ozone to increase mitophagy in the form rectal insufflation, ozone sauna or IV ozone while in a fasted state.

Phase 3 (Days 5-6) – StemTOR™, High Protein and Perfect Aminos to Maximize mTOR After a Fast.

1. Consume more protein. Break your fast with a shake versus steak, which might be too difficult to break down. Take 20 gm (4 scoops) of Perfect Aminos for 2 days and consume fish, chicken, or beef for 2 meals a day for 2 days.

7. **StemTOR™ is another MitoZen product that can support the mTOR signaling in Phase 3. Take StemTOR™ 2 times a day for 2-3 days following your fast.**

8. **Take supplements such as leucine, rhodiola, and HMB to further activate mTOR.**

I recommend this protocol weekly for 3 months, with a stronger 3-day fast one week each month. This longer fast is called the **Fast Track Fast™** and is done for 3 days for each of the 3 phases. Phase 2 is done with a 3-day water fast (a 4-hour feeding window is always an alternative).

Before you start this protocol, consult your health care provider, and use their guidance, as this article is not meant to be medical advice.

If you are looking to be better, think clearer, have more energy and function at a higher level, and have healthier ears, these metabolic-based strategies of health that lead to better and stronger mitochondria can't be ignored. Restoring youthful NAD+ levels, supplementing with methylene blue, using cellular clean up and recycling through fasting to support autophagy and mitophagy followed by a strong stem cell activation can be a great strategy. The Sensory Rejuvenation Protocol is easy to do and tolerated by most. The Sensory Rejuvenation Protocol for any inner ear program using endo-nasal therapy and or LumoMed can be done once a week for 3 months, then 1 time every 3-4 months.

Anti-Oxidant Theory for Inner Ear Health.

There have been many researchers who have proven that providing certain antioxidants in the diet can support improved inner ear function. The mitochondria can become dysfunctional with stress and buildup of senescent cells and old mitochondria can lead to a higher spillover of oxidation resulting is a need to quench

this oxidation. Many times, people with poor health, poor diet devoid of antioxidants can lead to a deficit that creates an environment that consists of high oxidation. Stack onto this poor sleep and lower melatonin as we age, and we have a perfect storm. See chapter 12 where I get into detail about melatonin and how it supports these type of stresses as well as my book **Melatonin: Miracle Molecule** which you can find at MelatoninBook.com. Let's consider some of the research on this subject.

Antioxidants like glutathione can be incredibly important in the support for the inner ear. The best way to support glutathione levels is to reduce stress in your life and consume glutathione as either a suppository or an IV at a doctor's clinic. Personally, I think the suppositories are going to be the best option for most people[20].

"Oxidative stress is an important mechanism underlying cellular damage of the inner ear, resulting in hearing loss. In order to prevent hearing loss, several types of antioxidants have been investigated; several experiments have shown their ability to effectively prevent noise-induced hearing loss, age-related hearing loss, and ototoxicity in animal models."[21]

In this study "Effects of antioxidants on the aging inner ear." The researcher found a diet containing antioxidants reduced the magnitude of cochlear degeneration.

Other Antioxidants that have been shown in research to support healthy ears.

Up regulator of Glutathione, D-methionine, the enantiomer of the amino acid l-methionine, is another potent antioxidant that has been considered in preclinical studies[22]. D-methionine can directly function as an antioxidant and as an adjuvant of the endogenous antioxidant system[23]. In fact, d-methionine increases intracellular GSH levels[24], specifically those of mitochondrial GSH[25], thereby preserving or improving the ratio of reduced to oxidized GSH in the cochlea[26].

Another up regulator of Glutathione, NAC is an acetylated l-cysteine that acts as an antioxidant in two ways. As a thiol, NAC can act directly as an antioxidant. Moreover, as an l-cysteine precursor, NAC stimulates the endogenous antioxidant system[27]. Previous reports have shown that NAC reduced the ototoxic effects of noise exposure in both animal models and humans[28-34].

Alpha-lipoic acid also contains thiol groups and has been shown to protect the cochlea from cisplatin-induced ototoxicity and noise in animal models[35, 36].

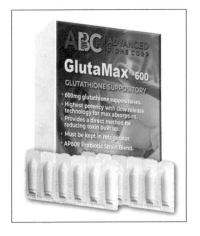

Korean red ginseng has anti-ROS and anti-apoptotic properties, and therefore may play a role in the prevention of noise-induced hearing loss[37].

CoQ10 is a component of the mitochondrial respiratory chain. It inhibits mitochondrial lipid peroxidation, induces ATP production, and is involved in ROS scavenging and prevention of oxidative stress-induced apoptosis[38].

Glutathione seems to be a great nutrient and since it's difficult to absorb orally we generally have our patients take this as a suppository in the form of GlutaMax in a 600 mg dose at nighttime. You can find this product at MitoZen.com

Enhanced Circulation Theory for Inner Ear Health. Herbs & PEMF.

Nutrients that support improved circulation such as vinpocetin and Glinko Biloba are two key nutrients that have been shown clinically to improve the inner ear function[39]. I always say you're either a swamp or a river. Tissues can be swampy or clean and clear like a river. This is the same for the inner ear as with any other part of the body. Enhanced circulation will bring in the groceries and take out the garbage. There are a variety of herbs that can help with circulation to explore with your health care provider.

I want to share one of my favorite therapies you can do right at home! It's called PEMF. I sleep on a PEMF MAT every night. It helps to reduce the stress or stickiness of the red blood cell which enhances circulation along many other benefits PEMF has to offer. PEMF stands for post-electromagnetic frequency. I personally use the Centropix PEMF MAT. I will share a link to the MAT this MAT with you. The Centropix Kloud MAT is a very advanced system which is much more effective than any other MATS due to the quality of pulses it produces. I have done my research and found that this mat is far superior, plus it has attachments for the ears, eyes, and acupoints. If you want to deep dive into this, you call always email me.

Here is the link to explore the Centropix Kloud PEMF mat as well as a discount when you buy through this link. https://centropix.us/advancedrejuvenation/pages/

Conclusion

We have covered a lot of ground in this chapter when it comes to caring for your inner ears. I always say that the inner ears are an extension of the health of the individual. Because the cells in the inner ear are so delicate and require such a high demand of continuous energy, they are a reflection of the overall health and vitality of the body. Therefore, treating the whole body with systemic applications, makes good sense geared towards metabolic care, specifically to enhance mitochondria or even more simply, the energy potential of the cell. In addition, circulation is important to bring those different nutrients into the tissues that reside in the inner ear. Things like PEMF, specific herbal preparations, cranial rhythm and removing restrictions and adhesions to the normal movement of the skull can all support healing in the inner ear. Protecting the ear from excessive sound stress is important just like a runner might have quality shoes to buffer the impact into the knee and hip from each time he lands on his foot. My hope is that at some point in the future there are more doctors that are treating the inner ear with the systems we described in this chapter. I anticipate doing more training in the future and will update at OutOfBoxDoc.com & SunaVae.com so continue to check in with me if you were looking for a practitioner that is in line with the principles outlined in this chapter.

References

1. Hack, Eugenio & Prosper, Joaquin. (2014). Effective Management of Meniere's and Vestibular Disorders with Photo-Biostimulation Light Laser. Otolaryngology -- Head and Neck Surgery. 151. P204-P204. 10.1177/0194599814541629a210.

2. Bartos A, Grondin Y, Bortoni ME, Ghelfi E, Sepulveda R, Carroll J, Rogers RA. Pre-conditioning with near infrared photobiomodulation reduces inflammatory cytokines and markers of oxidative stress in cochlear hair cells. J Biophotonics. 2016 Dec;9(11-12):1125-1135. doi: 10.1002/jbio.201500209. Epub 2016 Jan 21. PMID: 26790619.

3. Yamaguchi S, Yoshino J. Adipose tissue NAD^+ biology in obesity and insulin resistance: From mechanism to therapy. Bioessays. 2017 May;39(5):10.1002/bies.201600227. doi: 10.1002/bies.201600227. Epub 2017 Mar 15. PMID: 28295415; PMCID: PMC5469033.

4. Okur MN, Mao B, Kimura R, Haraczy S, Fitzgerald T, Edwards-Hollingsworth K, Tian J, Osmani W, Croteau DL, Kelley MW, Bohr VA. Short-term NAD^+ supplementation prevents hearing loss in mouse models of Cockayne syndrome. NPJ Aging Mech Dis. 2020 Jan 7;6:1. doi: 10.1038/s41514-019-0040-z. PMID: 31934345; PMCID: PMC6946667.

5. Activation of SIRT3 by the NAD+ Precursor Nicotinamide Riboside Protects from Noise-Induced Hearing Loss: Cell Metabolism

6. Hans von Euler-Chelpin – Biographical - NobelPrize.org

7. Covarrubias AJ, Perrone R, Grozio A, Verdin E. NAD^+ metabolism and its roles in cellular processes during ageing. Nat Rev Mol Cell Biol. 2021 Feb;22(2):119-141. doi: 10.1038/s41580-020-00313-x. Epub 2020 Dec 22. PMID: 33353981; PMCID: PMC7963035.

8. Schultz MB, Sinclair DA. Why NAD(+) Declines during Aging: It's Destroyed. Cell Metab. 2016 Jun 14;23(6):965-966. doi: 10.1016/j.cmet.2016.05.022. PMID: 27304496; PMCID: PMC5088772.

9. M. Wainwright & K.B. Crossley (2002) Methylene Blue - a Therapeutic Dye for All Seasons?, Journal of Chemotherapy, 14:5, 431-443, DOI: 10.1179/joc.2002.14.5.431

10. Srivastava S. The Mitochondrial Basis of Aging and Age-Related Disorders. Genes (Basel). 2017 Dec 19;8(12):398. doi: 10.3390/genes8120398. PMID: 29257072; PMCID: PMC5748716.

11. Srivastava S. The Mitochondrial Basis of Aging and Age-Related Disorders. Genes (Basel). 2017 Dec 19;8(12):398. doi: 10.3390/genes8120398. PMID: 29257072; PMCID: PMC5748716.

12. Glick D, Barth S, Macleod KF. Autophagy: cellular and molecular mechanisms. J Pathol. 2010 May;221(1):3-12. doi: 10.1002/path.2697. PMID: 20225336; PMCID: PMC2990190.

13. Ding WX, Yin XM. Mitophagy: mechanisms, pathophysiological roles, and analysis. Biol Chem. 2012 Jul;393(7):547-64. doi: 10.1515/hsz-2012-0119. PMID: 22944659; PMCID: PMC3630798.

14. Lee S, Lee JS. Cellular senescence: a promising strategy for cancer therapy. BMB Rep. 2019 Jan;52(1):35-41. doi: 10.5483/BMBRep.2019.52.1.294. PMID: 30526771; PMCID: PMC6386234.

15. Chen H, Li Y, Tollefsbol TO. Cell senescence culturing methods. Methods Mol Biol. 2013;1048:1-10. doi: 10.1007/978-1-62703-556-9_1. PMID: 23929093; PMCID: PMC3873382.

16. Ye B, Fan C, Shen Y, Wang Q, Hu H, Xiang M. The Antioxidative Role of Autophagy in Hearing Loss. Front Neurosci. 2019 Jan 9;12:1010. doi: 10.3389/fnins.2018.01010. PMID: 30686976; PMCID: PMC6333736.

17. Mathieu Laplante, David M. Sabatini; mTOR signaling at a glance. *J Cell Sci* 15 October 2009; 122 (20): 3589–3594. doi: https://doi.org/10.1242/jcs.051011

18. Schieke, S. M., Phillips, D., McCoy, J. P., Jr, Aponte, A. M., Shen, R. F., Balaban, R. S. and Finkel, T. (2006). The mammalian target of rapamycin (mTOR) pathway regulates mitochondrial oxygen consumption and oxidative capacity. *J. Biol. Chem.* 281, 27643-27652.

19. Durkalec-Michalski K, Jeszka J, Podgórski T. The Effect of a 12-Week Beta-hydroxy-beta-methylbutyrate (HMB) Supplementation on Highly-Trained Combat Sports Athletes: A Randomised, Double-Blind, Placebo-Controlled Crossover Study. Nutrients. 2017 Jul 14;9(7):753. doi: 10.3390/nu9070753. PMID: 28708126; PMCID: PMC5537867.

20. Jürgen Lautermann, Sherry A. Crann, John McLaren, Jochen Schacht, Glutathione-dependent antioxidant systems in the mammalian inner ear: effects of aging, ototoxic drugs and noise, Hearing Research, Volume 114, Issues 1–2, 1997, Pages 75-82, ISSN 0378-5955, https://doi.org/10.1016/S0378-5955(97)00154-8.

21. Pak JH, Kim Y, Yi J, Chung JW. Antioxidant Therapy against Oxidative Damage of the Inner Ear: Protection and Preconditioning. *Antioxidants*. 2020; 9(11):1076. https://doi.org/10.3390/antiox9111076

22. Pak JH, Kim Y, Yi J, Chung JW. Antioxidant Therapy against Oxidative Damage of the Inner Ear: Protection and Preconditioning. Antioxidants (Basel). 2020 Nov 2;9(11):1076. doi: 10.3390/antiox9111076. PMID: 33147893; PMCID: PMC7693733.

23. Clifford R.E., Coleman J.K., Balough B.J., Liu J., Kopke R.D., Jackson R.L. Low-dose D-methionine and *N*-acetyl-L-cysteine for protection from permanent noise-induced hearing loss in chinchillas. *Otolaryngol.-Head Neck Surg.* 2011;145:999–1006. doi: 10.1177/0194599811414496.

24. Yamasoba T., Pourbakht A., Sakamoto T., Suzuki M. Ebselen prevents noise-induced excitotoxicity and temporary threshold shift. *Neurosci. Lett.* 2005;380:234–238. doi: 10.1016/j.neulet.2005.01.047.

25. Kil J., Lobarinas E., Spankovich C., Griffiths S.K., Antonelli P.J., Lynch E.D., Le Prell C.G. Safety and efficacy of ebselen for the prevention of noise-induced hearing loss: A randomised, double-blind, placebo-controlled, phase 2 trial. *Lancet.* 2017;390:969–979. doi: 10.1016/S0140-6736(17)31791-9.

26. So H., Kim H., Kim Y., Kim E., Pae H.-O., Chung H.-T., Kim H.-J., Kwon K.-B., Lee K.-M., Lee H.-Y. Evidence that cisplatin-induced auditory damage is attenuated by downregulation of pro-inflammatory cytokines via Nrf2/HO-1. *J. Assoc. Res. Otolaryngol.* 2008;9:290–306. doi: 10.1007/s10162-008-0126-y.

27. Kil J., Pierce C., Tran H., Gu R., Lynch E.D. Ebselen treatment reduces noise induced hearing loss via the mimicry and induction of glutathione peroxidase. *Hear. Res.* 2007;226:44–51. doi: 10.1016/j.heares.2006.08.006.

28. Rushworth G.F., Megson I.L. Existing and potential therapeutic uses for *N*-acetylcysteine: The need for conversion to intracellular glutathione for antioxidant benefits. *Pharmacol. Ther.* 2014;141:150–159. doi: 10.1016/j.pharmthera.2013.09.006. [PubMed] [CrossRef] [Google Scholar]

29. Bielefeld E.C., Kopke R.D., Jackson R.L., Coleman J.K., Liu J., Henderson D. Noise protection with *N*-acetyl-L-cysteine (NAC) using a variety of noise exposures, NAC doses, and routes of administration. *Acta Oto-Laryngol.* 2007;127:914–919. doi: 10.1080/00016480601110188. [PubMed] [CrossRef] [Google Scholar]

30. Clifford R.E., Coleman J.K., Balough B.J., Liu J., Kopke R.D., Jackson R.L. Low-dose D-methionine and *N*-acetyl-L-cysteine for protection from permanent noise-induced hearing loss in chinchillas. *Otolaryngol.-Head Neck Surg.* 2011;145:999–1006. doi: 10.1177/0194599811414496. [PubMed] [CrossRef] [Google Scholar]

31. Coleman J., Huang X., Liu J., Kopke R., Jackson R. Dosing study on the effectiveness of salicylate/N-acetylcysteine for prevention of noise-induced hearing loss. *Noise Health.* 2010;12:159. [PubMed] [Google Scholar]

32. Doosti A., Lotfi Y., Moossavi A., Bakhshi E., Talasaz A.H., Hoorzad A. Comparison of the effects of *N*-acetyl-cysteine and ginseng in prevention of noise induced hearing loss in male textile workers. *Noise Health.* 2014;16:223. [PubMed] [Google Scholar]

33. Fetoni A.R., Ralli M., Sergi B., Parrilla C., Troiani D., Paludetti G. Protective effects of *N*-acetylcysteine on noise-induced hearing loss in guinea pigs. *Acta Otorhinolaryngol. Ital.* 2009;29:70. [PMC free article] [PubMed] [Google Scholar]

34. Kopke R., Slade M.D., Jackson R., Hammill T., Fausti S., Lonsbury-Martin B., Sanderson A., Dreisbach L., Rabinowitz P., Torre P., III Efficacy and safety of *N*-acetylcysteine in prevention of noise induced hearing loss: A randomized clinical trial. *Hear. Res.* 2015;323:40–50. doi: 10.1016/j.heares.2015.01.002.

35 Lo W.-C., Chang C.-M., Liao L.-J., Wang C.-T., Young Y.-H., Chang Y.-L., Cheng P.-W. Assessment of D-methionine protecting cisplatin-induced otolith toxicity by vestibular-evoked myogenic potential tests, ATPase activities and oxidative state in guinea pigs. *Neurotoxicol. Teratol.* 2015;51:12–20. doi: 10.1016/j.ntt.2015.07.004.

36. Fernández-Checa J.C., Kaplowitz N., García-Ruiz C., Colell A. *Seminars in Liver Disease.* Thieme Medical Publishers, Inc.; New York, NY, USA: 1998. Mitochondrial glutathione: Importance and transport; pp. 389–401.

37. Kaltenbach J.A., Church M.W., Blakley B.W., McCASLIN D.L., Burgio D.L. Comparison of five agents in protecting the cochlea against the ototoxic effects of cisplatin in the hamster. *Otolaryngol. Head Neck Surg.* 1997;117:493–500. doi: 10.1016/S0194-5998(97)70020-2. [PubMed]

38. Gurney J.G., Bass J.K., Onar-Thomas A., Huang J., Chintagumpala M., Bouffet E., Hassall T., Gururangan S., Heath J.A., Kellie S. Evaluation of amifostine for protection against cisplatin-induced serious hearing loss in children treated for average-risk or high-risk medulloblastoma. *Neuro-Oncology.* 2014;16:848–855. doi: 10.1093/neuonc/not241

39. Meniere's Disease: Herbal Treatments & Supplements - Menieres.org

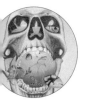

12

COMPLEX NEUROLOGICAL CONDITIONS TREATED USING ENDO-NASAL

Treating Complex Neurological Conditions

The clinical power of the therapeutic combination of Functional Neurology along with endo-nasal balloons in a clinical setting might best be described through my experience treating a rare neurological disease called palatal myoclonus (PM). I've now treated 60 cases of PM which is something I am very proud of as any other doctor in the world has only seen two or three in their career, if any at all. I was first approached about 10 years ago by a young lady who was suffering from the disease and found me online and although I had never treated this specific condition, I was optimistic that it may help. She agreed to come and be treated by me and flew from Arizona to Sarasota, Florida. The results were spectacular, and I videotaped them. At the time Google did not sensor like they do  now, and my video popped up on the first page when anybody would google palatal myoclonus. Unfortunately, it's hard to even find me online for this condition due to the pharmaceutical industry dominating everything that people read in media. This attracted more cases and there was more success treating these cases with this unique approach of endo-nasal balloons with functional neurology. I suppose that means I am the world's foremost expert in this condition.

What is PM?

Rhythmic palatal myoclonus (RPM) is a rare movement disorder consisting of continuous synchronous jerks of the soft palate. Patients with essential RPM usually have objective ear clicks as their typical complaint due to the pulling on the Eustachian tube. Head pressure is also common with PM. The cause of PM is not known but it is our opinion that a dysfunctional immune system is suspect and a genetic predisposi- 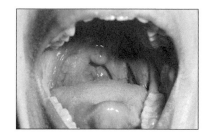 tion causing inflammation that favors a certain area in the brain stem. Toxins and infection are almost always at the root of diseases in general and this condition is no different.

With chronic neurological conditions such as PM it's important to understand the various ways to support the nervous system. We will do a synopsis at the end on this. The work itself using Functional Cranial Release (FCR) is utilizing the end-nasal releases and following up with specific neurological exercises to activate the brain in a precise way to calm down the "glitch" in the way the nerves are firing through the olivary nucleus which is the specific area of challenge in PM.

What is The Typical Medical Approach?

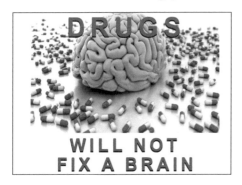

Mainstream medicine continues to attempt to inject Botox into these people's palate as well as giving them powerful "inhibition" medicines like Klonopin and benzodiazepines. The challenge with these two approaches is this; for one, Botox makes it difficult to swallow and speak in many cases I have seen that it's a less than ideal solution. There has been a couple of rare outliers that we're happy with that procedure and outcome. The next consideration is that medications will always globally excite or inhibit the central nervous system. Medicines do not allow for a specific activation of certain pathways in the brain. Imagine that I had you eat a strawberry and then imagine I tried to create a drug to give you the experience of what a strawberry tastes like. Once you taste the strawberry for the rest of your life you will know what that flavor tastes like because the nervous system has imprinted that with multiple neurological pathways that fire to give you that experience. There would never be a pill that could replace this just like there could never be a pill that can fix neurologic conditions like PM. Vestibular conditions are similar in the sense that once this complicated network of nerves is out of balance there needs to be activation to certain parts of the vestibular system to regain its proper function. Many of the drugs given to people to suppress their vestibular function will actually make things worse in the sense that it will take longer for their vestibular system to recalibrate because it has a brake applied to the entire system with the medicine.

Other Neurological Conditions Using Endo-Nasal

I have seen such a vast array of diseases in my 30 years of experience using endo-nasal techniques and find that most all neurological conditions have responded to my care. Because all brain-based conditions share the common theme of declining cellular energy,

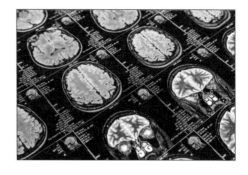

the application of these basic principles can be applied and used in a clinical approach to improve the brain's ability to heal and repair. Keep in mind the body has self-regulating and self-healing mechanisms in place that provide opportunity to restore balance so long as the energy is provided to drive this life force. The mitochondria are at the core of the cellular energy and when there is inefficient and poor energy production then the brain suffers the most. Inflammation due to stressors that lead to it are above the threshold of the adaptive abilities of the body, and the result is dis-ease or a lack of ease and the neurological system can break down and conditions develop based on environmental and genetic influences.

What is the main route that undo-nasal supports? First the sinus and nasal passages' health. The terrain within the nose can allow for microbial growth and sticky biofilm that traps toxins in the environment which causes them to be absorbed into the brain. Then you have the poor cranial rhythm that causes poor fuel delivery to the brain and poor detoxification of the brain. Next, we have poor oxygen utilization and absorption due to mouth breathing. You might go back and review all the ways mouth breathing interferes with oxygen use. When we have a lack of motion in the skull, we accumulate toxins due to the swamp vs river phenomenon which can further ramp up inflammation in the brain. Poor lymphatics and poor autophagy are also common with many neurological conditions which lead them to benefiting from fasting such as with Fast Track Fast and also improving sleep such as with Sandman and high dose melatonin approaches. See melatoninbook.com for more of this. Melatonin will also improve the adaptive ability within the brain against inflammation due to all forms of stressors including toxins like heavy metals, pesticides and environmental pollutants and infections such as with EBV, CMV, HHV-6 and Lyme.

Nasal Breathing & The Brain

In chapter 13 I take a super deep dive into this subject. Chronic blocked nasal breathing is a serious condition and there has been studies that show some of the negative impacts on the brain. Besides lack of oxygen there is also chronic inflammation that occurs from various microbial growth in the nasal passage and sinuses. One study suggested at least 11% of people in the US have chronic nasal inflammation which blocks nasal breathing and creates headaches and other symptoms and that this percentage is rising very fast with our children.[1] In this study researchers spotted a functional connectivity problem in the frontoparietal network. This

area of the brain is used for attention and problem-solving, higher functional connectivity specifically linked to self-reference and mind wandering or daydreaming, and lower functional connectivity in the salience network which manage external stimuli, communication and social behaviors. They discovered that people that had chronic sinusitis had problems in these networks and that they had subjective feelings of attention decline, difficulties to focus or sleep disturbances that a person with sinus inflammation experiences might be associated with subtle changes in how brain regions controlling these functions communicate with one another.[2] Current treatments are really aimed towards decreasing the inflammation versus addressing the problem with which is sinus hygiene. This is why we do a 30 -day sinus protocol with an anti-microbial nasal spray such as Glutastat. Like most medical procedures for chronic conditions taking these steroids or anti-inflammatories is like painting over rust and actually can make these problems worse over time. Compare this to addressing the core problem which is what we aim to do with our 30-day sinus protocol. Surgeries can also be performed and I find most unnecessary if a patient is able to receive endonasal balloon manipulations. Ultimately there needs to be some sort of effort for the person to start breathing through their nose such as using mouth taping as we discussed in prior chapters. We

also discussed some exercises to improve nasal patency such as the nose clearing exercises. The basics behind this is allowing carbon dioxide to accumulate which will reduce the blood vessel size in the nasal passage.

In this study the author states: The fact that the olfactory system is closely linked with limbic brain regions mediating emotion, memory, and behavior) suggests a robust pathway by which nasal breathing could even shape rhythmic electrical activity in downstream limbic areas, with corresponding effects on cognitive functions.[3,4,5,6]

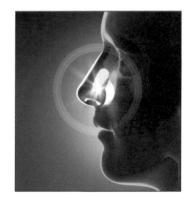

Functional Neurology & Endo-Nasal

Functional neurology can be a fairly complicated and difficult treatment for many doctors due to the extensive training and the vast knowledge required to understand how to apply this therapy to specific conditions. I have personally spent over two decades studying this work and still feel like a newbie. I have been humbled and honored to observe Professor Carrick work on many complicated neurologic conditions that have been considered untreatable. I've seen many of these cases have remarkable responses to functional neurology. I personally do not see functional neurology as the silver bullet to fix all conditions however it is necessary to bring balance back to the central nervous system as far as how it's firing through various pathways. I see the application of using endo-nasal balloon releases with functional neurology as an extremely powerful way to improve the health, functionality, endurance, fuel delivery through CSF through cranial rhythm, and general balance through the various networks of nerve pathways necessary for the brain to work properly. You're always going to want to consider improving "the ceiling" through the approaches explained in the chapter on Neurological Fitness.

Conclusion.

Consider your brain's metabolic capacity with the brains ability to make energy efficiently. Using a multi prong approach to healing makes the best sense when we consider all the stressors we face in modern times. Combining things like ozone, methylene blue, high dose melatonin, photobiomodulation (trans-cranial and Intra-nasal light therapy) can all be helpful in many neurological cases. Using Endo-nasal cranial releases allows for the cranium to support the brain that's held within it due to the negative effects our modern world has imposed upon it. Nasal breathing is extremely important for brain connectivity through the salient network and may result in significant cognitive and neurologic disturbances. See Chapter 14 for a deeper dive into this. Re-educating people on nasal breathing can be very important. Using endonasal balloon manipulations to enhance vestibular activation as a sensory stimulus through the trigeminal nerve can also be a great benefit by working with chronic neurological cases to allow improved neuroplasticity during brain-based therapy programs such as with Functional Neurology. Balancing mental emotional and behavioral aspects of cases through routes of self-identity is also an important aspect through which a more spiritual connection can also be helpful in an individual healing. See Chapter 13 for a deeper perspective on how I use this through guided meditations while performing endo-nasal.

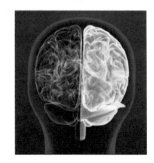

Weston Price discovered this many years ago and it should be something that all doctors pay close attention to especially when an individual is facing any neurological conditions. It's not the only consideration as you can see by reading through this book, however, it is extremely complimentary to any and all modalities in order for them to work better. Anybody treating neurological cases or if you were a patient suffering from any significant neurological cases balloon manipulations to the cranium can be very helpful added into whatever plan you were currently involved in.

References

1. Chen M, Reed RR, Lane AP. Chronic Inflammation Directs an Olfactory Stem Cell Functional Switch from Neuroregeneration to Immune Defense. Cell Stem Cell. 2019 Oct 3;25(4):501-513.e5. doi: 10.1016/j.stem.2019.08.011. Epub 2019 Sep 12. PMID: 31523027; PMCID: PMC6778045.

2. Jung J-Y, Park C-A, Lee Y-B, Kang C-K. Investigation of Functional Connectivity Differences between Voluntary Respirations via Mouth and Nose Using Resting State fMRI. *Brain Sciences*. 2020; 10(10):704. https://doi.org/10.3390/brainsci10100704

3. Zelano C, Jiang H, Zhou G, Arora N, Schuele s, Rosenow J, Gottfried J, Nasal Respiration entrains Human Limbic oscillations and Modulates Cognitive function; J. of Neuroscience 7 Dec 2016, 36 (49) 12448-12467; Doi: 10.1523/JNEUROSCI.2586-16.2016.

4. Eichenbaum H, Yonelinas AP, Ranganath C, (2007) The medial temporal lobe and recognition memory. AnnuRev Neurosci 30:123–152, doi:10.1146/annurev.neuro.30.051606.094328, pmid:17417939.

5. LeDoux JE, (2000) Emotion circuits in the brain. Annu Rev Neurosci 23:155–184, doi:10.1146/annurev.neuro.23.1.155, pmid:10845062.

6. Carmichael ST, Clugnet MC, Price JL, (1994) Central olfactory connections in the macaque monkey. J Comp Neurol 346:403–434, doi:10.1002/cne.903460306, pmid:7527806.

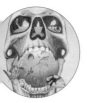

13

PINEAL GLAND, SPIRITUALITY & ENDO-NASAL THERAPY

A new direction I am going in with my work using endo-nasal cranial therapy is on a more spiritual level. Let me explain: when the cranium is released, it allows the CSF to affect the pineal gland in a positive way by using the piezoelectric effect of the crystalline structures within the pineal. I'm calling this new technique Bliss Release. It's different in the sense that the intention in this treatment is a pineal opening which is part of FCR as well. However, the set and setting are more guided and meditative. I have used this same set and setting when we have facilitated ketamine in our practice. There's a special music list that is played in order to bring about a calm, relaxed state and utilizes a positive intention to support powerful transformational spiritual work. The patient is coached through a process of manifesting their outcomes similar to what has been taught by my friend, Rhonda Byrne, who made the blockbuster film, "The Secret". The key here is to have gratitude for already receiving this outcome. Historically, praying is more petitioning for what you want, which sends the Universe, Divine Spirit, or God, the energy and message that you lack and don't yet have this outcome. The secret is to be grateful for already receiving it and doing so in a deep heart-centered space of meditation.

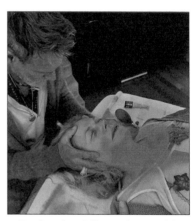

Performing Bliss-Release with Kelly with laser lights & guided mediation with intention.

I wrote a book on Melatonin called "*Melatonin: Miracle Molecule.*" You can find it on Amazon. In this Melatonin book, chapter 20 has much of the same information as this chapter does. However, we will focus on endo-nasal and cranial motion in this chapter versus on melatonin. I actually wrote both of these books at the same time; however, it was almost 1 year ago that I released my Melatonin book and I've been taking a deep dive into the work I will present in this chapter. I would like to thank Peter for his inspiration on this work. Peter would like to stay anonymous and works (with those lucky enough to find him) using unique healing breath work. I met Peter in 2020 and we have worked on each other. He used his unique skillset on my body, mind, and spirit, and I worked on his cranium using endo-nasal balloons. Peter has worked over the years with some of the world's top figures, from movie stars and elite athletes to politicians and public figures. And like most things in my life these days, it was a series of synchronicities that brought me to Peter's home in California. The outcome of these sessions over the last 2 years are brought together in my work I now call *Bliss Release*.

Shaped like a pinecone, the pineal gland is deeply seated within the brain. This small gland has ignited the imagination of philosophers, scholars as well as spiritual leaders from different cultures and religions.

The Romans called the pineal "the supreme gland", and Rene Descartes called it "the seat of our soul" in the 1600s. The pineal is referred to in Hinduism as the Eye of Shiva and in Buddhism as the Eye of wisdom and Compassion. In Egypt, the pineal is called the Eye of Osiris, Eye of Horus, and Eye of Ra, which is considered healing and regenerative[2,3,4]. There was an archaeological find in Ecuador, in La Mana,

where a black stone pyramid was found. This black pyramid was among many other items that somehow found its way to this site from several other faraway regions around the world. It contained an eye on the top which is represented on our US dollar bills. It is most notably thought of in each of these cultures as the Third Eye, or a sensory organ to detect. This is similar to the eyeball which detects our physical world and is represented by light reflections and the

visible light spectrum. Your third eye allows you to receive energy and information from a source that is thought to be creating our physical world. What is this "source energy" that all these religions are referring to that your pineal might be involved with? It's experienced by many as a near-death experience. For some it is a psychedelic experience, such as with a substance like Ayahuasca, psilocybin, DMT, ketamine, and MDMA, to name a few. It's a state

of consciousness where your pineal provides a sensory experience without any sensory input. The experience is surprisingly similar to those who have been through it, and they will describe it as a light and being completely one with and in a state of love that they have difficulty putting into words. I have found that in the right setting, many individuals have unique and powerful spiritual experiences with FCR or, as I now call it, a more spiritual and guided method of endo-nasal Bliss Release[5,6,7].

Interestingly, researchers have suggested that the pineal gland and its hormonal product, melatonin, are possibly associated with improved longevity. It was my friend and colleague Dr. Russell Reiter, who in the late 1960s, was the first to prove through modern-day science that the pineal actually has a significant physiological role[8]. He went on to be instrumental in discovering many of the marvelous health benefits of a healthy pineal and the melatonin it produces. Since the pineal makes melatonin, when

the pineal gland dysfunctions or fails, it can initiate or accelerate the aging process and disease.

This small gland is extremely vital for our health and lifespan. The pineal also releases DMT which is associated with feelings of love and connection to others. A paper published in 2018 by researchers in the U.K. purported that DMT simulates the near-death experience, wherein people report the sensation of transcending their bodies and entering another realm.

I was an expert guest on a film called Psychedelics Revealed and although I don't advocate using DMT (Dimethyltryptamine) recreationally, I am a proponent of using psychedelic medicines in the right setting to work through emotional trauma and to become more spiritually aware. These medicines can create a profound and mystical experience that many will refer to as the single most significant experience of their life! Many psychedelic medicines work through Melatonin & DMT pathways, and the pineal gland, and a healthy, structured cranium is supportive of this system![9,10,11,12]

What is "The Source Field"?

Simply called The Field, Source Field, Quantum Field, Torque Field, Morphogenic Field ,and Divine Oneness by many, this is the life force, the spark of life that we are infused with that animates us and the world around us. The Catholic and Christian religions call it Heaven. In the Indian religions, heaven is considered *Svarga Loka*,[13] and the soul is subjected to rebirth in different living forms according to its *karma*. This cycle can be broken after a soul achieves *Nirvana*. This is a very real and provable energy. It's been studied and there is hard proof of its existence. It's related to gravity, and gravity is actually "The Field", which when it moves through matter, creates time. I know this is difficult to wrap your head around at first, but the more you reflect on this the more reasonable it begins to sound.

Image of Onion Experiment

Alexander
Gavrilovich

Let's first talk about **Alexander Gavrilovich (**1874–1954), who was a Russian and Soviet biologist and medical scientist who originated the morphogenetic field theory and discovered the biophoton[14]. He conducted an experiment with onions and noticed that many lifeforms had both positive and negative sides to them, such as plants, eggs, animals, vegetables etc. He noticed a subtle energy coming out of the top of the onion which he then directed to the side of another onion. He observed a higher rate of mitosis, or cellular growth, occured in the area just adjacent to where the tip of the other onion was directed, which was not even touching, but at a distance. He concluded that this energetic field coming out of the tip of the onion was providing an environment for more robust growth. He saw this as a "life-generating field" or "life-giving radiation" which was emitting from the top of this onion. The key here is gratitude for already receiving a desired outcome. Historically, praying is more petitioning for what you want, which sends the Universe, Divine Spirit or God, the energy that you lack and don't have this outcome already. The secret is being grateful for already receiving it and doing so in a deep heart-centered space of deep meditation.

Now let's discuss **Nikolai Alexandrovich Kozyrev** (1908–1983), who was a Soviet astronomer and astrophysicist. When he was imprisoned by Stalin it was at a time when he was one of the top scientists in the country. While in prison,

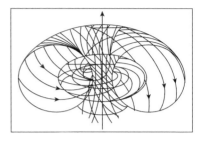

he had many hours to sit, reflect, and meditate. He began to have a deeper understanding of gravity, time, and the source field. He noticed that energy was in a spiral, which makes sense when you look at everything from the quantum all the way up to the planets, the solar system, the galaxies, and even the entire universe. Scientists see this pattern throughout history, and this is what Nikolai discovered when he saw the way bacteria were growing freely along the spiral pattern that prompted him to start to look more deeply into this[15].

Wilhelm Reich (1897-1957) was an Austrian doctor of medicine and a psychoanalyst, a member of the second generation of analysts after Sigmund Freud[16]. The author of several influential books, most notably *Character Analysis* (1933), *The Mass Psychology of Fascism* (1933), and *The Sexual Revolution* (1936), Reich became known as one of the most radical figures in the history of psychiatry[17].

Reich called the source field, Orgone. He postulated that the energy created during an orgasm was a magnification of this Source Field energy that would spontaneously create life. This was in contrast to the idea of the entire process being more of a chemical reaction or a reaction through DNA. His ideas were revolutionary, and he postulated that the field was creating life and not life creating the field. His electrophysiological experiments led to his "discovery" of microscopic vesicles (he called them "**bions**"), which **Reich** hypothesized were instrumental in originating life from nonliving matter. Reich went to a biology lab and discovered that culturing amoebas in sterile, autoclaved water that was heated and even frozen to destroy any precursors, could lead to the development of life. He did this using old, dead hay or grass in water that he let soak for a week to ten days. Surprisingly, tiny amoebas would grow spontaneously in the sterile solution. Where did this originate from? Did it spontaneously come from dead material? Does this change the narrative being taught in medical books on the origin of life? Why has this science been hidden from us?

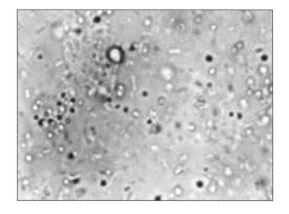

Viktor Grebennikov was a Russian insect specialist, and his work connects the dots showing that having an ideal cranial structure positively impacts how energy waves might interact with the skull shape. Victor S. Grebennikov: Insect Chitin Anti-Gravity & Cavity Structural Effect (CSE) (rexresearch.com)

"Cavernous structure effect" CSE gravitational waves or fractal waves moving through a structure begin to create swirling patterns like eddies is in a river. These waves can become more intense forms of energy and emit energy out from these caverns. Grebennikov was thought to have invented a small hover craft as seen in this image using this cavernous structure effect. He was noted to reference many ancient drawings from Egypt which suggested this effect and which are shown in the depictions, as well. Like beehives and insect bodies, the skull does the same when its shape is in its natural wide shape and not collapsed through the modern stressors of our industrial world.

Tibetan Buddhists would use meditation practices for extended periods of time. They believed this could provide access to higher levels of consciousness through tapping into this very Orgone field that Reich discovered[13]. Buddhists would practice these meditations for many hours. It is believed that one could achieve what's called *Rainbow Body* through this deep connection with the Source Field… *through an open and active pineal gland*[19].

In Taoism, the Source Field is referred to as Tao. Lau Tzu[20] lived in the 6th century BC and was the author of the famous book, Tao Te Ching. Taoism practices include meditation in caves in complete darkness. The Taoist perspective on this practice is described in the book *Darkness Technology*.

"The darkness actualizes successively higher states of divine consciousness, correlating with the synthesis and accumulation of psychedelic chemicals in the brain.

Melatonin quiets the body and mind in preparation for the finer and subtler realities of higher consciousness (Days 1 to 3).

Pinoline, affecting the neuro-transmitters of the brain, permits visions and dream-states to emerge in our conscious awareness (Days 3 to 5).

Eventually, the brain synthesizes the 'spirit molecules' 5-methoxy-dimethyltryptamine (5-MeO-DMT) and dimethyltryptamine (DMT), facilitating the transcendental experiences of universal love and compassion (Days 6 to 12)."

In the late 1980s, the neurochemist, James Callaway, in his paper called 'Pineal Gland, DMT & Altered State of Consciousness' proposed that pineal melatonin is converted into DMT (along with Pinoline and 5-MeO-DMT) just before the onset of REM (rapid eye-movement) sleep, when we dream. Are these natural, endogenous and psychoactive molecules literally fueling our dreams?[21] Consider the imagination of children, dreamers, people who are using plant medicine or psychedelics, telepaths, remote viewers, UFO abductees, shamans, meditators in deep states of meditation,  birthing mothers and babies, those who have had a near-death experience, and schizophrenics, and what they might all have in common. The *hypnagogic* imagery state occurs just before you fall asleep, and it is fueled by melatonin's conversion to DMT during an *activation* of the pineal gland. This also seems to be the same thing Tibetan, Taoist and Kabbalistic masters and religious prophets share. In his courses, Dr. Joe Dispenza teaches the technique of waking up at 4 am, when melatonin peaks, to meditate. In fact, when I did his training, we woke up twice for a 4 am meditation and I have kept this practice alive ever since. This window immediately before falling asleep seems to be a natural gateway into a spiritual and divine world. Certain psychedelic medicines such as psilocybin, LSD, ketamine, ayahuasca and 5-MAO, can be an opening for some to understand this. The medicines work by *waking you up* or *uncovering a veil* to a more heightened reality than what we experience in the physical world.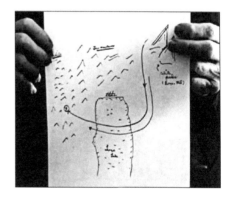

Through these dream states, some experience contact with purported 'entities' transmitting information or "channeling" wisdom from within the Source Field. This has been recorded by the founder of the Theosophical Society, Helena Blavatsky, who wrote *The Secret Doctrine*[22]. This was also reported in secret government agencies that conducted remote viewing for the CIA where these remote viewers would state they would experience interactions with what they called "Divine Entities". Jimmy Carter once stated that the most unexplainable experience while he was president was in 1979. A plane went down in Zaire, Congo and one of the CIA remote viewers gave them the exact GPS coordinates to the plane's position. This was one of the earliest examples of an operational success claimed by the US Government's sponsored remote viewing team. Remote viewing was popularized in the 1990s upon the declassification of certain documents related to the Stargate Project, a $20 million research program that had started in 1975. It was sponsored by the U.S. government in an attempt to determine any potential military application of psychic phenomena. Your pineal is the receiver of this source field, which carries information, and remote viewers have learned to access this through deep states of meditation. My understanding of this "channeling" is that one needs to be so totally present in the now moment that you can relax and allow this information to be the only thing rising in your awareness. You have a totally silent-thinking mind and all you are aware and conscious of is the present.

Is it possible that the pineal gland – the 'Eye of Shiva' which in many of us has atrophied as a result of toxins and chronic stress – is integral to the evolution of our consciousness? This was a wide held Hindu philosophy which considered an opened third eye to be a reawakened pineal gland. Is it possible that our healthy activated pineal could enable amazing abilities such as out-of-body experiences, near-death experiences, connection with divine beings, access to universal intelligence, remote viewing and astral travel, and ultimately our spiritual evolution?

It's thought that with work, the pineal could be more active which could allow it to potentially be a stronger 'radio antenna' for our perception into Source Field.

Many spiritual practitioners meditate with the goal of a complete dissolution of all fear. There are only 2 states; fear and love. Through enough practice, they could drop all fear and live through pure love, thus filtering their entire experience of the physical world through love. This would be considered enlightenment. The term "enlightenment" is equal to the term "awakening" or "self-realization".

Ram Dass said the following about his experience when he was in the presence of an enlightened being:

"The universe disappears. Only his eyes exist. A flow of love, wisdom, consciousness passes between you. It is just his stillness, his presence, the incredible love that flows from him, the deep compassion you feel. You feel as if you were naked before his glance. He sees through you, he knows all – past, present, and future. He does not judge, but simply acknowledges how it all is. Even a moment of such compassion can be liberating."[23].

This awake state seems to be transmissible to others in close proximity through this Source Field. To me this is like the onion experiment onion that Gavrilovich conducted.

There have been many enlightened beings that have achieved this state. A few of them were Amma, Jesus Christ, Buddha, Jiddu Krishnamurti, Krishna, Muhammad, Moses, Rumi, Socrates, St. Catherine of Siena, Osho, Yeshe Tsogyal, Lao-tzu, Mother Theresa, and St. John of the Cross.

Why do I get into source fields in a book on Endo-Nasal? It's in an attempt to open your eyes to the idea that your pineal is involved in more than melatonin production, and its health may have a direct relationship to your cranial function. When properly functioning, the pineal can open you up to experience a higher power which has the ability to support your health, vitality, and life span.

The precursor to melatonin is serotonin, a neurotransmitter derived from the amino acid tryptophan. Within the pineal gland, serotonin is acetylated and then methylated to yield melatonin. Serotonin regulates various states of consciousness. Serotonin is a feel-good hormone that increases alertness and happiness, but it also supports a relaxed state. Serotonin's energizing effects are what get you up in the morning washing away the fatigue that would otherwise keep you in bed.

Swami Karananda Saraswati[24], a well know guru from India once said:

"The ropes that prevent the perception of reality in which you are infinite seems to be related to the level of serotonin in the brain."

The 3rd eye sees the spirit world or ethereal world and translates it into a meaningful understanding of or physical world.

In 1943, the same year the first atomic bombs were being ignited, **Albert Hoffmann** discovered the molecule LSD-25. Serotonin is very similar to LSD-25 and it occupies the same receptor as serotonin. In this study, he discovered that 'Melatonin and LSD induce similar retinal changes in the frog'[25]. It seems that there is a close relationship that LDS has to a deep state most experienced meditators and notable spiritual leaders describe in which they are more fully connected to the 'Divine Oneness' or "The Source Field". We will dive more into The Source Field later.

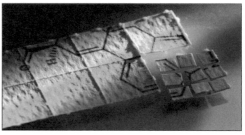

Cranial and Dural blockages can initiate a sympathetic stress response in the body, and block CSF flow that activates the pineal's piezoelectric field. More on this later. In order to be in a state to appreciate Divine Oneness, the volume on the stress response system must be turned down, otherwise the body and nervous system are in a state if survival. This requires calming the stress response or the sympathetic nervous system (fear) and activating the parasympathetic nervous system (love & bliss) which is associated with resting and digesting. Notably, digestion is the assimilation of nutrients and substance. It is in this state that we can assimilate wisdom, compassion, and understanding. I find it interesting to reflect on how melatonin is the ultimate buffer of stress in the body. It is in these deep states of relaxation that the body enters a heavy parasympathetic state. It's this same state that is associated with sleep, deep states of meditation, and as we will explore

> ## Dr Joseph Dispenza
>
> *Dr. Joe Dispenza[26] teaches his students to use a particular type of breathing to improve the pressures around the pineal gland. I've taken his advanced course and it is something very powerful that creates a similar experience to being on psychedelics. There is a feeling of universal connection, love, and gratitude for being alive. This connection with the "divine source" is the experience I assume all religions speak about. Becoming more aware of this energy or "doorway" can allow you to be connected to something that many religions speak of that unites us all. However, this is an energy that is not yet detectable with modern science. That's the best I can do to explain, as I know some might read this and think it's a bit "woo-woo", but there is no denying the events taking place at these events and the studies soon to be published through the research conducted on Joe Dispenza's meditators.*

Hemal Patel, MD & Dr John in 2021

later, the potential for spontaneous healing through the release of exosomes & VSEL stem cells. More on that soon.

NASA scientists, like my friend Hemal Patel, MD, are seeing changes in the blood levels of these meditators. They took blood samples from experienced meditators and found something that surprised us all. They found tiny vesicles in much higher amounts in the blood of the meditators which could be either exosomes or VSEL stem cells, or both. They conducted an experiment where they used these small particles found in the plasma of the meditators and mixed them with epithelial cells. They then introduced the COVID-19 virus and compared the results in both samples of epithelial cells, one with and one without the meditator's healing particles. Shockingly, the COVID-19 virus was unable to enter the epithelial cells mixed with the meditator's plasma. In contrast, the control tissues without the particles were infected severely with COVID-19[27].

What are Exosomes?

Exosomes are packets of RNA which carry information to other cells and parts of the body. Scientists are attributing some of the remarkable changes within these meditators to these exosomes. These changes include the healing of diseases that range from virtually all known conditions, including cancer.

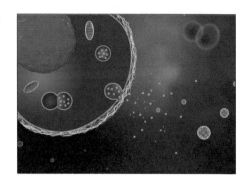

What I'm speaking of is spontaneous healing that occurs due to this heightened connection of source through the pineal gland, through a properly functioning cranial structure. Ultimately, it's the pineal and the other energy centers that run through the body.

We use exosomes and VSEL stem cells in my practice to heal various injuries and degenerative conditions that occur in the body, such as osteoarthritis and even damage from a stroke. Exosomes can be injected just like stem cells, as exosomes are the healing substances delivered by stem cells once they arrive at their target. Think of these exosomes as the stem of the stem cell. Therefore, by bypassing the need for the stem cells to deliver the exosomes, they can simply be isolated and injected by themselves with great results in many applications.

Our clinic began using stem cell therapy in 2005, in which we extracted them from both fat or adipose tissue, as well as bone marrow. In 2015, exosomes became commercially

available to doctors for clinical use in regenerative medicine. These exosomes, which can be derived from placental stem cells, carry the information to repair and heal through messenger RNA. They can be injected into the central nervous system through an intrathecal injection, as an intravenous injection, into soft tissue such as rotator cuff or other tendon injuries, or into joints to rebuild cartilage.

In our clinic, we do this under high-definition ultrasound. As of late, we are even using them to repair the inner ear for hearing loss and tinnitus with a system called SunaVae. You can learn more about this at SunaVae.com. SunaVae uses a regenerative injection which was pioneered by Dr. Minbo Shim in Korea and taught to me and my staff, and this technique is called ShimSpot. SunaVae also utilizes LumoMed which is a series of laser treatments pioneered by Dr. Amon Kaiser in Germany, which our clinic has been using since 2015 with great success for tinnitus, hyperacusis, and hearing loss.

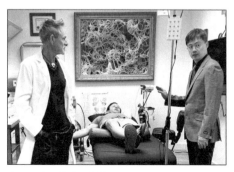

Dr John & Dr Shim: SunaVae Stem Cell Therapy to the Inner Ear, Florida.

VSEL Stem Cells "Can Become Anything & Small Enough to Go Anywhere."

Very small embryonic-like stem cells (VSELs) are pluripotent stem cells, meaning they are able to turn into any cell type needed for repair by your body. In other words, they are at the top of the cell differentiation tree. There are numerous reports demonstrating that there are rare stem cells that express early-development markers and are endowed with broader differentiation potential[44, 45, 46, 47, 48]. The size of a dormant VSEL is only 1-2 microns. After stimulation with the QiLaser, they expand to a size of 4-5 microns within 4 days. VSELs have an average diameter of 1-5 microns. In order to gain access to the entire body, substances need to pass through the lung tissue (pulmonary capillary beds) which must be smaller than 6 microns. VSELs have that ability and are able to turn into any cell type. They are small enough to go anywhere and powerful enough to turn into any cell type to support a regenerative effect throughout the body.

Dr John & Dr Todd Ovokaitys during VSEL clinicals in 2022

I studied with Todd Ovokaitys, MD at his center in Carlsbad, California, and we are among a few centers in the world using VSELs. Mike Tyson was recently treated by Dr. Ovokaitys and his return to boxing was so impressive that he responded in his interviews about how VSELs were an important part of his conditioning. Nature has equipped us with the means to heal. Doctors never heal patients; it is the patient that heals themselves. The doctor simply removes the interference to that expression of health, which is the body's natural state. VSELs are revolutionary in their therapeutic use and, in my opinion, are the next big technological breakthrough in stem cell therapy and healing. VSELs even show efficacy in regenerating all tissues in the body; eyes, brain, joints, organs, glands and the inner ear (see SunaVae.com for more on Inner Ear Regeneration).

They are administered in our clinic by drawing several tubes of blood and we then spin them down to remove all the red blood cells. This leaves all the healing components within the blood including the VSELs. These tubes, once spun down, are then activated using a special system created by Dr. Ovokaitys. A blocking protein is removed using laser that is thought to activate the VSELs as well as to stimulate the VSELs to multiply 2-3 fold. There are 1-2 million VSELs per cc of blood after they have been activated with our system, which we learned from Dr. Todd. Once the blood components are ready, they are placed into syringes which are either injected into a joint or tendon or given as an IV route of administration. The local injections are done in the same way Platelet Rich Plasma (PRP) or

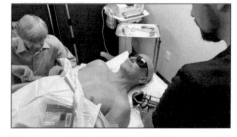

Harry receiving VSELs to his lower neck area: Sympathetic Ganglion.

> Dr. Todd remarks that, "In the 2 years since the accurate testing has been available, with repeated treatments there's a growing number of recipients that are 10-15 years younger than their pre-treatment baseline, and up to 18 years younger than their chronological age."

a stem cell treatment might be done. In our clinic, we use high-definition ultrasound to place the cells so we can both accurately see where the damage is and direct the injection into the perfect spot. The IV is simply a slow push into a vein. Once the IV and injections are completed, then there is special laser device we use to further activate the VSELs or to draw them into a specific area. Here is an example: if a shoulder or knee was injected, we would then laser the knee and or shoulder. If the IV was done, then we would use the laser to target them to areas such as the eyes, brain, glands, or any area we would like to direct them to.

Perhaps the most profound effect is reversal of the biological age clock at the DNA level. The most accurate testing of this clock that exists is called the *epigenetic DNA methylation biological age clock* developed by Dr. Steven Horvath of UCLA. With VSELs, the typical age reversal is about 3 years per treatment.

Results can be immediate or they can also take time as the tissues can take up to 2-4 months to fully repair. This is similar to what is seen in the Joe Dispenza research with Hemal Patel, MD. Dr. Ovokaitys believes the regeneration and cancer effects have more to do with VSELs then exosomes. I feel more research should be done to look into these mechanisms.

Healing Potential

Is it possible that when we connect with our pineal with certain intentions, such as to heal a foot or your brain, that the body responds by releasing these stem cells & healing particles like exosomes which will carry the information you intend?

I believe this is what's happening. If you look at a graph of all the energy spectrums and what a small part of it is the "visible light," you can appreciate there are so many frequencies and wavelengths we cannot see visually and that we must use a different

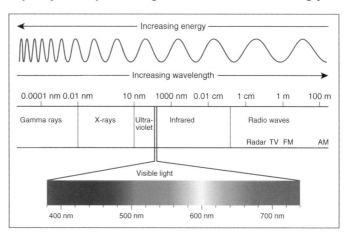

receiver than the eyes to detect them. Maybe that receiver is the 3rd eye which is, of course, the pineal gland?

Is it possible the pineal is more of a radio receiver? Crystals within the pineal can become activated through a piezoelectric effect (more on this soon) resulting from the force created by the CSF that normally pumps throughout your brain and spinal cord. This pressure against the crystals of the pineal allows us to tap into the Source Field, opening the opportunity to create powerful changes in our health. In the next section, I'll discuss endo-nasal and how it might enhance the pineal's "radio receiver" abilities.

Pineal & CSF Flow

This image of the flow of CSF shows how the circulation goes through the ventricles in the brain. These ventricles are like canals carrying life-giving nutrients that the CSF delivers to the brain and spinal cord. The pineal sits right at the end of the 3rd ventricle, and the CSF has most of its pressure around both the pineal and pituitary gland. Restricted motion in the cranium can alter this flow, and by using endo-nasal adjustments, we can support this flow to more fully move and activate your pineal.

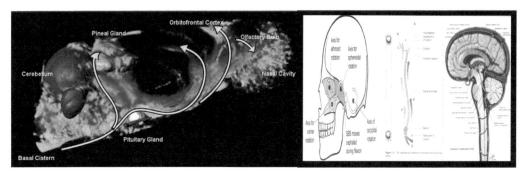

Take a look at this MRI showing the red areas as the most active

What Dr. Dispenza teaches is that breathing or 'breaths' directs your CSF into the pineal by locking down your muscles from the base of your pelvis or perineum up the spine and throat towards the pineal. There is a pumping action upon a full inhalation with intentionality to the pineal gland. This is creating hydrostatic pressure to the pineal, which Dr. Dispenza explains is involved in an activation of the crystalline structure inside the pineal.

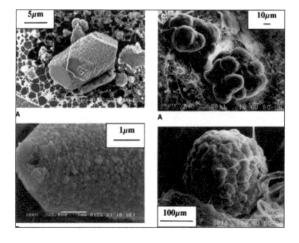

There seems to be a piezoelectric effect from the hydrostatic pressure of CSF as it interacts with the crystalline structures within the pineal.

Piezoelectric is defined as the ability of certain materials to generate an electric charge in response to applied mechanical stress[28]. I always say you're either a swamp or a river and this means better circulation and better health, and the pineal can become a victim or a victor dependent on the quality of circulation.

Doing things like this pineal breath which Dr. Dispenza teaches might hold some promise to improving pineal health. Is it possible that by simply unlocking the restrictions in the cranial

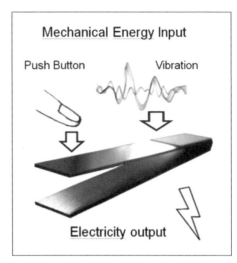

bones that this might work more automatically even without the breathwork? Maybe the breathwork would be more effective with the cranium released? These are questions we hope to discover with some collaboration with the Dispenza group. Toxins and chemicals such as fluoride that interfere with pineal gland function should be avoided because it has been proven to create calcifications. Dr. Dispenza's work, along with a pineal-friendly lifestyle and endo-nasal might be the answer to greater awareness. We will get into how to better care for your pineal later.

Still Point Breathing

Another teacher of mine, Dr. Michael Ryce,[29] does work synthesizing several disciplines, has created a profoundly powerful tool called Stillpoint Breathing. This is a technique that he created through his studies of the ancient Aramaic New Testament. This was the original scripture taught directly by Yeshua or Jesus Christ to his disciples in his native Aramaic language.

The Greek translation in the creation story says God sent out his spirit, whereas in Aramaic, the original language, when properly translated said, "God Sent out his breathe." There seems to be a spiritual opening that occurs with doing breathwork and certain breathing styles. Many plant medicine techniques and psychedelic protocols such as with ketamine, MDMA, and psilocybin therapy, utilize breathing techniques, like holotropic breathing, during their ceremonies. There are also groups that strictly rely on breathing and intention, such as with Dr. Dispenza's and Dr. Ryce's protocols. How does this all tie into VSEL stem cells and exosomes, and how does prayer and meditation affect them? We will dive more into these tiny particles and how your microbiome might be involved.

Information, Exosomes & The Micro-Biome (Bliss-Tides)

What seems to be within this Source Field is information. This information may explain the dramatic changes in the blood of meditators who achieve a certain peak experience. Then, there is the release of healing particles and stem cells discovered by Dr. Patel with meditators. These small healing particles are the source of information exchange in the body where stem cells use exosomes to transmit the effect to your tissues for repair and regeneration through the RNA codes contained within them. The exosomes can also be from your microbiome that also release exosomes[30]. I would offer that many of the positive effects in healing seen through prayer and meditation are in fact through the complex collection of bacteria that numbers in the trillions within each of us. Your microbiome is quickly adaptable and can be influenced by our behaviors, thoughts, and even emotions. Healthy thoughts might lead to healthy substances released by your microbiome.

Environmental influences can have profound influences on the various strains of bacteria as well as neuropeptides that they release. In other words, your environment such as diet, thoughts, emotions, and sleep can have an influence on the level of the good bacteria and what they release that might support a healthy mental emotional state as well as a healthy body. This makes sense when we consider that in the early days of man, we would feel uncomfortable in areas where the food didn't support our microbiome so we would feel uneasy and desire to move to an area where the environment would better support the microbiome. Your thoughts, emotions, and foods can have a strong influence on your microbiome and the neuropeptides they produce. Your microbiome will help by releasing things like exosomes and specific neuropeptide that I call Bliss-Tides.

BLISS-TIDES & My Experiments with Them.

The exosomes and VSELS can support the physical body by clearing inflammation and regenerating your cells. Bliss-Tides, through your microbiome and through a healthy lifestyle and a positive and blissful mental/emotional state, can turn around and further promote even more of these positive and blissful mental/emotional states. I am working on producing these through culturing rare and exquisite probiotics. So far, my experiments are suggesting that supplementing with them can lead to profound peace in the body and mind, and feelings of love and oneness. Make sure you are signed up for our newsletter to keep in the loop on this as we may be having this available in our events in Sarasota as well as to our patient population. Next, let's dive into breathing and how it opens you up to your subconscious and beyond.

The Unconscious Mind, Breath & the Pineal

I have personally greatly benefited from a regular breathwork practice and found that breathwork when properly done, has accelerated my physical, mental, emotional, and spiritual healing process. I often wake up at 4 am and do one or two hours of meditation that utilizes many of the tools I learned through various teachers I've worked with.

The first breathwork experience was in the late 1990's with Stillpoint breathing through Dr. Michael Ryce. When I asked Michael to explain the rationale and method of Stillpoint breathing, he shared that he had gathered information from many sources before he could "see" what all of these sources of information were actually saying. With his unique history and personal experimentation, he discovered and pieced together this amazing breathing method.

He explained the background of his technique like this. "Many years of inner work and study, especially from the first century Aramaic language, gifted me with a foundation from which to comprehend the healing power of the breath. The "secret" has been hidden in plain sight for centuries if you have, "the eyes to see," and "the ears to hear."

A foundation is needed to understand what the... "eyes to see... ears to hear" even means. In essence, to understand what another says, you have to generate your perception of what they are saying through a set of "brain cells" which match those of the meaning originating from their minds. If my perception of their conversation is built out of a different set of brain cells than theirs, my meaning for the exact words they use will be different. Simply put, I have a different perspective.

For example, if I hand a map to someone who just arrived to a new city, for the first time, and ask them to navigate to an address on the other side of town, what might be their response? Without using an app on your phone, it might be bewilderment. They

look at the same map but, with, "no eyes to see" and no "brain cells," the mind generates a senseless blob of lines and colors, certainly nothing they can make any sense of compared to someone familiar with the city.

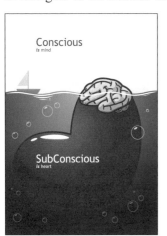

I look at the map, and with the "brain cells" for reading a map, I will understand the directions on the map. It would require me to see the map through the perspective of the map maker to follow their directions. If my "brain cells"

> *The word **Salience** (also called **saliency**) is that property by which something stands out. Salient events are an attentional mechanism by which organisms learn and survive; those organisms can focus their limited perceptual and cognitive resources on the pertinent (that is, salient) subset of the sensory data available to them.*

for north on a map with a northern orientation tell me to go south, I have no way to accurately navigate efficiently.

One of the networks within the brain responsible for this construct of reality includes the Salient Network (SN). The salient network contributes to a variety of complex functions, including communication, social behavior, and self-awareness through the integration of sensory, emotional, and cognitive information.

The Salient Network is the network that allows us to have a bit of control over what we place our attention on. The SN is upstream to another network called the Default Mode Network (DMN) in the sense that the SN allows the DMN to operate.

The DMN is best known for being active when a person is not focused on the outside. It's active when the brain is at wakeful rest, such as during daydreaming and mind-wandering. The DMN can also be active when the individual is thinking about others, thinking about themselves, remembering the past and planning for the future. This network houses the self, the assumptions about the self, and the stories we tell about ourselves to ourselves. The DMN is where our sense of self becomes our reality. *Keep in mind that nasal breathing (nasal openness) has a powerful impact on these brain networks, and we dive deep into this in chapter 12.*

> *Endo Nasal Therapy can open the nasal passages to allow better activation to the limbic oscillations, default mode network and salient networks. This can have a profound impact on how we process information and build our constructs of reality and our identity of self. Limbic Oscillations are intimately connected through nasal breathing which drives our emotions and is hardwired into the SN & DMN.*

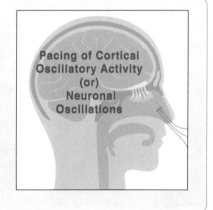

Pacing of Cortical Oscillatory Activity (or) Neuronal Oscillations

> *There might be an entirely different way to look at the world by breaking free from the constraints of these brain networks. There may also be subconscious and unconscious information available that we may not have access to that is driving these networks through deep limbic (emotional) triggers. The breath holds the key to activating this information (thought energy) where we can access it and make some decisions as to whether these thoughts are giving us the mental, emotional, and physical support we would like or if they are causing negative thoughts and behaviors.*

Limbic Oscillations also play a role in this story of building brain cells and our construct of identity of self. Respiratory rhythms that draw air through the nose are hard wired into your brains "need to breathe". At a pace of 2-12 Hertz, these rhythms regulate cortical excitability and coordinate network interactions. This helps to shape olfactory coding, memory, and behavior. Limbic oscillations are hard linked to the human respiratory cycle and this respiration control creates pacing for the cortical oscillatory activity. Endo-nasal therapy, as well as intra-nasal and trans-cranial light therapy, can play a role to enhance these systems.

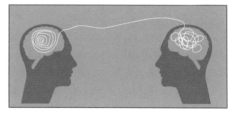

In order for accurate communication to occur, especially on complex topics, our mind must be building its perception of reality and self-identify through the SN (what we choose to place our attention on) and DMN (how our reality is constructed based on all the data points highlighted through the SN). So indeed, it's through our thoughts that we create our individual meanings. So often, we might think we understand another but, in fact, we are living in different perceptual constructs of reality.

The ancient Aramaic language, which was Jesus' original language and is the root language of at least 5 of the world's major religions, is not a religious language. It comes from a deep understanding of the function and inter-relationship of physics, physiology, genetics, and psychology. Often scripture is filtered through primitive religious precepts, often reflective of a deeply disturbed mind that functions out of fear, hostility, and control. The Aramaic version of the Bible describes how the world really works, and how to harmonize with life and your fellow humans. There is also a description of neurology that resonates strongly with what we're just now learning about the human brain.

Michael arrived at his conclusions with breath and the Stillpoint process through decades of working with people where each time a memory of unresolved trauma began to surface, people radically altered their breathing patterns, or stopped breathing all together.

> *There may also be unconscious information available we may not have access to and the breath may hold the key to accessing both. Take care of hidden thoughts within your unconscious because this is what your life is created from!*

In the Greek Scriptures, there is a passage that states, "keep thy heart with all diligence; for out of it are the issues of life". In Aramaic, this might translate into "take care of the unconscious." Since it is the unconscious that is hidden from us, I offer this, "Take care of hidden thoughts within your unconscious and subconscious because this is what your life is created from!"

How do I do that? Another Greek passage refers to a tearing of a purple curtain in a church, "The veil of the temple must be 'Rent in Twain!' "Rent in Twain" means opened into two. Understood in its original sense, it says (long form), "Your body is your temple, and you have built a barrier to hide what you do not want to look at or deal with. This has been going on for generations. You have been driven and controlled by your unconscious generational patterns."

Breath is the key! It's how the veil is built and through breath we can break it down? We commonly hold our breath and create a veil when unconscious pain began to surface.

The veil of the temple is the barrier between the conscious and the subconscious/unconscious. That barrier is built by holding the breath. This barrier (the veil) is opened by proper use of the breath. I also offer that these subconscious and unconscious patterns become locked into our tissues such as dense connective tissue and there is no other such dense tissue then the Dura Mater or "Tough Mother" that surrounds our brain and spinal cord and it is the main structure released with endo-nasal balloons. Our "Tough Mother" is built to protect us just like mothers do, however, sometime mothers become overly protective and don't allow the full expression of the child (life force).

There's more to this story as there are specific chemicals at play here that are released during specific breathing, meditation, and prayer. Next, let's dive into DMT and its relationship to melatonin.

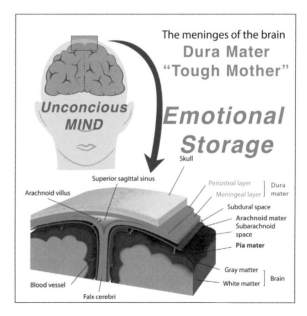

DMT, The Spirit Molecule

DMT or N, N-Dimethyltryptamine is so powerful that it was dubbed the "spirit molecule" for its spiritual awakening–type effects. It's defined as a chemical substance that occurs in many plants and animals and is a derivative and a structural analog of tryptamine. DMT is used as a recreational psychedelic drug and prepared by various cultures for ritual purposes as an entheogen such as with Ayahuasca. Ayahuasca is traditionally prepared using two plants called *Banisteriopsis caapi* and *Psychotria Viridis*. The latter contains DMT while the former contains MAOIs, which prevent certain enzymes in your body from breaking down DMT.

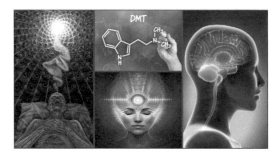

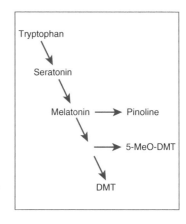

DMT may also be released when we dream. It's also believed to be released during birth and death. This release of DMT at death may be responsible for those mystical experiences seen with Dispenza's work and psychedelic drugs such as psilocybin and LSD. Trace amounts of DMT have been shown in rat pineal glands[31].

The pineal gland in humans produces a small amount of DMT, but it's uncertain if the pineal is a large enough source of DMT to be psychoactive. My personal belief is that DMT can be released by a healthy pineal. Keep in mind 80% of us have calcified pineal glands, and therefore, a healthy pineal is fairly rare, thus meaning that studies on typical pineal glands might not reflect the potential in certain individuals. In fact, it's quite possible that the pineal can produce more DMT than what scientists have seen thus far, given the right circumstance.

Dr. Ryce's and Dr. Dispenza's work, as well as other anecdotal methods to activate your "third eye" such as breathing methods, yoga, meditation, taking certain supplements, doing a pineal detox or cleanse, using crystals and various vibrations tuned to certain frequencies, might hold the answers.

Dr. Rick Strassman wrote a book on DMT called "The Spirit Molecule: A Doctor's Revolutionary Research into the Biology of Near-Death and Mystical Experiences"[32]. In this amazing

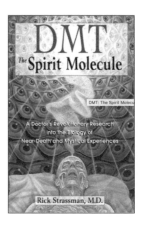

book, Strassman sees DMT consistently producing near-death and mystical experiences with his volunteers. any reported encounters with intelligent nonhuman presences, aliens, angels, and spirits. Nearly all felt that the sessions were among the most profound experiences of their lives.

The Pineal Gland Commonly Becomes Inadequate & Calcified as We Age.

In 80% of adult humans, the pineal gland contains calcifications defined as "corpora arenacea" or "brain sand"[33].

One of the defense mechanisms protecting the body against the effects of fluoride toxicity seems to be its deposition in calcified tissues. The symptoms of excessive fluoride accumulation in bones and teeth are known and well documented, classified as skeletal fluorosis and dental fluorosis, respectively.

Calcium deposition into the pineal gland is similar to that found in bones. The process of calcium accumulation in the pineal gland is initiated in childhood and even in newborns.

Calcification is accompanied by a reduction in melatonin synthesis. Pineal gland calcification has an indirect effect on the production and secretion of melatonin. The image here shows the severe calcification of the pineal.

In light of this science, it may make sense to limit fluoride intake by avoiding drinking most municipal water sources, which have been fortified with fluoride, as well as many conventional toothpastes.

Researchers have studied a potential connection between increased fluoride exposure and pineal gland calcifications. Fluoride is a naturally occurring mineral that some areas add to their water supply to reduce tooth decay. The mineral is present in most toothpaste because it's thought that it necessary to maintain and strengthen tooth enamel. Yet, fluoride is naturally attracted to calcium, and researchers believe increased fluoridation leads to increased pineal gland calcification.

A study in 2019, 'Fluoride-Free Diet Stimulates Pineal Growth in Aged Male Rats'[34], found those who were placed on a fluoride-free diet for 4 to 8 weeks experienced a greater increase in the number of pineal gland cells compared with those who consumed fluoridated food and drinking water. See the chapter on pineal for more details on this subject.

> 66
>
> *Endo-Nasal can support a healthy pineal.*
>
> *The stagnation and chronic swampy state of the pineal from a locked up cranial structure can be improved using endo-nasal cranial work.*

These are my favorite natural alternatives to fluoride toothpaste.

1. OZONE Toothpaste

The disinfecting power that ozone has can be used to kill many different types of bacteria that cause certain diseases, pain, and tooth decay. Ozone is dissolved into tooth paste and can penetrate areas of the teeth, gums, and mouth. This is my go-to tooth paste. Ozone tooth paste

2. MINERAL CREMES/MOUTHRINSES

You can use a mineral creme which coats your teeth in a protective film. This film can release natural calcium and phosphate minerals into the enamel. A mineral mouth rinses can provide bioavailable minerals in high concentrations to naturally strengthen enamel.

3. TOOTH POWDER

Therapeutic tooth powder can be used daily to neutralize acidity in the mouth and provide naturally occurring minerals to strengthen your enamel.

4. MCT Oil Pulling

Oil pulling with MCT coconut oil can be an excellent way to support your teeth. Coconut oil contains monolaurin, which has antibiotic properties and naturally occurring minerals. Oil pulling involves swishing oil around the mouth, using it like a mouthwash. Put a tablespoon of MCT oil in your mouth, then swish it around for 15–20 minutes. Try adding a few drops of peppermint or tea tree essential oil to create it even more effective and it tastes better as well.

5. XYLITOL

Xylitol is a natural sugar and tastes sweet. This 2003 study[35], shows that xylitol is effective at re-mineralizing enamel. Make sure to chew it after or between meals to get the maximum remineralization benefits.

Support Your Pineal Gland

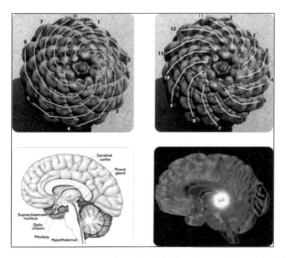

Pineal calcification is calcium deposition in the pineal gland, which has long been reported in humans. The occurrence of pineal calcification depends on environmental factors, such as sunlight exposure, toxins like fluoride, and increased metabolic activity. This calcification is seen in many chronic conditions.

Studies have found that the more metabolically active the pineal gland is, the more likely it is to form calcium deposits. Furthermore, researchers have conducted animal studies where gerbils who were exposed to less light than others had higher amounts of pineal gland calcifications[36]. Darkness strongly influences the pineal to release melatonin. If the pineal gland has to work harder to produce your melatonin as a consequence of less sunlight exposure, calcification can occur.

Certain chronic medical conditions will increase the likelihood of pineal gland calcifications. Pineal calcification causing lower melatonin levels can lead to a lowering of the body's ability to be resilient to stress adaptation. Examples of these medical conditions include Alzheimer's disease, migraine headaches, kidney disease, and schizophrenia. One consideration about all degenerative neurological conditions is the glymphatic connection. The glymphatic system is the primary detoxification mechanism used by the central nervous system. Deep sleep is the strongest activator of this system and is enhanced or inhibited from a properly functioning cranial structure.

Considering the swamp/river relationship to cellular health, it's easy to see how poor cleansing leads to accumulation of waste. This leads to proteins like beta amyloid, such as with Alzheimer's disease, that build up and entangle the nerves within the brain. Reading through this book you can see how vast of an influence melatonin has on all of your organs and cells. Sleep is more important than nutrition for pineal health, and the body needs to have a strong circadian rhythm, both of which rely on a healthy pineal and cranial function.

Can you decalcify your pineal gland?

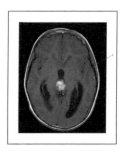

Besides cranial work, sun, and breathwork, you need to stop consuming fluoridated water. If you're on a public water system, you can request support from your water supplier, which will contain information about fluoride and chlorine, which is another mineral that may contribute to calcifications. As an alternative, some people will have a whole house water filter that is a reverse osmosis system at the sink to have pure water to drink. Quality bottled water can be another way to avoid drinking toxins. Avoid toothpaste that contains fluoride. Fluoride is also used in pesticides and some chemicals used to create non-stick compounds for pots and pans. Eat organic foods and avoid processed foods to reduce fluoride consumption. Calcium supplementation consumed in excess could be problematic, especially if you're low in vitamin D and K-2. Another issue could be taking too much vitamin D and not enough vitamin K-2, as the K-2 is needed to prevent the calcium from depositing into your tissues. Either way, to answer the question: Yes, it is possible to decalcify the pineal gland.

Nutrients To Detox Your Pineal Gland

Spending more time in the sun each day and limiting the use on sunglasses, regular meditations, prayer, and breathwork are all great ways to detoxify your pineal. Breathing that works on the hydrostatic pressures in your CSF may have the strongest effect to detoxify the pineal. Recall my analogy about the swamp versus the river and consider that circulation brings in nutrients and takes out garbage. There are also supplements and foods that can help. Besides melatonin, there are a few others that can be helpful. Here are the ones I found to be most relevant:

- *Iodine* is a mineral found in sea vegetables, like seaweed or kelp. This vital mineral assists the thyroid gland in regulating hormones and is one of the most efficient removers (chelators) of heavy metals from the body. Iodine chelates heavy metals such as mercury, lead, cadmium, and aluminum, as well as fluoride.

- *Shilajit* is plant material produced over millions of years from plants preserved in dark crevices of the Himalayan Mountains. Shilajit forms a thick resin that's packed with 85 different trace minerals including fulvic acid. Fulvic acid helps eliminate toxins and heavy metals, supporting the decalcification process.

- *Turmeric* is another excellent supplement for your pineal gland detox. This study in Pharmacognosy Magazine shows that curcumin, the active ingredient in turmeric, can prevent and potentially reverse the damage from fluoride exposure[38].

- *Chaga Mushrooms:* The Chinese call it the "King of Plants." In Siberia, it's the "Gift from God", and for the Japanese, it's the "Diamond of the Forest." Not bad for wood-rotting fungus! Hundreds of scientific studies have demonstrated the potent effects of the Chaga mushroom on the immune, hormonal, and central nervous systems. Studies in Finland and Russia found that Chaga is an efficient anti-tumor agent as well as antiviral. Chaga provides us with phytochemicals, nutrients, and melanin. The pineal gland uses melanin to help shield us from UV light. Siberian Chaga may be the most potent with the highest recorded levels of antioxidants according to the ORAC Scale[39, 40, 41].

- **_K2 or factor X:_** Intestinal microflora in animal tissues produces vitamin K1 & K2. You can find it in organ meats, fermented dairy products, like cheese or butter (grass-fed butter), sauerkraut, and marine oils.

- In 1945, the "Isaac Newton of Nutrition," a former dentist named Weston Price, described a vitamin-like compound that plays a major role in:

  - Growth

  - Reproduction

  - Brain function

  - Tooth decay prevention

  - Protection against calcification of the arteries

- **_Tamarind:_** One study and a follow-up study from the early 2000s demonstrated that tamarind increased the excretion of fluoride in urine compared to the control group. The researchers believe tamarind may even be able to reverse the effects of skeletal fluorosis caused by ingesting fluoride[42, 43].

- Green Superfoods: Finally, eating raw, green foods that are rich in chlorophyll will also help chelate heavy metals from your blood while nourishing it. Chlorophyll-dense foods like chlorella, spirulina, and wheatgrass also increase oxygen levels, repair damaged tissue, and boost the immune system.

Agnihorta & Sun Gazing

Dr Alan Macy

This year, while traveling in California I was blessed to spend time with Dr Alan Macy, a biological engineer who shared the American Indian practice called Agnihorta which is where you stare at a specifically made fire for 10 minutes in the morning around sunrise and 10 minutes around sunset. He explained that the flames have a frequency and pattern that they "beat". The frequency at the base of the fire produces frequencies that activate areas in your nervous system that relate to your lower root chakra energy centers, which supplies life force to your organs and glands in the lower pelvis. The top of the fire produced frequencies that relate to the upper chakras and energy centers which support the head. And, there are frequencies all the way between the root and crown through the entire fire. This can be a powerful practice to create a strong signaling to the circadian rhythm and allow a powerful balance between the 2 parts of your autonomic nervous system; the sympathetic and parasympathetic nervous system. Another method I am finding helpful and is very easy to integrate into your activities with little effort is using the SaunaSpace bulbs for 20-30 minutes in the morning and evening around sunset and sunrise. The bulbs made by SaunaSpace are unique and amazing. My good friend Brian Richards developed this bulb which has 40% Near InfraRed! I set 1-2 lamps in my living area which extends into my kitchen. I'm then exposed to the light without any downtime. I try to wear only a little amount of clothing during this time. Brian is giving out a 5% off coupon which is "LIEURANCE5". Calming down the stress  responses (or sympathetics) is very important for general health and vitality. Stressors which exceed our ability to adapt resulting in excessive inflammation, are the primary factors driving disease in modern times. Sometimes we are unable to reduce the stressors in our life, however we can increase energy at the cellular level which will give our bodies the ability to adapt. This is the case with the use of light therapy and PBM.

Sun Gazing can also be very powerful when done at sunrise and sunset. My good friend and well-known podcaster, Luke Story, recently visited me and shared this technique with me. He stated that this practice has helped him feel more vital during the day and sleep more peacefully at night. I have been doing this myself and love the effects as well. It is totally safe to look at the sun without sunglasses in these times of day where the sun is close to the horizon. It  may even be safe to do some in more extreme times of sun, however, I would suggest you work with your health care provider or study under someone that understands sun gazing before starting a sun gazing practice.

Genesha, the Lord of Doorways, Sits on a throne of Skulls.

In Hindu mythology, Ganesh is the scribe of the Mahabharata[49], one of two epics of ancient India that includes the Bhagavad Gita. Ganesh (also spelled Ganesa or Ganesha, and known as Ganapati, Vinayaka and Pillaiyar) is the Lord of Good Fortune who provides prosperity, fortune, and success.

Ganesha sits on an Asana of skulls or Throne of Demon Skulls. Ganesha is the remover of Obstacle's, Lord of Beginnings and Doorways, and is one of the most beloved and recognized Hindu Gods. They say Ganesha is the remover of obstacles, and doors are the obstacle to what's behind them and to new beginnings. Ganesha's ultimate purpose is laya, or ultimate liberation from Maya Rupa or the illusory state of samsara.

In Hindu, they will chant to Ganesha or Ganapati (Ganna Party) to be let through the doorway to the Divine. Like a bouncer at a club, Ganesha sits at the doorway to the Divine Oneness and lets those through the doorway that are in harmony with the divine. To be in Harmony, means to be in a state of Bliss, Gratitude, and Love. In Hinduism, demons often

represent ignorance, hostility, fear, anger, and jealousy, as well as other bad characteristics, and hence the various Hindu Gods and Goddesses often conquer demons. So, in this statue, Ganesha is sitting on top of a throne with demon skulls and represents overcoming our own inner demons. In other words, these are the same ideas Yeshua brought forth in the original Aramaic Scripture regarding the veil of the temple, which is the barrier between the conscious and unconscious. That barrier is represented in Hindu as demon skulls. The barrier, the veil, or skull structures can be opened by proper use of the breath and function of the cranium. Here is Ganesha holding a skull or empty inverted Kapala to signify the emptiness of mind and perception. Drinking from skull cups, you are taking in the nectar of pure perception and imagining without boundaries, where the mind creations emanate from the primordial void of pure possibilities, like the aureoles of flames from a fire.

'Maya Rupa' Refers to an Illusion of Form.

Maya is the Goddess of Illusion, and Rupa means 'form' so, it is Illusion of Form. All of our illusions are based on our filters of reality which we create based on what we are taught by others, through our experiences, relationships, and genetic imprints. These filters alter our perception, so we experience the world in our own unique way. This is why multiple people can experience the same things and have radically different objective views of the same event. We all have our own Maya Rupa experiences that can either support a blissful, positive and vital experience of life or it can take us into fear and hostility. Uncovering these filters that hide under the veil, locked in by the breath and stored in our tissues, such as within the dura

> " *We hold our breath when fear and hostility come up. Thought forms come from the mind, are unconscious & subconscious, and they get stored and/or are retrieved to build our identity of self. These thought forms are only energy stored and this storage occurs, in our body's connective tissues such as in the Dura Mater.*

DURA MATER

"Tough Mother"

mater, is the key that has been brought forth in several religions. Within Hindu and Buddhism, and based on the original Aramaic scripture, there is also Jesus or Yeshua. Is Evil (unripe or missing a target) really a demon with horns or a black figure with a pitchfork, or is it something we create within ourselves that is largely hidden from us within our unconscious and subconscious mind?

An interesting fact that puts this in perspective from a scriptural point of view is that the word 'sin' is used by the Catholic church to suggest an act that results in going to a fiery hell where you burn for infinity. Actually, sin was described in the original Aramaic scripture as an archery term that means you missed your shot (Evil) and try a new shot (Sin). The word Evil meant that you missed the mark, and sin meant give it another go. Yeshua also referred to Evil many times, and his true meaning in Aramaic was "not ripe" He would say, "sufficient for the day are the evils thereof." In other words, don't set too many goals for your day that you cannot complete and retire with un-ripened goals. It is similar to closing out extra programs running on the computer before sleep because you know this is a good way to live.

Yeshua said "Fear Not" 100's of times throughout scripture, so it seems he was not intending us to be in a state of fear. In the scriptures, He says, "The Beginning of Wisdom is Fear of God." Fear creates a threatening reality and I offer this is a misinterpretation of Yeshua's true meaning. Yeshua spoke about Rakhma as the filter that is through love, and that filters out hostility and fear. Love is our natural state and without Rakhma, intentions that are key to love are blocked. Intentions are the key to drive our goals, so ask what are our goals based on? If Yeshua's intention was to teach us to live through Rakhma, then the goal of spiritual growth is to drop all fears and live from a place of pure love. When we live from love, we experience life totally different from that of fear and hostility. Yeshua

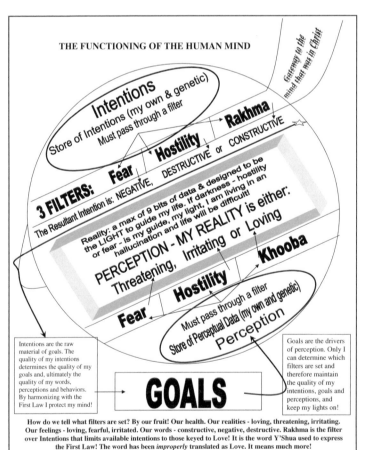

spoke about an area of the mind he called Rakmah which filters reality through pure love, and that this was something to work towards. The Greeks translated the Aramaic scripture from this fear/hostility perspective as well as a filter to control the public through fear-based religious teachings. Many of the scriptures have not been interpreted through Rakhma, and Michael Ryce is one of the few individuals who discovered what was the true message given by Yeshua. When he brought this up during his time as a deacon in the Catholic church, he was told to be quiet about this and thus he went his own way.

A Diagram out of the book Why Is This Happening To Me...Again. See WhyAgain.org to purchase Michael's book or to learn about his teachings.

Conclusion

The pineal is an important gland due to its connection to melatonin production and spiritual connectiveness. It serves as a connection to a "source" or a divine oneness, and its ability to be healthy relies on a properly functioning cranium with a wider structure.

It has now been scientifically proven that the pineal, via its piezoelectric effect through the pressures CSF imposed upon it, and that with breath and cranial rhythm, the pineal may be like activating a radio receiver. Moreover, the pineal may allow us to have the ability to access information in the spectrum of very high frequencies and allow us to perceive and interact with the Source Field. This gateway seems to allow for health and healing in the body through tiny particles that are released, such as VSEL stem cells and exosomes. Also, remote viewing that many prophets and religions speak of, means receiving information from the quantum and divine states of complete love and oneness.

In other words, the pineal gland may serve as a connection with a force we might classify as mystical, holy, divine, God or the creator. Whatever one chooses to call this force or energy; it's difficult to deny its existence.

As you have learned from past chapters, endo-nasal cranial work can be a powerful supporter to the CSF flow and the cavernous effect, due to a wider cranium, which amplifies source field. Breathwork is one of the best ways to strengthen and support the CSF flow as well as the autonomic parasympathetics. Both can also lead to DMT production and access to a divine and a mystical oneness experience. Endo Nasal Therapy, by opening the nasal passages, allows for better activation to the limbic oscillations, default mode network and salient networks. This can have profound impact on how we process information and build our constructs of reality, and our identity of self, which is hardwired into the SN & DMN.

Melatonin supplementation, such as with Sandman, can be very supportive to the body and pineal in high doses as discussed in the book Melatonin: Miracle Molecule. Anyone inter-

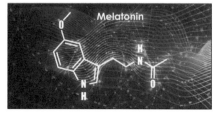

ested in pineal health should consider including cranial work, prayer, meditation and breathing techniques into their daily ritual. I prefer to do these early in the morning as this seems to be the best time due to melatonin levels. Doing these techniques before bed would be the next best time.

Early morning and late afternoon sungazing and ditching the shades while driving will support less calcification of the pineal. Also, microbiome support might be the next gold rush for mental, emotional, and spiritual health with the new Bliss-Tides.

Ultimately what we are speaking about is a deeper connection to Source. That connection might be the most important one we make in our lifetime. You can own all of the real estate, fancy boats and cars, and you can have many degrees, but none of this will really help you on your spiritual journey. In fact, it is often a hindrance as it gets you more into your mind and focused on material things. As Dr. Ryce explained, this further disconnects you from your subconscious, allowing those less empowering thoughts and beliefs to run the show behind the scenes. Working to uncover them may also uncover a calmer and more present state that could greatly enhance your life experience. In addition to these benefits, some might find something even more profoundly amazing within the source field. It's a simple process of moving the "Nos" in our mind and saying "Yes" to the present moment, and fully being in this openness. This spacious "Now Moment" is where we experience our true nature as love.

Although the material in this chapter is related to endo-nasal, I veered off of the scientific conversation in some parts into more ethereal ideas. I hope that this has given you the "eyes to see" and the "ears to hear" the potential for a higher level of consciousness. May it spark a journey into deeper exploration into your own consciousness and unconscious mind, and create a more loving empathetic filter or Rakhma to see life through.

Retreats with Advance Rejuvenation

I will be holding workshops from time to time on this subject in Sarasota, Florida, so please check with our website OutOfBoxDoc.com or AdvancedRejuvenation.us and click retreats to learn about:

How to create the most vital body and brain, breathwork, psychedelic medicine journeys with ketamine and endo-nasal (Bliss Release), Bliss-Tides, improving the body's vitality to achieve higher levels of consciousness, achieving a direct experience of Divine Oneness, and accessing the unconscious/subconscious mind, thoughts and belief patterns that are driving unwanted emotions and behaviors in order to remove these from your operating system.

References

1. Guan, J.-L. (2010), Integrin signaling through FAK in the regulation of mammary stem cells and breast cancer. IUBMB Life, 62: 268-276. https://doi.org/10.1002/iub.303

2. Booth FM. The human pineal gland: a review of the "third eye" and the effect of light. Aust N Z J Opthalmol. 1987 Nov;15(4):329-36. doi: 10.1111/j.1442-9071.1987.tb00092.x. PMID: 3435677.

3. Hormones.gr

4. ReFaey K, Quinones GC, Clifton W, Tripathi S, Quiñones-Hinojosa A. The Eye of Horus: The Connection Between Art, Medicine, and Mythology in Ancient Egypt. Cureus. 2019 May 23;11(5):e4731. doi: 10.7759/cureus.4731. PMID: 31355090; PMCID: PMC6649877.

5. Booth FM. The human pineal gland: a review of the "third eye" and the effect of light. Aust N Z J Ophthalmol. 1987 Nov;15(4):329-36. doi: 10.1111/j.1442-9071.1987.tb00092.x. PMID:3435677.

6. Masters, A., Pandi-Perumal, S. R., Seixas, A., Girardin, J. L., & McFarlane, S. I. (2014). Melatonin, the Hormone of Darkness: From Sleep Promotion to Ebola Treatment. Brain disorders & therapy, 4(1), 1000151. https://doi.org/10.4172/2168-975X.1000151

7. Romijn HJ. The pineal, a tranquillizing organ? Life Sci. 1978 Dec 4;23(23):2257-73. doi: 10.1016/0024-3205(78)90191-1. PMID: 366320.

8. Russel J. Reiter, Pineal Melatonin: Cell Biology of Its Synthesis and of Its Physiological Interactions, Endocrine Reviews, Volume 12, Issue 2, 1 May 1991, Pages 151–180, https://doi.org/10.1210/edrv-12-2-151

9. Ketamine Assisted Psychotherapy In Sarasota | Mental Health Treatment (advancedrejuvenation.us)

10. Srinivasan V, Cardinali DP, Srinivasan US, Kaur C, Brown GM, Spence DW, Hardeland R, Pandi-Perumal SR. Therapeutic potential of melatonin and its analogs in Parkinson's disease: focus on sleep and neuroprotection. Ther Adv Neurol Disord. 2011 Sep;4(5):297-317. doi: 10.1177/1756285611406166. PMID: 22010042; PMCID: PMC3187674.

11. Oaknin-Bendahan S, Anis Y, Nir I, Zisapel N. Effects of long-term administration of melatonin and a putative antagonist on the ageing rat. Neuroreport. 1995 Mar 27;6(5):785-8. doi: 10.1097/00001756-199503270-00020. PMID: 7605949.

12. Rozencwaig R, Grad BR, Ochoa J. The role of melatonin and serotonin in aging. Med Hypotheses. 1987 Aug;23(4):337-52. doi: 10.1016/0306-9877(87)90054-5. PMID: 2889131.

13. Heaven - Wikipedia

14. Alexander Gurwitsch - Wikipedia

15. Article 113: Physics - Aether, Space & Time - Part 3 - Kozyrev, Ginzburg, Shnoll & Dematerialization- Cosmic Core (cosmic-core.org)

16. Wilhelm Reich - Wikipedia

17. Wilhelm Reich - Wikipedia

18. The_Bions (weebly.com)

19. Rainbow Body Phenomenon - The Highest Level Of Attainable Consciousness & Enlightenment — MOT MAG

20. Lao-Tzu - World History Encyclopedia

21. Pineal Gland, DMT & Altered State of Consciousness | Miller | Journal of Consciousness Exploration & Research (jcer.com)

22. The Secret Doctrine - Vol. II (theosociety.org)

23. Ram Dass - Wikipedia

24. Dayananda Saraswati (Arsha Vidya) - Wikipedia

25. Kemali M, Milici N, Kemali D. Melatonin and LSD induce similar retinal changes in the frog. Biol Psychiatry. 1986 Aug;21(10):981-5. doi: 10.1016/0006-3223(86)90276-3. PMID: 3488766.

26. The Official Website of Dr Joe Dispenza – Unlimited with Dr Joe Dispenza

27. Barberis, E., Vanella, V. V., Falasca, M., Caneapero, V., Cappellano, G., Raineri, D., Ghirimoldi, M., De Giorgis, V., Puricelli, C., Vaschetto, R., Sainaghi, P. P., Bruno, S., Sica, A., Dianzani, U., Rolla, R., Chiocchetti, A., Cantaluppi, V., Baldanzi, G., Marengo, E., & Manfredi, M. (2021). Circulating Exosomes Are Strongly Involved in SARS-CoV-2 Infection. Frontiers in molecular biosciences, 8, 632290. https://doi.org/10.3389/fmolb.2021.632290

28. Piezoelectric Effect - an overview | ScienceDirect Topics

29. Dr. michael ryce - Why Is This Happening To Me... AGAIN?! (whyagain.org)

30. Teng, Y., Ren, Y., Sayed, M., Hu, X., Lei, C., Kumar, A., Hutchins, E., Mu, J., Deng, Z., Luo, C., Sundaram K., Sriwastva, M. K., Zhang, L., Hsieh, M., Reiman, R., Haribabu, B., Yan, J.m, Jala, V. R., Miller, D. M., Van Keuren-Jensen, K., … Zhang, H. G. (2018). Plant-Derived Exosomal MicroRNAs Shape the Gut Microbiota. Cell host & microbe, 24(5), 637–652.e8. https://doi.org/10.1016/j.chom.2018.10.001

31. LC/MS/MS analysis of the endogenous dimethyltryptamine hallucinogens, their precursors, and major metabolites in rat pineal gland microdialysate (umich.edu) article_5713_34b0cf-778cb423c5cc4fc28672805c32.pdf (ekb.eg)

32. Rick Strassman MD – DMT: The Spirit Molecule

33. Article_5713_34b0cf778cb423c5cc4fc28672805c32.pdf (ekb.eg)

34. Mrvelj A, Womble MD. Fluoride-Free Diet Stimulates Pineal Growth in Aged Male Rats. Biol Trace ElemRes. 2020 Sep;197(1):175-183. doi: 10.1007/s12011-019-01964-4. Epub 2019 Nov 12. PMID: 31713773.Pineal Gland 329

35. Miake Y, Saeki Y, Takahashi M, Yanagisawa T. Remineralization effects of xylitol on deminer-alized enamel. J Electron Microsc (Tokyo). 2003;52(5):471-6. doi: 10.1093/jmicro/52.5.471. PMID: 14700079.

36. Tan, D. X., Xu, B., Zhou, X., & Reiter, R. J. (2018). Pineal Calcification, Melatonin Production, Aging, Associated Health Consequences and Rejuvenation of the Pineal Gland. Molecules (Basel, Switzerland), 23(2), 301. https://doi.org/10.3390/molecules23020301

37. Jessen NA, Munk AS, Lundgaard I, Nedergaard M. The Glymphatic System: A Beginner's Guide. Neurochem Res. 2015 Dec;40(12):2583-99. doi: 10.1007/s11064-015-1581-6. Epub 2015 May 7. PMID: 25947369; PMCID: PMC4636982.

38. Sharma, C., Suhalka, P., Sukhwal, P., Jaiswal, N., & Bhatnagar, M. (2014). Curcumin atten-uates neurotoxicity induced by fluoride: An in vivo evidence. Pharmacognosy magazine, 10(37), 61–65. https://doi.org/10.4103/0973-1296.126663

39. Lemieszek MK, Langner E, Kaczor J, Kandefer-Szerszeń M, Sanecka B, Mazurkiewicz W,Rzeski W. Anticancer effects of fraction isolated from fruiting bodies of Chaga medic-inal mushroom, Inonotus obliquus (Pers.:Fr.) Pilát (Aphyllophoromycetideae): in vitro studies. Int J Med Mushrooms. 2011;13(2):131-43. doi: 10.1615/intjmedmushr.v13.i2.50. PMID:22135889.

40. Melanin Complex from Medicinal Mushroom Inonotus obliquus (Pers.: Fr.) Pilat (Chaga) (Aphyllophoromycetideae) - International Journal of Medicinal Mushrooms, Volume 4, 2002, Issue 2 - Begell House Digital Library

41. ORAC: Scoring Antioxidants? - Dr. Weil (drweil.com)

42. Khandare AL, Rao GS, Lakshmaiah N. Effect of tamarind ingestion on fluoride excretion in humans. Eur J Clin Nutr. 2002 Jan;56(1):82-5. doi: 10.1038/sj.ejcn.1601287. PMID:11840184.

43. Khandare AL, Kumar P U, Shanker RG, Venkaiah K, Lakshmaiah N. Additional beneficial effect of tamarind ingestion over defluoridated water supply to adolescent boys in a fluorotic area. Nutrition. 2004 May;20(5):433-6. doi: 10.1016/j.nut.2004.01.007. PMID: 1510503

44. Beltrami AP, Cesselli D, Bergamin N, Marcon P, Rigo S, Puppato E *et al*. Multipotent cells can be generated *in vitro* from several adult human organs (heart, liver, and bone marrow). *Blood* 2007; 110: 3438–3446.

45. D'Ippolito G, Diabira S, Howard GA, Menei P, Roos BA, Schiller PC . Marrow-isolated adult multilineage inducible (MIAMI) cells, a unique population of postnatal young and old human cells with extensive expansion and differentiation potential. *J Cell Sci* 2004; 117: 2971–2981

46. Kogler G, Sensken S, Airey JA, Trapp T, Muschen M, Feldhahn N *et al*. A new human somatic stem cell from placental cord blood with intrinsic pluripotent differentiation potential. *J Exp Med* 2004; 200: 123–135.

47. Jiang Y, Jahagirdar BN, Reinhardt RL, Schwartz RE, Keene CD, Ortiz-Gonzalez XR *et al*. Pluripotency of mesenchymal stem cells derived from adult marrow. *Nature* 2002; 418: 41–49.

48. Ling TY, Kuo MD, Li CL, Yu AL, Huang YH, Wu TJ *et al*. Identification of pulmonary Oct-4+ stem/progenitor cells and demonstration of their susceptibility to SARS coronavirus (SARS-CoV) infection *in vitro*. *Proc Natl Acad Sci* 2006; 103: 9530–9535.

49. Mahabharata - Wikipedia

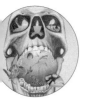

14

NASAL BREATHING &
BRAIN FUNCTION

This was one of my favorite chapters to write as the concepts are so important as to the potential for endo-nasal therapy to create positive changes in the brain! I will be dive deep into the neurological systems within the brain that are hardwired to breathing through the nose. How adequate airflow through the nasal passage has deep primitive, survival connections through limbic centers (emotional) which can effect attention, cognition, memory and our sense of self or identity. It seems to matter which side of the nostril is the dominant side that air flows through. We are going to discuss numerous studies about what happens with each nostril and how this might play a role in cognition, behavior, and information processing. This chapter goes deep into science, so it might be more for the health care practitioners or serious biohacking group to geek out on.

Alternate Nostril Breathing (Yoga)

In this study,"EEG signatures change during unilateral Yogi nasal breathing," the researchers sought to further explore nasal breathing laterality by controlling nasal airflow and observing patterns of cortical activity through encephalographic (EEG) recordings [1].

The researchers found airflow through each side of nostril breathing can entrain "endogenous nasal cycle" which is paced by both poles of the hypothalamus. Yogic practices suggest, and scientific evidence demonstrates, that right-nostril breathing is involved with relatively higher sympathetic activity (arousal states), while left-nostril breathing is associated with a relatively more parasympathetic activity (stress alleviating state). The objective of this study was to further explore this laterality by controlling nasal airflow and observing patterns of cortical activity.

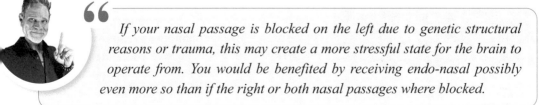

If your nasal passage is blocked on the left due to genetic structural reasons or trauma, this may create a more stressful state for the brain to operate from. You would be benefited by receiving endo-nasal possibly even more so than if the right or both nasal passages where blocked.

> *Left nostril breathing can activate a more restorative and meditative state. Breathing patterns can have a powerful role in brain function.*

In this context, our study adds to the limited research into elucidating the effects of nasal breathing laterality and brain function, as our results suggests that general breathing patterns and specific nostrils, influence brain activity.

The left-nostril is usually the non-dominant breathing side and is associated with greater power in posterior areas of the brain. Increased posterior power occurs during eyes-closed / meditative activities related to relaxation and restoration[2].

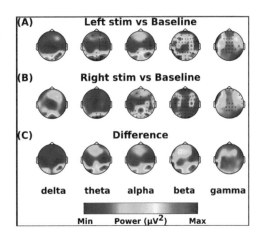

Nasal Breathing, Stimulus Processing & Behavior

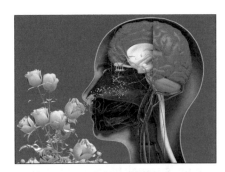

This study indicated that the limbic system is dominate in regulation during the voluntary mouth breathing compared to nasal breathing. This could be a problem as it can be a source of stress response as the limbic system is the system that is involved in emotionality. When the limbic system is overly activated, it can trigger over exaggerated emotional responses. An example is road rage or becoming triggered and is thought to be related to the phrase "short fuse"[3].

There is a network in the higher levels of the brain which create our sense of self as it relates to our surroundings and those around us. Called the default mode network (DMN)[4], it is best known for being active when a person is not focused on the outside world and the brain is at wakeful rest, such as during daydreaming and mind-wandering. The DMN can also be active when the individual is thinking about others, thinking about themselves, remembering the past and planning for the future. This network houses the self and the assumptions about the self and the stories we tell about ourselves to ourselves.

Just like psychedelics such as LSD and psilocybin which also down regulate the DMN, endo nasal has a similar mechanism of action.

Another interesting brain network that is active through nasal breathing is the Salient network (SN). The salient network contributes to a variety of complex functions, including communication, social behavior, and self-awareness through the integration of sensory, emotional and cognitive information. The SN is the network that allows us to have a bit of control over what we place our attention and is upstream to the DMN in the sense that the SN allows the DMN to operate. The DMN is where our sense of self becomes our reality. This study ties this all together in one statement "Mouth breathers exhibited abnormal functional connections between the DMN, SN, and central executive network (CEN)". (2.5)

Nasal breathing has an impact on these brain networks and the nasal side seems to matter. Therefore, I always like to inflate the left side last to end with a parasympathetic effect.

Consider this study, "Nasal Respiration Entrains Human Limbic Oscillations and Modulates Cognitive Function" The researcher discover that the need to breathe is inextricably linked to the olfactory system relating to respiratory rhythms that draw air through the nose[5]. At a pace of 2-12 Hertz, these rhythms regulate cortical excitability and coordinate network interactions. This helps to shape olfactory coding, memory, and behavior. There is a brain phenomenon called cortical oscillatory activity. This is hard linked to the human respiratory cycle and the respiration control through pacing the cortical oscillatory activity or neural oscillations. This study demonstrates that natural

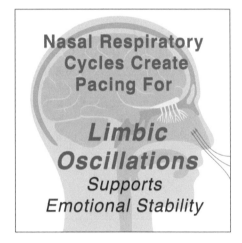

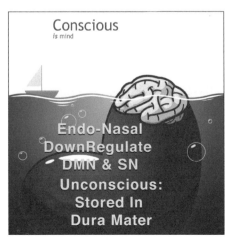

breathing synchronizes pacing activity through the olfactory bulb and piriform cortex (PC) into the limbic-related brain areas such as amygdala and hippocampus. They found during inspiration the pacing signal was at its peak and it was suppressed when breathing was diverted from nose to mouth. Experiments showed that nasal breathing enhances fear discrimination and memory retrieval. These oscillatory rhythms regulate cortical excitability, synchronize activity within cell assemblies, and coordinate network interactions, helping to shape olfactory sensory

coding, memory, and behavior. These findings demonstrate another role of nasal breathing in coordinating cortical oscillatory activity or neuronal oscillations to support stimulus processing and behavior through the default mode network and salient networks. These cortical oscillations can be desynchronized through the influence of the inspiration pacing signal which is more pronounced when we breath more fully through the nose.

Robert Fulford, D.O. was onto something when he stated "Breathing enlivens and vitalizes the physical body with life energy, and also balances the flow of life energies within the body. The pumping action, which circulates the cerebrospinal fluid, is created by the cranial bones in the skull, in conjunction with our breathing. A man is only half alive unless he is breathing through his nose." This was before this neurology was more known.

Robert Fulford, D.O.

Desynchronization vs Synchronization.

Desynchronization is a process inverse to synchronization, where synchronized oscillating systems desynchronize as part of learning and plastic changes the brain encounters during learning and other changes due to sensory and thought input through the ascending reticular activating system (ARAS). Desynchronization is important where disease in the brain cause a strong synchronization of neurons may severely impair brain function such as in Parkinson's disease or epilepsy. Synchronization can also be an important phenomenon that can be entrained through the oscillatory pacing to synchronize activity within cell assemblies as well as to coordinate network interactions such as within ARAS. This is sculpting our sense of identity based on sensory and mind energies in which we focus on via the SN.

A variety of emotional and cognitive states such as fear and anxiety can influence the rate and depth of breathing. The alternative idea, that respiratory rates and quality can exert a direct impact on emotion and cognition is Newley discovered in science. The fact that the olfactory system is closely linked with limbic brain regions mediating emotion, memory, and behavior suggests a robust pathway by which nasal breathing could activate cortical pacing activity thus influence limbic areas, with corresponding effects on emotional, cognitive and behavioral functions.(12)

The Powerful Brain effect of Sensory input through the Trigeminal Nucleus

Let us try and understand the DMN a bit more and how the nasal breathing and endo-nasal therapy might work within it. All of our sensations from our body climb up to the brain though what's called the ascending reticular activating system (ARAS) as well as the Locus Coeruleus (LC) which controls the level of attention and alertness.

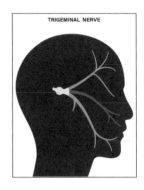

LC neurons also influence our brains metabolic activity, gene expressions, and inflammatory processes. As you can see, this is hugely important for many reasons. One of the main sensory channels that fires into this network is the trigeminal nerve. I found this study very interesting 'Trigeminal, Visceral and Vestibular Inputs May Improve Cognitive Functions by Acting through the Locus Coeruleus and the Ascending Reticular Activating System: A New Hypothesis'[6]. Activation of a sensory channel such as the trigeminal nerve, which integrates the face, mouth and nasal/sinus areas, may potentially influence neuronal activity and a healthy state within the brain. This has been shown to support cognitive functions and exerting a neuroprotective action on the brain[7].

These researchers also discussed how mouth breathing can lead to an asymmetric hemispheric excitability, leading to an impairment in cognitive functions. Keeping in mind that the trigeminal nucleus is a primary source of input from the nasal passages which are involved in such an intimate way to brain function. It's easy to conclude that these findings can be a function of poor nasal breathing causing this brain asymmetry through the ARAS/LC.

There are 3 main inputs that may drive LC neurons and ARAS[8]

1) Trigeminal Region

2) Visceral Organs

3) Vestibular which regulating their activity.

Improving trigeminal, visceral, and vestibular control of ARAS/LC activity may explain why these input signals: (1) Affect sensorimotor and cognitive functions even though

> *LC are the primary pathways that begin to get activated when a girl becomes a woman, or a boy becomes a man where there is a maturation and an enhanced identity with oneself. This is a maturation of the DMN.*

> *Mood, motivation, attention, and arousal are behavioral states having a profound impact on cognition. Behavioral states are mediated though our senses which move through the ARAS and that attention is based on SN and LC networks in the brainstem. These are all paced through the respiratory cycles. Peripheral activation such as with endo-nasal balloon therapy can provide sensory input into LC neurons and the ARAS as a complementary approach for the treatment of cognitive impairments and neurodegenerative disorders.*

it is not directly related to the information carried (2) Effective in relieving the symptoms of some brain conditions involved in memory and executive function.

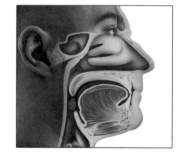

Peripheral activation (such as with as with endo-nasal therapy) can provide a sensory input into *LC neurons and the ARAS* as a complementary approach for the treatment of cognitive impairments and neurodegenerative disorders [9].

The Trigeminal Nerve & Vestibular Function

For most of us, there is very little that is more important than our vestibular function. One bout of vertigo or dizziness is enough to bring anyone to their knees. Likewise, even subtle challenges with this delicate system can create many challenges. We discussed how the vestibular ocular reflex or the VOR is important as it relates to muscle balance in the neck and spine. As mentioned in chapter 10, I found much success in chronic neck conditions by rebalancing the vestibular ocular reflex with therapies such as

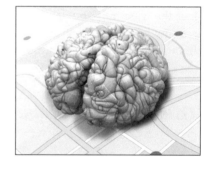

gaze stabilization, improving gaze holding, and working on retinocollicular maps with saccadic exercises. Here is a great article to understand retinocollicular maps[10]. In addition to the information already discussed, endonasal balloon adjustments can be of great benefit to assist in improving the vestibular system. Doing the endo-nasal balloon therapy and then beginning vestibular rehab has been a bit of a mainstay in my practice for many years with much success. In this paper, 'Trigeminal Stimulation Elicits a Peripheral Vestibular Imbalance in Migraine Patients,' the authors describe how sensory activation to the trigeminal nucleus improved migraines through balancing the vestibular system[11]. The small study I did on the balance plate before and after endo-nasal therapy is also convincing evidence that these pathways are doing just that. Clinically, Endo-Nasal Therapy addresses migraine headaches quite well and, in fact, it works great for many types of headaches.

Zen Meditation Mist

Zen meditation mist is a nasal mist which I developed in 2019 based on my inspiration from an Amazonian snuff called 'Hape'. One of the actions of Zen or hobby is that there is a burn in the nasal passage, and this is part of its action along with the herbal preparation in the Zen product. With the information contained in this chapter, you can see that there could be a different effect if Zen was applied to the right versus the left nostril. I will often recommend people use the Zen on the left side in order to produce a more calming, centered, and relaxed state, whereas if someone is interested in more of an analytical and mathematical mind, then the right nostril would be better. In addition, Zen can be used prior to meditation as well as during breath work or at any point where one feels it would be beneficial. To learn more about Zen you can check ZenNasalSpray.com or MitoZen.com

Conclusion

Many mental illnesses are a subconscious defense reaction to uncertainty. This is in order to give oneself more of a sense assuredness in the world. Even if this means you develop behaviors that might be destructive or result in danger or poor health. An example is if one becomes a drug addict, he is certain he can take this drug and get this certain feeling state. You have a sense of control over your sense of identity. In breaking the DMN down you would be breaking down the sense of self. One might think that might not be so good, right? Things could get chaotic. The benefit here is the opportunity to see things differently and to move different beliefs and biases out of the way. It is almost like being able to zoom out like an astronaut seeing the bigger picture of our planet which can place things in more perspective. One can let go of various maladaptive strategies that are not serving you. Both psychedelics and endonasal balloon therapy seem to work on similar areas in the brain and I believe there should be research into the combination of these together. I have been asked to provide this treatment in settings with psychedelic medicines and almost 100% of the participants have stated that the balloon inflation was the highlight of their experience.

The studies referenced in this chapter show what I have been seeing in the clinic for the last 27 years. Besides, it is interesting to consider these important actions of nasal breathing and the importance of this system (open nasal breathing) to be free from obstruction even if it's not a noticeable blockage. When you look at the work by Westin Price and the fact that we all have this shrinking skull phenomenon, which is when our face becomes narrow compared to those of our ancestors and those that are living off the land outside of industrial cultures such as aborigines and Amazonian tribes. Due to the impact on the DMN and SN, there seems to be an application for integration of endo-nasal into mental health, children with learning disabilities *(I wish I had access to it when I was a kid in learning disability classes),* and even in spiritual settings.

This section should open conversation on the use of endo-nasal balloon therapy as well as coaching to use methods such as mouth taping to keep form mouth breathing. All brain-based treatments might benefit due to it far reaching effects throughout the brain.

References

1. Niazi IK, Navid MS, Bartley J, Shepherd D, Pedersen M, Burns G, Taylor D, White DE. EEG signatures change during unilateral Yogi nasal breathing. Sci Rep. 2022 Jan 11;12(1):520. doi: 10.1038/s41598-021-04461-8. PMID: 35017606; PMCID: PMC8752782.

2. Barry, R. J., Clarke, A. R., Johnstone, S. J., Magee, C. A. & Rushby, J. A. EEG differences between eyes-closed and eyes-open resting conditions. *Clin. Neurophysiol.* **118**, 2765–2773 (2007).

2.5. Aberrant brain functional connectome in patients with obstructive sleep apnea

Li-Ting Chen,[#1,*] Xiao-Le Fan,[#2,*] Hai-Jun Li,[1] Cheng-Long Ye,[1] Hong-Hui Yu,[1] Hui-Zhen Xin,[1] Hong-Han Gong,[1]De-Chang Peng,[1] and Li-Ping Yan[3]

3. Resting-State Functional Connectivity during Controlled Respiratory Cycles using Functional Magnetic Resonance Imaging - Basic and Clinical Neuroscience (iums.ac.ir)

4. Raichle ME. The brain's default mode network. Annu Rev Neurosci. 2015 Jul 8;38:433-47. doi: 10.1146/annurev-neuro-071013-014030. Epub 2015 May 4. PMID: 25938726.

5. Zelano C, Jiang H, Zhou G, Arora N, Schuele S, Rosenow J, Gottfried JA. Nasal Respiration Entrains Human Limbic Oscillations and Modulates Cognitive Function. J Neurosci. 2016 Dec 7;36(49):12448-12467. doi: 10.1523/JNEUROSCI.2586-16.2016. PMID: 27927961; PMCID: PMC5148230.

6. Zhang S, Hu S, Chao HH, Li CS. Resting-State Functional Connectivity of the Locus Coeruleus in Humans: In Comparison with the Ventral Tegmental Area/Substantia Nigra Pars Compacta and the Effects of Age. Cereb Cortex. 2016 Aug;26(8):3413-27. doi: 10.1093/cercor/bhv172. Epub 2015 Jul 28. PMID: 26223261; PMCID: PMC4961017.

7. Zhang S, Hu S, Chao HH, Li CS. Resting-State Functional Connectivity of the Locus Coeruleus in Humans: In Comparison with the Ventral Tegmental Area/Substantia Nigra Pars Compacta and the Effects of Age. Cereb Cortex. 2016 Aug;26(8):3413-27. doi: 10.1093/cercor/bhv172. Epub 2015 Jul 28. PMID: 26223261; PMCID: PMC4961017.

8. Zhang S, Hu S, Chao HH, Li CS. Resting-State Functional Connectivity of the Locus Coeruleus in Humans: In Comparison with the Ventral Tegmental Area/Substantia Nigra Pars Compacta and the Effects of Age. Cereb Cortex. 2016 Aug;26(8):3413-27. doi: 10.1093/cercor/bhv172. Epub 2015 Jul 28. PMID: 26223261; PMCID: PMC4961017.

9. Zhang S, Hu S, Chao HH, Li CS. Resting-State Functional Connectivity of the Locus Coeruleus in Humans: In Comparison with the Ventral Tegmental Area/Substantia Nigra Pars Compacta and the Effects of Age. Cereb Cortex. 2016 Aug;26(8):3413-27. doi: 10.1093/cercor/bhv172. Epub 2015 Jul 28. PMID: 26223261; PMCID: PMC4961017.

10. Sterratt DC, Hjorth JJJ. Retinocollicular mapping explained? Vis Neurosci. 2013 Jul;30(4):125-8. doi: 10.1017/S0952523813000254. Epub 2013 Aug 23. PMID: 23968139; PMCID: PMC3836172.

11. Marano, E., Marcelli, V., Stasio, E.D., Bonuso, S., Vacca, G., Manganelli, F., Marciano, E. and Perretti, A. (2005), Trigeminal Stimulation Elicits a Peripheral Vestibular Imbalance in Migraine Patients. Headache: The Journal of Head and Face Pain, 45: 325-331. https://doi.org/10.1111/j.1526-4610.2005.05069.x

12. Carmichael et al., 1994; LeDoux, 2000; Eichenbaum et al., 2007

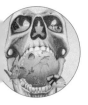

15

LIGHT THERAPY & PHOTO-BIO-MODULATION

Imagine a single therapy that has been proven to do the following: Improve Circulation / Blood Flow, Angiogenesis, Synaptogenesis (Neuroplasticity), Increase NeuroTrophins such as BDNF, NGF, & GDNF, increases SOD Antioxidant System, Neuron Progenitor Cells (Stem Cell Activation) enhance Mitochondria function and as an Ant-Inflammatory. These are all the benefits that light has been used for therapeutically.

I have been using lasers and devices that emit photons for many years both personally and in my clinic. In my younger days as a doctor, I had chronic canker sores that I later found was related to chronic Epstein-Barr infections that I subsequently treated and then no longer had this problem anymore. However, anybody that suffers from canker sores knows that it can be quite life altering as the pain can be quite severe and can affect eating and speaking. One of the things I found at a tradeshow was these red light-emitting diodes that I could then treat my mouth with and found that it gave me a great deal of relief and would allow the canker sores to heal up very quickly. This was my first experience with photo biomodulation. Later, I was an early adopter of using lasers in my practice for musculoskeletal conditions in order to relieve pain and aid in healing damaged and inflamed tissues.

My Stand-Up Desk with 8 Mito-Light panels. Allows me to do work on my computer while receiving therapy!

Later, I was to discover that lasers could be used on various reflex points in the body to clear different blockages that related to everything from organs, emotions and other stress responses created by the body. Using the combination of kinesiology and applying the laser to various points became a common practice I used to balance the body's energy systems. I continue to use these methods as I find them quite useful clinically.

Each morning I use my red-light panels or my SaunaSpace lights to enjoy charging up my cells for 10-15 minutes. I also enjoy intra-nasal laser most days and find them to move the needle for me personally.

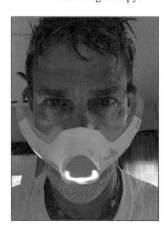

Around a decade ago our clinic began using trans cranial, intranasal as well as intravenous applications of light therapy. In this chapter we're going to dive into all of the ways that light therapy can be used both clinically in general and also in combination with endonasal balloon therapy. We will also explore a compound called methylene blue in combination with light therapy for a more powerful effect.

What is Light?

All matter, so you, a house or a flower, are composed of energy charges that constantly appear and disappear. These potentialities all come from what some call the zero point.

Energized polarity is the cause of all motion, information, and light. Physical matter is really just a set of information. When light acts as if it were a stream of particles, we call these particles photons and this is laser technology.

What is PhotoBiomodulation

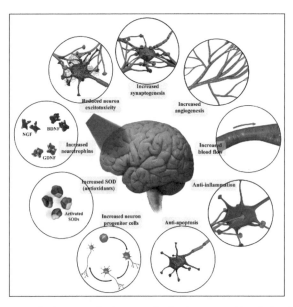

Photobiomodulation therapy (PBM) is based on the use of specific light parameters to promote tissue repair. Studies suggested that cellular energy, healing and repair are all enhanced by both red and near-infrared light[1]. PBM involves the activation of cellular energy pathways (mitochondrial respiratory chain) by activating the enzyme Cytochrome *C with Photons*. Electrons are physical particles that the mitochondria use, however, a photon is a non-physical unit of energy that has no mass or physical property and is only a unit of light energy. I love considering the difference between photons and electrons as it relates to the physical and non-physical states of matter.

What's interesting is the relationship between heme and chlorophyll which is what plants use to convert sunlight into energy. The only difference being chlorophyll is bound by an atom of magnesium as opposed to heme being bound by iron.

Mitochondria & Cyto-Chrome C Oxidase

"Cyto" is for Cell and "Chrome" is for Light! This is where we absorb light, and our bodies literally have the ability to use the energy contained within the light to make energy. Not just any light but very specific light. Red is between (600–700 nm) and near-infrared is between (760–940 nm) spectral regions, and are

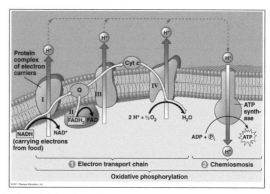

the Goldilocks Zone for our cells. Red light is within the visible and the near-infrared is outside of the visible spectrum.

The mechanism of action of PBM centers around the enzyme cytochrome c oxidase (CCO), which is a unit with four steps or proteins (5 really but 4 main) of the mitochondrial electron transport chain. This movement of electrons through this "chain" causes the reduction of glucose and oxygen into water or H_2O[2]. CCO enzyme activity is inhibited by nitric oxide (NO) (especially in hypoxic conditions or cells dealing with excessive inflammation). This is where methylene blue comes into play which we will get into next. What's amazing here is that the inhibitory NO can be dissociated by photons of light that are absorbed by CCO *(containing copper & heme centers which we will discuss later)*[3].

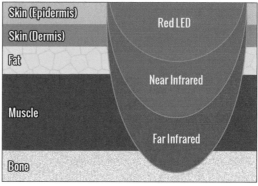

These absorption peaks are mainly in the red (600–700 nm) and near-infrared (760–940 nm) spectral regions. When NO is cleared, the energy produced across the membrane of the mitochondria becomes more charged. This allows even more oxygen and glucose to be used and results in more energy output or ATP production by the mitochondria.

What's amazing is that both methylene blue and light work through reducing NO's interference, yet we have millions of fitness enthusiasts as well as elderly men for erectile dysfunction taking substances to increase NO.

> *The NO that is blocking the mitochondria from making energy can be removed by photons of light that are absorbed by CCO in the red (600–700 nm) and near-infrared (760–940 nm) spectral regions so more oxygen and glucose are metabolized and more ATP is produced by the mitochondria.*

Why IF & Near IR Lights is the Key.

A major benefit we have not yet discussed regarding PBM is Near IR's ability to stimulate what's called extra-pineal melatonin. I wrote a book on melatonin called *Melatonin: Miracle Molecule* that takes a deep dive into how melatonin works to protect and heal the body. Very few people understand that melatonin is made in

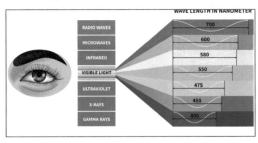

every mitochondrion throughout the body to maintain our energy production through stressful events. We will get more into this later.

NASA scientists have discovered that near-infrared, or Near-IR Lights in the 630nm to 880nm range are the most effective in promoting cell growth and thus stimulating faster healing. For surface healing of the skin, researchers found that the most suitable wavelength is around 660nm and for deeper penetration for wound healing and joint tissues, 880nm appears to be most effective.

The spectrum of solar radiation reaching the Earth is divided as follows: 6.8% UV, 38.9% visible, and 54.3% near infrared radiation (NIR)[4].

Near-IR light therapy accelerates cell growth 150 to 200 percent when compared to non-treated cells. This is why SaunaSpace Lights area so special as they put out 40% Near IR light which is way more than LED's or any other bulb available on the market.

Melatonin as a Key to PBM's Effects.

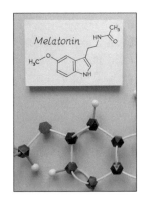

NIR light is the main stimulator for our pineal to produce melatonin and store it. In the absence of light, the pineal releases this melatonin into circulation which is the primary activator of the sleep cycle. In fact, every cell in your body responds by increasing melatonin production through exposure to near infrared light. In a paper by my good friend Dr. Russel Reiter, he discusses how the body produces and maintains a melatonin

> *Near IR accounts for approximately 54.3% of the Sun's radiation reaching Earth. God must feel this light spectrum is kind of important!*

reservoir that is separate and apart from the circulatory melatonin generated by the pineal gland. He states that the NIR portion of natural sunlight stimulates an excess of melatonin in each of our healthy cells and that the cumulative effect of this antioxidant reservoir is to enhance the body's ability to deal with changing conditions rapidly and locally throughout the day. This is the ability of the body to deal and adapt to stress.

In this research paper called, 'Melatonin as a principal component of red-light therapy' their report focuses on how melatonin is a potential mediator of red light's therapeutic effects[5].

Using PhotoBioModulation to Heal the Body.

The healing effects of light therapy was first used in the late 1800s to treat skin tuberculosis (TB), and NASA used it in the 1980s to grow plants in outer space.

NIR light therapy works by stimulating color-sensitive chemicals in the mitochondria of body tissues' cells. Adding a color-sensitive substance like methylene blue can drive this reaction even further as we will discuss later.

PBM has been used to *improve wound healing*[6] reduce pain[7],and many other healing and regenerative applications. The light can be supplied by lasers or light-emitting diodes (LEDs). Transcranial PBM and intra-nasal both have amazing therapeutic uses in various neurological and psychological conditions, including ischemic stroke, chronic traumatic brain injuries, and depression[8,9]. Using endo-nasal along with transcranial PBM is a promising upgrade. A study using a PBM to the forehead, Barrett and Gonzalez-Lima demonstrating that PBM to the forehead benefits cognition in healthy humans, including enhanced attention, working memory, and executive functions[10]. Remember though the red light only works on the cytochrome oxidase (CCO) complex IV. What if we can get all 4 complexes to activate using methylene blue along with light? We will discuss ways to further enhance this using this magic bullet for even greater benefit.

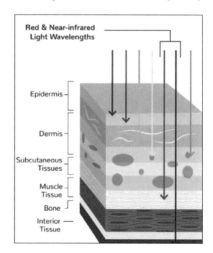

Red light as a treatment is considered bio-active in human cells and can directly and specifically affect and improve mitochondria function through the CCO[11]. Red light photons are absorbed by our cells and converted to energy. This energy produced can then stimulate the production of collagen, elastin, and adenosine triphosphate (ATP), which is great for skin. However, it goes much deeper and can have diverse positive effects on all aspects of health and vitality due to its mitochondrial-enhancing properties.

A case study at UCSF found light therapy had positive effects for a pro hockey player with persistent post-concussive symptoms, and several VA Boston case studies showed good outcomes from light therapy for former pro football players with symptoms due to repetitive head impacts. In addition, researchers are studying light therapy for PTSD, Parkinson's Disease (see also Dr. John Mitrofanis' book, Running in the Light), Alzheimer's Disease, and dementia. The effects include increased cerebral blood flow, increased (ATP) energy production, increased neuroprotection, brain repair, and reduced inflammation. A 2019 study found that using light therapy applied to the head (transcranial) and intra-nasally has a positive effect on brain wave patterns in just one treatment; read more about the study[12].

Age reversal of the thymus gland has been shown using PBM which these researchers claim through enhancing melatonin and stimulating stem cells in the bone marrow[13].

TransCranial PhotoBiomodulation

The idea of applying light to areas of the skull in order to affect the brain through skin and bone might seem hard to wrap your head around. In this paper, 'Quantitative analysis of transcranial and intraparenchymal light penetration in human cadaver brain tissue' the researchers discussed the work they did on how deeply the light therapy penetrates into the skull to affect the brain[14]. They concluded that 808 nm wavelength light demonstrated superior CNS tissue penetration. In another review of literature paper, they also concluded penetration of 808 nm was best through the scalp plus the number of photons penetrating the skull was between 0.11% and 1.75%.[15]. This means that we can get enough photons through the skull, due to the porousness of the skull bone whereas the most difficult

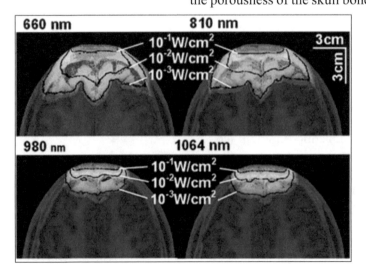

aspect is the skin penetration. Once the photons get through the skin, they can travel through many other types of tissues much easier. Therefore, when we perform intranasal or place the lasers over the wrists or carotid arteries; a place where there are areas of more superficial blood vessels, we might have a higher probability to affect photon penetration into the blood.

Trans-Cranial PhotoBiomodulation & Depression.

Transcranial PBM has been proven to relieve depression as described in this paper, 'Transcranial PBM For The Management Of Depression: Current Perspectives'[16]. With the understanding that PBM works to dislodge NO in the mitochondria and NO has been linked to depression, this seems to be a reasonable mechanism of action. Methylene blue also has significant effect on depression and large trials demonstrate this. I dive deep into this in my book on methylene blue called Magic Bullet. Also, laser therapy applied to the cranium has shown to improve glymphatic activation which is the gutter system in the brain which we covered in chapter 8. Increasing overall energy production through mito-chondrial support, in combination of clearing waste, would certainly move the needle for depression based on those concepts, but then you add in methylene blue and the actions of endo-nasal therapy, you might have a world class protocol for depression. Of course, I would also consider high dose melatonin into this conversation.

Trans-Cranial PhotoBiomodulation & Glymphatics

In this research paper 'PBM Therapy and the Glymphatic System: Promising Applications for Augmenting the Brain Lymphatic Drainage System,' they concluded that PBM Therapy did increase the blood–brain barrier permeability with a subsequent rise in beta amyloid plaque, this is the protein associated with Alzheimer's disease. They found PBM Therapy induced relaxation of lymphatic vessels via a vasodilation process and promoted cranial and extracranial lymphatic system function[17].

Trans-Cranial Light Therapy for Concussion

Here is a paper from my friend Dr. Naeser, 'New research on light therapy shows promise for patients who have suffered repetitive head impacts and may have CTE based on their medical history.'[19]. She feels 'connectivity' between areas of the brain can become dysfunctional after a brain injury; A 2018 study found that *light therapy improves brain con-nectivity and cognition*[18]. Proper functioning of the Default Mode Network (DMN) is related to cognition, includ-ing executive function. We covered this in chapter 14 and how endo-nasal has an impact on this system. Transcranial and Intra-Nasal light therapy combined with Endo-Nasal Therapy have an enhanced benefit from both a sensory and structural effect through the balloons as well as through the PBM.

Dr John with Dr Naeser
in 2022.

Intra-Nasal PhotoBioModulation

The intra-nasal approach for light therapy works well due to the rich nasal blood supply that is superficially exposed so that the light has very little tissue to penetrate before it directly exposes the light to the blood.

In one study, they found that red light at 633 Hz for 25 minutes relaxed RBCs and made them more flexible so more heme was exposed, thus increasing oxygen absorption into the blood and activation of the Salience Network[20]. Intranasal Photobiomodulation significantly modulates Neural Oscillations as

well[21]. These Neural Oscillations or Limbic Oscillations can support better moods and sensory processing which can have a positive effect of how we behave. Our identity is created through this process and how we identify with our 'selves' is key to how we feel and treat others. Let's dive into the Salience Network, Default Mode Network, ascending reticular activating system (ARAS) as well as the Locus Coeruleus (LC) as a review here from Chapter 14 because its super important.

Intra-Nasal PhotoBioModulation, Brain Networks & Our Identity.

In chapter 14, we did a deep dive into the effects of endonasal therapy and its effect on the Default Mode Network DMN and the Salience Network SN. Recall The Default Mode Network (DMN) it is active when a person is not focused on the outside world and the brain is at wakeful rest, such as during daydreaming and mind-wandering. The DMN can also be active when the individual is thinking about others, thinking about themselves, remembering the past, and planning for the future.

Just as nasal breathing and endo-nasal therapy might activate the ascending reticular activating system (ARAS) as well as the Locus Coeruleus (LC), which controls our attention and alertness, so might intranasal PBM working through this mechanism based on the conclusions of many studies.

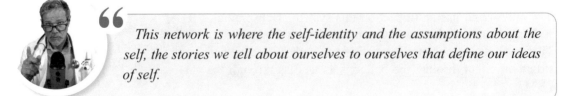

This network is where the self-identity and the assumptions about the self, the stories we tell about ourselves to ourselves that define our ideas of self.

Also recall psychedelics work to down regulate the DMN! Transcranial and intranasal light therapy, endo nasal therapy, and breathing patterns through the nasal passages all have a similar mechanism of action through specific networks. These are self-identity pathways and pathways that create our focus, attention, and our emotionality on those objects of attention.

Recall the Salient Network (SN) which contributes to communication, social behavior, and self-awareness through the integration of sensory, emotional, and cognitive information. This is the network that allows us to have a bit of control over what we place our attention on, and is upstream to the DMN in the sense that the SN allows the DMN to operate. The DMN is where our sense of self becomes or reality.

The specific nasal side the light is applied doesn't seem to matter like it does in the endo-nasal therapy or transcranial light therapy because of the lights ability to cross through the nasal tissue.

Intra-Nasal PBM & Neurological and Neuropsychiatric Disorders.

In the paper called, 'Therapeutic potential of Intranasal PBM Therapy for Neurological and Neuropsychiatric Disorders: A Narrative Review,' the researchers point out that intra-nasal light therapy has shown to improve cerebral metabolic activity, blood flow, and provide neuroprotection via anti-inflammatory and antioxidant pathways. They also point out that intranasal light therapy has become an attractive and potential method for the treatment of brain conditions[22].

As you can see there are many reasons to include intra-nasal light therapy during endo-nasal sessions. Two of my top reasons are to improve neurological circulation and it helps settle down any inflammation in the nasal passages.

Agnihotra, SunGazing Circadian Rhythm, Chakra's & Photo-BioModulation

I was recently traveling in California and was introduced to one of the most interesting scientists I've met, named Dr Alan Macy, who is a biomedical engineer. As we sat and chatted around a fire Sunday morning at the restaurant at the Ritz hotel in Santa Barbara, our attention to the flames started an interesting conversation about

Dr Alan Macy

Agnihortra. What he revealed to me is that this is an ancient practice from the Vedic traditions whereby one would create a small fire that they would then stare into in the morning and then at night. It is thought that the different sections of the fire had frequencies that correlated to the energy centers in the body. An example would be that the lower aspects of the flame, which have lower frequencies of flicker, would be more related to the root chakra or root energy centers versus the top of the flames, with a higher frequency of flicker, would be more related with those frequencies related to higher energy centers. I'm sure most people reading this might be a bit confused as some of these concepts related to energy centers in the body and the chakra system are not necessarily main stream medi-

cine or main stream to most people at all. The concept of energy centers or chakras in the body is a concept that arose in the early traditions of Hinduism[23], Buddhism, and is in early Sanskrit texts. Within Kundalini yoga, the techniques of breathing exercises, visualizations, mudras, bandhas, kriyas, and mantras are focused on manipulating the flow of subtle energy through chakras. I've had opportunities to practice many of these through various teachers with the most recent being Joe Dispenza who is becoming very popular for his intensive meditation retreats. His retreats focus on meditating and connecting these energy centers to allow for better energy movement and stronger energy sourcing through our root in order to have a more vital physical body as well as to heal various aspects of

disease. I have witnessed many spontaneous healings through my involvement with these methods and I practice focusing my attention on meditation, and outside of meditation to pull energy from the route up through the heart and higher. This practice seems to have brought balance to me energetically and emotionally. I feel overall healthier and more connected with my body when I do this regularly.

Back to Alan Macy and the idea that we can start this Agnihortra fire by doing a mediation which might act to balance our energy centers through the light and frequency of the fire. What really perked my attention was the idea that the near-infrared light within the fire would mimic the sunrise and sunset. I had also recently spent time with my friend, Luke Storey, who is a well-know podcaster on health, spirituality, and biohacking. While visiting me, he

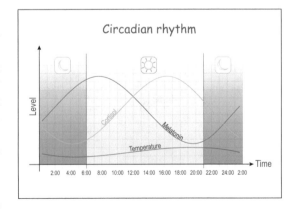

had me join him during sungazing. He had made the statement
about how much it has helped
his sleep and overall health to
spend a short time watching the
sunrise and sunset each day. I
admittedly have been through
stages in my life where I was

actively doing a lot of Sungazing myself, so I was familiar with the process. You stare
directly at the sun with your eyes. There is controversy around whether this is safe or not
and I think that the dangers of this have been over exaggerated. I have seen people stare at
the Sun for five minutes at a time during noon hours. This one individual stated that they
do that most days and their vision is improved from this process. Most recommendations
in this setting would be to point your head in that direction with your eyelids closed.
This was the most extreme example of Sungazing I've ever witnessed personally. This
is something that one obviously needs to become adapted to, but it is a very interesting
way to utilize photo bio modulation. It's very reasonable to see Sungazing as a viable and
interesting way to utilize PBM due to the fact that there is direct exposure to your blood
circulating through the retina and an opportunity for direct exposure of near infrared spectrum light that could support various positive physiological outcomes as seen throughout
this chapter regarding how the power of photo biomodulation can affect various aspects
of cellular health through the mitochondria and improve signaling through our circadian
rhythm. I wrote a book on melatonin last year called *Melatonin: Miracle Molecule* and in
this book, we discussed the importance of this sleep wake cycle I would highly encourage
anyone to explore how important this is to our health and vitality. In essence, the release
of cortisol in the morning to get us up and get us moving countered by the release of
melatonin at night to allow us to rest and restore is not something that is supported in
modern times. Many people are suffering from disease states as a result of this system
being in poor harmony. I feel that the Agnihortra practice as well as the sunset and sunrise
Sungazing practice are so beneficial as much of its benefit is through the activation of
these circadian rhythm signaling. I might have found an alternative to either Sungazing

or Agnihortra that is super easy to do in a busy lifestyle
like mine. I've discovered the sauna space lamps, which
produce 40% near infrared light, can be placed around
my living space where I get ready in the morning. I can
turn them on both in the morning and in the evening
around sunset. It might not be as powerful as either
Sungazing or Agnihortra, however, it's something that
I have easily adopted into my routine and I am noticing
some nice benefits from this practice.

Next, we dive into how you can enhance all 4 cytochrome
subunits with Methylene Blue to really drive healing
and regeneration.

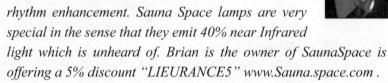

> Sauna Space lamp is on in my room for 20-30 minutes in the morning and evening around sunset and sunrise, so I achieve both a mitochondrial boost as well as a circadian rhythm enhancement. Sauna Space lamps are very special in the sense that they emit 40% near Infrared light which is unheard of. Brian is the owner of SaunaSpace is offering a 5% discount "LIEURANCE5" www.Sauna.space.com .

PBM With Methylene Blue for Neurological Wellness

I wrote an entire book on methylene blue, and felt it was important to discuss it in some detail in this book especially as it relates to photo bio modulation. I use methylene blue regularly with many of my cases that I am also treating with endonasal balloon therapy. Methylene blue is a brilliant blue salt, methylene blue or MB was first used as is a dye. It is now known that MB improves mitochondria respiration and might be a magic bullet within metabolic medicine. In 1870, MB was discovered and used as an industrial dye. Soon after MB was found to be a great way to stain human tissues and microbes for microscope examination. They found that MB would even inactivate certain microbes. An anti-microbial that virtually leaves cells and tissues unharmed. That's right, it is a powerful antimicrobial![24] It gets even more impressive so stay with me. MB was one of the first chemotherapeutic medications ever tested in humans. It was used to treat malaria in 1891. Of course, it was replaced by antibiotics when they first came on the scene even though MB is superior to them. With heavy marketing by big pharma to doctors, a shift was made to these new "superior" anti-microbials. Are they really superior? We have now found that antibiotics can have negative effects to our health through killing our microbiome and that many bugs can become resistant to the antibiotics. The treatment of malaria with antibiotics has proven that this is not the best way as many of the antibiotics have created resistant strains, making them useless. With MB, there has been no detection that the micro-organism has resistance to MB unlike antibiotics. Your microbiome is an incredibly important diverse group of bacteria that coexists in your body, mostly your gut. The malarial parasites, *Plasmodium falciparum*, is now showing an increased resistance to common antimalarial drugs. As a result, methylene blue is being considered a better option.

Methylene Blue: The Magic Bullet.

The term **magic bullet** is a scientific concept developed by a German Nobel laureate Paul Ehrlich in 1900. Ehrlich formed an idea that it could be possible to kill specific microbes (such as bacteria), which cause diseases in the body, without harming the body itself. He named this agent

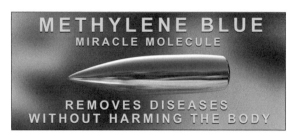

as *Zauberkugel*, the "magic bullet."[25]. This magic bullet was methylene blue! Methylene blue does seem to have few negative effects and is extremely safe to consume, and since it works on the upstream aspect of health, which is the energy production or metabolism, it supports the body in a wide range of conditions. If you give energy reserves that the body needs to work, it will correct disease much better than any man-made chemical such as with virtually all pharmaceutical approaches to health and disease.

Methylene Blue & Mitochondria

Methylene blue is anti-inflammatory and neuroprotective showing promise with treatment of diseases such as stroke, Alzheimer's disease and Parkinson's disease.[26].

Remember your mitochondria works through the electron transport chain where it shuffles electrons which releases chemical energy which the body uses to make ATP, which is the energy currency in our cells. Methylene blue is an electron carrier and even recycles electrons, which allows it to improve mitochondrial function. It basically turns your mitochondria into super mitochondria! It is highly beneficial in toxic situations in the brain as it encourages cellular oxygen consumption and decreases anaerobic glycolysis. This fits into the melatonin conversation where stress induces cytokines (inflammation) and causes the cell to switch to the inefficient, anaerobic glycolysis. We will dive into melatonin in another section. How methyl-

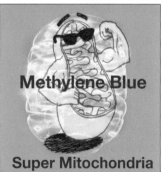

ene blue really shines is that it improves the electron transport chain in the mitochondria such that it recycles electrons. This shifts your cells into very efficient energy production.

Methylene Blue is Anti-Viral.

Besides improving mitochondrial function, methylene blue also has antiviral properties. It displays broad-spectrum virucidal activity in the presence of UV light and has been shown to be effective at inactivating various viruses in blood products prior to transfusions[27].

Methylene blue displays virucidal preventive and therapeutic activity against influenza virus H1N1 and SARS-CoV-2[28].

A recent French publication on a cohort of 2500 end stage cancer patients treated with MB during the first wave of CoviD-19 mentions a possible protective role of MB against respiratory viruses, as in this cohort, there were no reported cases of influenza or SARS-CoV-2 infections[29].

Having been treating mini degenerative neurological conditions, I've come to the conclusion that it's either toxins or infections that are at the root of the disease. New science is demonstrating that many of the proteins such as beta-amyloid and alpha- synuclein are the immune system's response to these toxins and or infections and most often they are both involved. I have found virtually all of the patients that have come to

me test positive for at least one but typically two different viruses. I often test for Epstein bar, cytomegalovirus, and HHV6, as well as an immune marker called CD57. A lab called Cyrex runs an array of 12 tests for 25 different microbes. Things like ozone and methylene blue have qualities to both improve mitochondrial status as well as having an antiviral/anti-microbial effect which makes them great therapeutic substances for any brain-based conditions.

Methylene Blue is an Anti-depressant

In higher doses, methylene blue seems to be a powerful anti-depressant. Keep in mind, in higher doses, MB acts as an MAO inhibitor. This is why it can be dangerous to take antidepressants along with higher doses of MB. In one study, methylene blue at 15 mg/day, was compared to placebo in treatment of severe depressive illness. The 3-week trial showed that the improvement in patients receiving methylene blue was significantly greater than in those receiving placebo. Methylene blue at a dose of 15 mg/day appears to be a potent antidepressant, and further clinical evaluation is essential[30].

Methylene blue increases autophagy which is cellular cleaning and recycling. This study showed MB induced neuroprotection by enhancing autophagy[31].

Due to this, methylene blue might be considered something helpful during fasting. We will get into fasting in this chapter a little later.

Methylene Blue & Memory Consolidation

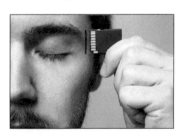

What are the primary benefits I see of utilizing methylene blue during treatment plans for patients utilizing endonasal therapy is that it can enhance learning and neuroplasticity by consolidating memory as described in this study.

They took people with phobias and they gave them one dose of methylene blue the day of the therapy and the results were significantly better in the group that took the methylene blue which the researchers felt was due to enhanced mitochondrial support to the nerves which resulted in enhanced memory consolidation[32]. What this means is that people will enjoy enhanced learning. When I'm using functional neurology for cases presenting with vestibular dysfunction, autonomic dysregulation, as well as movement disorders, having an extra boost is welcomed. Next, I'll discuss how one would take MB under a health care providers guidance.

Guidelines to Methylene Blue Use

Always use pure, clean pharmaceutical grade (USP grade) methylene blue as there can be contaminants within cheaper methylene blue which can be dangerous for your health. Consumption of Methylene Blue has been studied from ½ -100 mg per kilogram of body weight. According to experts, the dosage window for methylene blue is between ½ - 4 mg per kilogram. The half-life is 12 ½ hours for methylene blue. Always use pure, clean pharmaceutical grade (USP grade) methylene blue as there can be contaminants within cheaper methylene blue which can be dangerous for your health. Consumption of Methylene Blue has been studied from ½ -100 mg per kilogram of body weight. According to experts, the dosage window for methylene blue is between ½ - 4 mg per kilogram. The half-life is 12 ½ hours for methylene blue. MB metabolized by the urine, so be prepared for a blue or green urine for a day or two after a higher dose. If an intervention is desired, such as in the case of poisoning or toxicity, a higher one-time dose of 4mg/kilo is given. This would apply with methemoglobinemia, when such a higher dose might be given orally. ½ -1 mg per kilogram can be given every day safely if breaks from dosing are performed. 1-2,000 mg ascorbic acid can be helpful to take along with methylene blue. Silver and gold can be combined with the MB for greater photodynamic effects. Gold is difficult to find but silver is very easy in the market. See MitoZen.com for oral gold/silver products. Higher doses of MB can be used in unusual circumstances such as infection into the higher end of the dosage schedule 2-4 mg/kilo of body weight for short periods of days to a week. Since MB builds up within the mitochondria it is important to take breaks from taking methylene blue such as 2-3 days off every 10 days of daily dosing. The buildup of MB within the mitochondria can create a diminishment in effect for mitochondrial support. In my own clinic I have found each person has their own sweet spot at a specific dose. One needs to do experiments with various doses to see what works best for them. It is important that MB dosing be monitored through a healthcare practitioner. These suggestions are not meant to be medical advice.

Methylene Blue & SSRIs

One of the concerns with methylene blue consumption is a serotonin storm when methylene blue is taken with SSRIs, SNRIs or drugs that increase serotonin levels, such as anti-depressants and other MAO inhibitors. The contraindications for methylene blue and SSRIs are based on a handful of cases (x5) where extremely high doses of methylene blue

were used to stain the parathyroid gland during a surgical procedure to remove part or all this gland due to disease. The patients that were on SSRIs experienced a serotonin storm and did not do as well. The doses used during this procedure where much higher than the therapeutic doses discussed in this book. This concern was rescinded by Mayo Clinic, and the FDA in Canada does not have this warning associated with methylene blue except as it relates to this surgical procedure. The FDA in the United States has not removed this contraindication to date. To my knowledge, there have never been any issues with methylene blue and SSRIs besides these 5 cases. If you research methylene blue, you will find a lot of negative and scary articles and papers saying it is a dangerous substance to take, when in fact, it is amazingly safe. In fact, methylene blue has been around before the FDA was formed. It was grandfathered in due to its safety record; therefore, it did not need to go through any studies to prove its safety.

At high doses (>10mg/kg or about 6-700mg), methylene blue may cause some potential side effects including hypertension, methemoglobinemia, dizziness, GI distress, altered pulse oximeter readings, and it can induce hemolytic anemia in people with a genetic condition called G6PD.

It is important that you source pharmaceutical grade methylene blue as any other level of quality may carry significant heavy metals and other toxins. Sublingual methylene blue, according to the expert Francisco Gonzalez-Lima is a poor route of administration with little absorption and will turn your mouth completely blue which may look strange. MitoZen.com has created an oral bar both called Lumetol Blue, which may provide better absorption because methylene blue mixes with stomach acid and is well-absorbed. When taken orally, this product will leave no blue stain in your mouth. Suppository delivery is particularly good as well as a direct absorption that is over a 5-7-hour period of time. MitoZen's 60 mg suppositories can be used with good results and combined with light therapy as well. Suppository dosing should be about 30-45 minutes prior to the light therapy.

> *I have been using methylene blue intravenously in my clinic along with light therapy. Methylene blue is considered photodynamic, meaning that it has a response to light. Red light in the 660 nm range seems to be the sweet spot for methylene blue. We use an IV protocol called LumeBlue which is an intravenous laser along with the methylene blue. We also use red light panels that you stand in front of and receive the light therapy through the skin.*

We will then use either hyperbaric oxygen therapy or the CVAC pod. We call this IV protocol LumeBlue. This protocol, combined with endonasal balloon therapy to allow for proper cerebral spinal fluid flow, carries nutrients to the cells and tissues of the central nervous system as well as caring waste products away, thus demonstrating some

LumeBlue IV Protocol. IV Laser After IV Magnesium / Methylene Blue & Prior to CVAC

synergy. I have been working with a protocol that can be done at home using methylene blue and red-light panels. For home application, you can take an

Lumetol Blue 175mg Bar's

oral methylene blue bar called Lumetol Blue and use red light panels that put out 660 nm called MitoLights. I also feel the SaunaSpace Lights are very powerful as they provide a high amount of the deep penetrating and highly photodynamic near infrared spectrums. These can be a powerful system to integrate into a routine at home to get all the benefits of mitochondrial support through photobiomodulation.

SunaVae Inner Ear Care & PhotoBioModulation

The use of laser for inner ear regeneration has been a significant part of my practice for the last seven years. I originally studied with Dr. Amon Kaiser in Baden-Baden, Germany and have been the only USA location to use the treatment LumoMed. Please refer to chapter 11 on inner ear treatments for more detail on this and other methods.

What is SunaVae?

LumoMed is a series of laser treatments, and ShimSpot is a safe and effective injection of stem cells. Combined, they become SunaVae Therapy!

What is Our History with Inner Ear Regeneration?

Dr. John Lieurance and the team at Advanced Rejuvenation have been focusing on inner ear regeneration for many years. They have been seeking out the best options for treatments aimed to regenerate the inner ear for conditions such as tinnitus, hearing loss, hyperacusis and even balance disorders which can all be due to inner ear damage. We brought LumoMed to the USA almost a decade ago and are currently the only providers for LumoMed in the USA. Our clinic became certified in ShimSpot this year and we are currently offering the combination of both techniques.

Why Laser Stem Cells?

Stem cells are fragile, and there is a risk called senescence where they can go into a permanent state of sleep. This is the major focus of many studies on improving stem cell results by scientists working in the field of regenerative medicine. Laser also enhances the mitochondria within both the stem cells introduced into the area and also the existing cells that are to be repaired also receive an energy boost to do the work of regeneration.

Additional Support at Home Also Advised.

Advanced Rejuvenation and Dr John Lieurance have been working on a home-based protocol. together the most cutting-edge protocol for inner ear health we call the "Sensory Rejuvenation Protocol". This protocol focuses on specific lifestyle modifications, nutritional support, and removing all triggers causing inflammation in the nervous system and/or the inner ear. Read Dr John's Article on Sensory Rejuvenation find it at OutOfBoxDoc.com.

CONCLUSION

Who wouldn't want to: Improve Circulation / Blood Flow, Angiogenesis, Synaptogenesis (Neuroplasticity), Increase NeuroTrophins such as BDNF, NGF, & GDNF, increases SOD Antioxidant System, Neuron Progenitor Cells (Stem Cell Activation) and have more ant-inflammatory effects? Both light therapy and methylene blue should be used with the direction of a healthcare provider ideally. Many of the suggestions in this chapter are just references to various therapies and not meant as a prescription for anybody to begin doing these at home without the guidance of the healthcare practitioner. With that said, many responsible individuals can begin to unpack this information and design a program with their healthcare provider to introduce both light therapy and methylene blue into a routine. The use of the SaunaSpace lights, Sungazing or Agnihorta are all great options for folks to utilize photo biomodulation as it relates to improving circadian rhythm and all the wonderful benefits that can provide.

For the purpose of this book, which is on the topic of endona-sal therapy, it makes sense that once you open up and release the cranial structures, it will allow more oxygen available for the electron transport chain, which, when combined with photo biomodulation and enhanced mitochondrial function through methylene blue, you may provide an optimal environment for many individuals to heal from various diseases. As doctors, we do nothing to "heal" our patients! It is always the patient that heals themselves through the innate intelligence within the body that made the body and continues to self-regulate the body. We simply remove the obstacles and interference to this divine force.

See MitoZen.com for MitoLights & Lumetol Blue products. Also find my Methylene Blue Book at MethyleneBlueBook.com

If you're looking for a trained practitioner for this condition then go to www.NasalTherapyBook.com or www.OutOfBoxDoc.com or if you're a clinician wanting to learn how to do endonasal to treat sleep apnea then please go to www.LearnEndoNasal.com

References

1. Wang X, Tian F, Soni SS, Gonzalez-Lima F, Liu H. Interplay between up-regulation of cyto-chrome-c-oxidase and hemoglobin oxygenation induced by near-infrared laser. Sci Rep. 2016 Aug 3;6:30540. doi: 10.1038/srep30540. PMID: 27484673; PMCID: PMC4971496

2. Michael R. Hamblin, Shining light on the head: Photobiomodulation for brain disorders, BBA Clinical, Volume 6, 2016, Pages 113-124, ISSN 2214-6474, https://doi.org/10.1016/j.bba-cli.2016.09.002. (https://www.sciencedirect.com/science/article/pii/S2214647416300381)

3. IBID

4. Daniel Barolet, François Christiaens, Michael R. Hamblin, Infrared and skin: Friend or foe, Journal of Photochemistry and Photobiology B: Biology, Volume 155, 2016, Pages 78-85, ISSN 1011-1344, https://doi.org/10.1016/j.jphotobiol.2015.12.014. (https://www.sciencedirect.com/science/article/pii/S1011134415300713)

5. Ronnie L. Yeager, Deanna A. Oleske, Ruth A. Sanders, John B. Watkins, Janis T. Eells, Diane S. Henshel, Melatonin as a principal component of red light therapy, Medical Hypotheses, Volume 69, Issue 2, 2007, Pages 372-376, ISSN 0306-9877, https://doi.org/10.1016/j.mehy.2006.12.041.(https://www.sciencedirect.com/science/article/pii/S030698770700028X)

6. Avci P, Gupta A, Sadasivam M, Vecchio D, Pam Z, Pam N, Hamblin MR. Low-level laser (light) therapy (LLLT) in skin: stimulating, healing, restoring. Semin Cutan Med Surg. 2013 Mar;32(1):41-52. PMID: 24049929; PMCID: PMC4126803.

7. Chung H, Dai T, Sharma SK, Huang YY, Carroll JD, Hamblin MR. The nuts and bolts of low-level laser (light) therapy. Ann Biomed Eng. 2012 Feb;40(2):516-33. doi: 10.1007/s10439-011-0454-7. Epub 2011 Nov 2. PMID: 22045511; PMCID: PMC3288797.

8. Hamblin MR. Shining light on the head: Photobiomodulation for brain disorders. BBA Clin. 2016 Oct 1;6:113-124. doi: 10.1016/j.bbacli.2016.09.002. PMID: 27752476; PMCID: PMC5066074.

9. Hamblin MR. Photobiomodulation for traumatic brain injury and stroke. J Neurosci Res. 2018 Apr;96(4):731-743. doi: 10.1002/jnr.24190. Epub 2017 Nov 13. Erratum in: J Neurosci Res. 2019 Mar;97(3):373. PMID: 29131369; PMCID: PMC5803455.

10. Hipskind SG, Grover FL Jr, Fort TR, Helffenstein D, Burke TJ, Quint SA, Bussiere G, Stone M, Hurtado T. Pulsed Transcranial Red/Near-Infrared Light Therapy Using Light-Emitting Diodes Improves Cerebral Blood Flow and Cognitive Function in Veterans with Chronic Traumatic Brain Injury: A Case Series. Photobiomodul Photomed Laser Surg. 2019 Feb;37(2):77-84. doi: 10.1089/photob.2018.4489. PMID: 31050928; PMCID: PMC6390875.

11. Low-level red and infrared light increases expression of collagen, elastin, and hyaluronic acid in skin - Journal of the American Academy of Dermatology (jaad.org)

12. Zomorrodi, R., Loheswaran, G., Pushparaj, A. *et al.* Pulsed Near Infrared Transcranial and Intranasal Photobiomodulation Significantly Modulates Neural Oscillations: a *pilot exploratory* study. *Sci Rep* **9,** 6309 (2019). https://doi.org/10.1038/s41598-019-42693-x

13. Odinokov, D, Hamblin, MR. Aging of lymphoid organs: Can photobiomodulation reverse age-associated thymic involution via stimulation of extrapineal melatonin synthesis and bone marrow stem cells? *J. Biophotonics.* 2018; 11:e201700282. https://doi.org/10.1002/jbio.201700282

14. Tedford CE, DeLapp S, Jacques S, Anders J. Quantitative analysis of transcranial and intraparenchymal light penetration in human cadaver brain tissue. Lasers Surg Med. 2015 Apr;47(4):312-22. doi: 10.1002/lsm.22343. Epub 2015 Mar 13. Erratum in: Lasers Surg Med. 2015 Jul;47(5):466. PMID: 25772014.

15. Salehpour F, Cassano P, Rouhi N, Hamblin MR,De Taboada L, Farajdokht F,Mahmoudi J,(2019), Penetration Profiles of Visible and Near-Infrared Lasers and Light-Emitting Diode Light Through the Head Tissues in Animal and Human Species: A Review of Literature Photobiomodulation, Photomedicine, and Laser Surgery, doi: 10.1089/photob.2019.4676, 10.1089/photob.2019.4676

16. Askalsky P, Iosifescu DV. Transcranial Photobiomodulation For The Management Of Depression: Current Perspectives. Neuropsychiatr Dis Treat. 2019 Nov 22;15:3255-3272. doi: 10.2147/NDT.S188906. PMID: 31819453; PMCID: PMC6878920.

17. Salehpour F, Khademi M, Bragin DE, DiDuro JO. Photobiomodulation Therapy and the Glymphatic System: Promising Applications for Augmenting the Brain Lymphatic Drainage System. *International Journal of Molecular Sciences*. 2022; 23(6):2975. https://doi.org/10.3390/ijms23062975

18. Forbes D, Blake CM, Thiessen EJ, Peacock S, Hawranik P. Light therapy for improving cognition, activities of daily living, sleep, challenging behaviour, and psychiatric disturbances in dementia. Cochrane Database Syst Rev. 2014 Feb 26;(2):CD003946. doi: 10.1002/14651858. CD003946.pub4. PMID: 24574061.

19. Hamblin MR. Photobiomodulation for traumatic brain injury and stroke. J Neurosci Res. 2018 Apr;96(4):731-743. doi: 10.1002/jnr.24190. Epub 2017 Nov 13. Erratum in: J Neurosci Res. 2019 Mar;97(3):373. PMID: 29131369; PMCID: PMC5803455.

20. Photobiomodulation as a promising new tool in the management of psychological disorders: A systematic review (pbmfoundation.org)

21. Zomorrodi, Reza & Loheswaran, Genane & Pushparaj, Abhiram & Lim, Lew. (2019). Pulsed Near Infrared Transcranial and Intranasal Photobiomodulation Significantly Modulates Neural Oscillations: a pilot exploratory study. Scientific Reports. 9. 10.1038/s41598-019-42693-x.

22. Salehpour, Farzad, Gholipour-Khalili, Sevda, Farajdokht, Fereshteh, Kamari, Farzin, Walski, Tomasz, Hamblin, Michael R., DiDuro, Joseph O. and Cassano, Paolo. "Therapeutic potential of intranasal photobiomodulation therapy for neurological and neuropsychiatric disorders: a narrative review" *Reviews in the Neurosciences*, vol. 31, no. 3, 2020, pp. 269-286. https://doi.org/10.1515/revneuro-2019-0063

23. Chakra - Wikipedia

24. Hampden-Martin A, Fothergill J, El Mohtadi M, Chambers L, Slate AJ, Whitehead KA, Shokrollahi K. Photodynamic antimicrobial chemotherapy coupled with the use of the photosensitizers methylene blue and temoporfin as a potential novel treatment for *Staphylococcus aureus* in burn infections. Access Microbiol. 2021 Oct 27;3(10):000273. doi: 10.1099/acmi.0.000273. PMID: 34816092; PMCID: PMC8604179.

25. Heynick, F. (2009). The original 'magic bullet' is 100 years old. *British Journal of Psychiatry, 195*(5), 456-456. doi:10.1192/bjp.195.5.456

26. Wainwright M, Crossley KB, (2002) Methylene Blue - a Therapeutic Dye for All Seasons?, Journal of Chemotherapy, 14:5, 431-443, DOI: 10.1179/joc.2002.14.5.431

27. Steinmann E, Gravemann U, Friesland M, Doerrbecker J, Müller TH, Pietschmann T, Seltsam A. Two pathogen reduction technologies--methylene blue plus light and shortwave ultra-violet light--effectively inactivate hepatitis C virus in blood products. Transfusion. 2013 May;53(5):1010-8. doi: 10.1111/j.1537-2995.2012.03858.x. Epub 2012 Aug 21. PMID: 22905868.

28. Cagno, V., Medaglia, C., Cerny, A. *et al.* Methylene Blue has a potent antiviral activity against SARS-CoV-2 and H1N1 influenza virus in the absence of UV-activation in vitro. *Sci Rep* 11, 14295 (2021). https://doi.org/10.1038/s41598-021-92481-9

29. Cagno, V., Medaglia, C., Cerny, A. *et al.* Methylene Blue has a potent antiviral activity against SARS-CoV-2 and H1N1 influenza virus in the absence of UV-activation in vitro. *Sci Rep* 11, 14295 (2021). https://doi.org/10.1038/s41598-021-92481-9

30. Naylor, G.J., Smith, A.H., & Connelly, P. (1987). A controlled trial of methylene blue in severe depressive illness. *Biological Psychiatry, 22*, 657-659.

31. Jiang Z, Watts LT, Huang S, Shen Q, Rodriguez P, Chen C, Zhou C, Duong TQ. The Effects of Methylene Blue on Autophagy and Apoptosis in MRI-Defined Normal Tissue, Ischemic Penumbra and Ischemic Core. PLoS One. 2015 Jun 29;10(6):e0131929. doi: 10.1371/journal.pone.0131929. PMID: 26121129; PMCID: PMC4488003

Websites

To find a doctor near you that has been trained in Endo-Nasal see www.NasalTherapyBook. com

If you are a practitioner and would like to learn Endo-Nasal and are looking to enroll in a course see www.LearnEndoNasal.com

Dr John's Educational site: www.OutOfBoxDoc.com

Functional Cranial Release (FCR) Site: www.FunctionalCranialRelease.com

Clinic Site: www.AdvancedRejuvenation.us

Instagram: @YourOutOfBoxDoc

Youtube: www.youtube.com/OutOfBoxDoc

Resources for Melatonin, Zen Mist, Methylene Blue and Glutathione: MitoZen.com

For information on treatment in our Sarasota Clinic- Info@AdvancedRejuvenation.US

Take a photo of you holding this book and use the #Endonasal So I can see it and share it with my community.

JOHN LIEURANCE, ND, DC

Made in the USA
Columbia, SC
24 September 2024

42857476R00126